Africans on the Land

THIS BOOK HAS BEEN PREPARED UNDER THE AUSPICES OF THE CENTER FOR INTERNATIONAL AFFAIRS, HARVARD UNIVERSITY

Created in 1958, the Center fosters advanced study of basic world problems by scholars from various disciplines and senior officers from many countries. The research at the Center, focusing on the processes of change, includes studies of military-political issues, the modernizing processes in developing countries, and the evolving position of Europe. The research programs are supervised by Professors Robert R. Bowie (Director of the Center), Alex Inkeles, Henry A. Kissinger, Edward S. Mason, Thomas C. Schelling, and Raymond Vernon.

A list of Center publications will be found at the end of this volume.

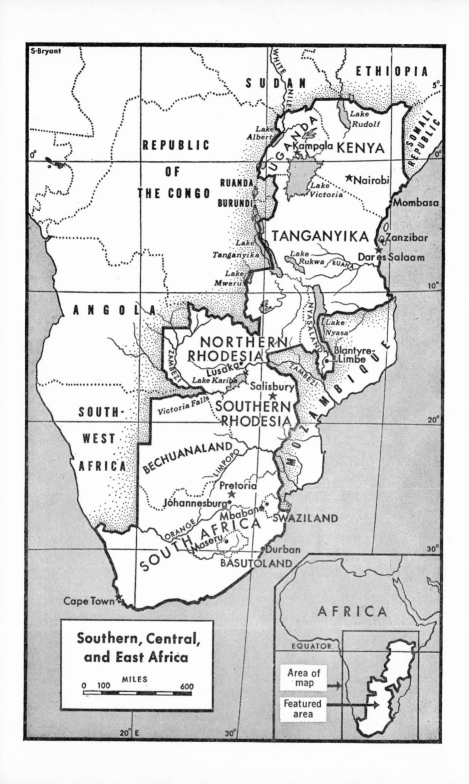

S·Bryant

SUDAN

ETHIOPIA

5°

Lake Albert

Lake Rudolf

REPUBLIC

OF

THE CONGO

UGANDA

Kampala

KENYA

0°

0°

RUANDA

BURUNDI

★Nairobi

Lake Victoria

SOMALI REPUBLIC

Mombasa

TANGANYIKA

Zanzibar

Lake Tanganyika

Lake Rukwa

Dar es Salaam

RUAHA

Lake Mweru

10°

ANGOLA

NYASALAND

Lake Nyasa

NORTHERN RHODESIA

Blantyre-Limbe

ZAMBEZI

Lusaka

ZAMBEZI

Lake Kariba

Salisbury

MOZAMBIQUE

SOUTH-

Victoria Falls

SOUTHERN RHODESIA

20°

WEST

BECHUANALAND

AFRICA

LIMPOPO

Pretoria

Johannesburg

Mbabane

SWAZILAND

ORANGE

SOUTH AFRICA

Maseru

Durban

30°

BASUTOLAND

Cape Town ★

AFRICA

Southern, Central, and East Africa

EQUATOR

0   100   MILES   600

Area of map

Featured area

20° E

30°

20° E

30°

Africans on the Land

Economic Problems of African Agricultural Development in Southern, Central, and East Africa, with Special Reference to Southern Rhodesia

MONTAGUE YUDELMAN

HARVARD UNIVERSITY PRESS

Cambridge, Massachusetts

1 9 6 4

To
E. S. M.

Foreword

BY EDWARD S. MASON FOR THE
CENTER FOR INTERNATIONAL AFFAIRS

One of the central problems of economic development in low-income, predominantly agricultural societies is how a farming population producing principally for self-subsistence is brought, or brings itself, into the market economy. Production for the market is usually a necessary condition to an adaptation of land use to more productive purposes. Production for the market can provide the wherewithal to purchase the fertilizers, insecticides, and tools required to increase productivity. The establishment of relations with the exchange economy is apt to stimulate an interest in, and knowledge of, other and better ways of doing things. But the process by which a group of tribally organized and self-sufficient peasants, sowing and reaping in accordance with age-old tradition, and possessing limited and easily satisfied wants, becomes a collection of risk-taking individuals, responsive to price and income incentives, and interested in conserving their land and improving its productivity, is a complicated socioeconomic phenomenon.

Dr. Yudelman's experience has been principally in Southern, Central, and East Africa, and what he has to say about this major problem of development applies in varying degree to all these areas. He concentrates, however, on Southern Rhodesia in order to make a detailed examination of the subject. Southern Rhodesia, along with South Africa and Kenya, is a "dual" society in which there exist, side by side, "European agriculture" and "African agriculture." On the one hand are large-scale, capital-intensive, highly efficient farming units producing for the market under European direction. On the other are small-scale, labor-intensive, and mainly self-sufficient African farming enterprises. Within the last few years the attention of white-dominated governments in those countries has been directed toward improving the productivity of African farmers and bringing them to a greater degree into the market economy. One of Dr. Yudelman's principal concerns is to examine and assess the probable consequences of government attempts to increase African productivity.

This study is one of several designed to throw light on the relative roles of private enterprise and government in the process of economic development. These studies, undertaken at the Center for International Affairs, were made possible by a generous grant from the Ford Foundation. Some of them focus attention on a wide range of government-private relations in particular countries. The first of the country studies to be published was Professor Raymond Vernon's *The Dilemma of Mexico's Development*. Others, in preparation, deal with Brazil, Iran, Pakistan, and Nigeria. Additional studies, however, are concerned with important problems of development common to a number of countries. Dr. Yudelman's analysis of the ways and means of increasing agricultural productivity is one of those.

Author's Preface

The political map of Africa is changing rapidly. Between the time of completing the manuscript and the date of this preface, the "winds of change" have swept through both East and Central Africa and have extended to Southern Africa as well. Uganda has become independent, Kenya will be independent, important constitutional changes have taken place in the British protectorates of Basutoland, Bechuanaland, and Swaziland, and the Federation of Rhodesia and Nyasaland has been scheduled for dissolution in December 1963. Both Nyasaland and Northern Rhodesia are soon to be independent; the future and status of Southern Rhodesia hangs in the balance.

The future of Southern Rhodesia — the country with which I am most concerned in this book — is problematical and has become a matter of international concern. The ruling European minority is sternly resisting the tide of African nationalism. It faces a difficult choice, either to modify its policies — some of which are outlined in this book — in order to accommodate the demands of the African majority for majority rule, or to resist change by force of arms. Force begets force, but there are many in the embattled minority who want to resist all pressures. They make this choice because they fear being "swamped" by the less sophisticated African majority and they wish to maintain the privileges of their position as an elite European ruling group. This may well lead them to establish a close link with the like-minded administration in the Republic of South Africa. Such a move may also be encouraged by the economic consequences of the breakup of the Federation. Losing free access to the markets of Northern Rhodesia and Nyasaland may make it necessary for Southern Rhodesia to find an alternative source for the revenue formerly provided by the rich output of the copper mines of Northern Rhodesia.

However, whether the European minority meets the African demands for rapid change or whether it defies them, the country is going to have to place increasing emphasis on raising the productivity of the agriculture carried on by its African majority.

If African demands are met fully or even partially, there may very well be an exodus of Europeans, especially of European farmers, and this will have serious consequences for the predominantly agricultural economy of Southern Rhodesia. As I discuss in this book, the European producers, with their skills and capital, have provided the leading edge of economic growth. If they leave, the burden of maintaining and expanding the economy will fall on the African producers, many of whom produce very little above subsistence levels, and the economy may well decline and stagnate as a result, unless there is a compensating and substantial increase in the productivity of African agriculture.

On the other hand, if the European minority defies the African demands, there will be other difficulties following from certain political turbulence. Even if the government of Southern Rhodesia is aided by the Republic of South Africa, it will have to rely more heavily on its own resources than it did when it was a member of the Federation. There will be need of a sustained effort on the part of the entire economy, especially the African sector, which embraces about half of the country's land resources and the bulk of its population.

No matter what happens, agriculture will have to yield a substantial surplus to replace the revenues lost through the breakup of the Federation. The government is going to have to provide certain services, without which there can be little hope of increased agricultural productivity, such as the spread of knowledge and the provision of cooperant factors of production. The government will have to adopt well-conceived economic policies in order to stimulate the incentive to increase output. In this respect the problems of raising productivity in the African sector are not dissimilar to those in many other parts of Southern, Central, and East Africa.

Some such steps are in progress it must be noted here. In Southern Rhodesia there have been modifications in the marketing system and there have been shifts in the policy on the allocations of land by race and on the provision of development services in East Africa, especially in Kenya and Tanganyika. On the larger scene it is gratifying to note that the International Bank for Reconstruction and Development has announced its intention to lend for development services as well as capital works. This should facilitate progress in agricultural development in much of Africa.

In my view there is an urgent need for closer cooperation between economists and other social scientists in dealing with the problems of raising agricultural productivity in traditionally oriented societies. Economists and cultural anthropologists, for example, have much to learn from one another. I attempt to point this out in the latter part of this book when I deal with the "concept of security." At the same time I borrow from the anthropologists when I suggest that a distinction be drawn between additive and substitutive actions in considering the most appropriate strategy for developing African agriculture.

Many of the recommendations in this book have been made already to the government of Southern Rhodesia. The field work on which this study is based was begun in 1956, and in 1959 and 1960 I collaborated with Dr. Sam Makings, the Economic Adviser to the Secretary for Native Affairs, in writing a long note on problems of African agricultural development. This note was mimeographed by the government and circulated among members of the Legislative Assembly and others interested in this topic. Much of the content of the note was later included in the "Second Report of the Select Committee on Resettlement of Natives," 16 August 1960, which recommended far-reaching changes in land policy in Southern Rhodesia.

These recommendations included the modification of some of the strictures on allocation of land by race. They were endorsed by the government of the day and became an element in the Southern Rhodesian elections of 1963, in which the principal issues were African advancement and the rate of change in current policies, including those that pertained to African and European rights to land. The electorate, predominantly European, rejected the government party and returned a party committed to maintaining the status quo to power. This result reinforced the resolution of the Africans in Northern Rhodesia and Nyasaland to dissolve the Federation of Rhodesia and Nyasaland. The Federation was already doomed — largely because the Africans in Northern Rhodesia and Nyasaland felt that it worked to their disadvantage and to the advantage of the Europeans in Southern Rhodesia. Had the then government party won the 1963 elections in Southern

Rhodesia, it is conceivable that the Africans in the two northern states might have looked more favorably on any proposals to maintain some form of looser political association with Southern Rhodesia. However, with the victory of the opposition party in Southern Rhodesia this prospect became wholly unacceptable.

In undertaking this study I have been helped by the Ford and Rockefeller Foundations. I am grateful to these organizations for their generous support. I am also grateful to the Center for International Affairs at Harvard University for providing me with facilities for writing this study. I would like to express a special word of thanks to Professor E. S. Mason for his critical advice. I also wish to thank Barbara Ward (Lady Jackson), Dr. Andrew Kamarch of the International Bank and Dr. E. O. Berg of Harvard University for their comments on my manuscript.

Many persons in Southern Rhodesia assisted me in my field work. They are too many to name in person, but I would like to acknowledge, with special thanks, the help given me by two economists, Dr. Sam Makings and Mr. Arthur Hunt, who kindly shared some of their research findings with me. I would also like to acknowledge the generous assistance of Mr. Philip Laundy, the librarian of the Legislative Assembly in Southern Rhodesia, and of Mr. Mervyn van Ryneveld, on the staff of the Legislative Assembly in Southern Rhodesia. In making these acknowledgments I should stress the point that the views expressed in this book do not necessarily coincide with their views — they are my own.

MONTAGUE YUDELMAN
Nicosia, Cyprus
5 November 1963

Contents

MAPS

These maps have been adapted by Samuel H. Bryant for the purposes of this book from material supplied by the Federal Director of Trigonometrical and Topographical Surveys (Salisbury) and by the Minister of Agriculture and Lands (Salisbury).

Part I: Introduction

Chapter 1

Africans, Europeans, and the Land

More than 80 percent of the Africans south of the Sahara depend on the land for the greater part of their livelihood. Land is relatively plentiful, but productivity is low: output per acre is far below the world average, and output per capita is only slightly greater than in the densely populated areas of Asia.[1] Noncommercial tribal traditions are strong, and much of the produce does not enter the exchange economy but is used for subsistence. As a result, at a time when economic aspirations are rising, little salable surplus is produced in African agriculture, that is, in agriculture carried on by *Africans* rather than by people of European stock or of some other ethnic background. Therefore, disposable incomes are extremely low. Clearly, if the rising aspirations of this region are to be satisfied, the rate of economic growth must be expanded, and this cannot be done unless the agricultural resources of the area are used to greater advantage than they are at present.

This book is devoted to examining the problem of raising the productivity of African agriculture and to discussing policies and programs that might foster this development. The principal geographic focus is on Southern Rhodesia, a self-governing British colony that, at the time of writing, is part of the Federation of Rhodesia and Nyasaland. Though many of the factors that influence African agricultural productivity in Southern Rhodesia are peculiar to that country, many of them are common to other countries in Southern, Central, and East Africa. Some of the characteristics of this larger area, particularly those that relate to Africans, Europeans, and the land, are examined in the first part of this book. Then the emergence of a dual economy in Southern Rhodesia is discussed, with emphasis on the political, social, and economic factors that have influenced the over-all use of resources in that country. A third section is devoted to the specific problems involved in raising African agricultural productivity in Southern Rhodesia. Finally there is a general discussion of policies and programs, and in Chapter 9 some of the findings that pertain to Southern Rhodesia are related to the wider area that encompasses the following contiguous countries and territories:

Southern Africa: The Republic of South Africa, the Protectorates of Basutoland, Bechuanaland, and Swaziland (Southwest Africa is not included).

Central Africa: The Federation of Rhodesia and Nyasaland, consisting of Southern Rhodesia, Northern Rhodesia, and Nyasaland.

East Africa: Kenya, Uganda, and Tanganyika.

These countries display a wide range of physical, social, and economic conditions. Together they are seven times the size of France and have a population of more than 47 million. Though there are many differences among them, they also have many common characteristics. The major differences pertain to resource endowment, population composition, and level of economic development; the major similarities relate to the backwardness of African agriculture and to the fact that all of these countries have a heritage of British colonial rule.

None of them is "developed" by the most widely used measure of economic development, that is, the level of average per capita income. The Republic of South Africa has the most highly developed economy with an average per capita income close to $400 per year. It is the only country in Southern, Central, or East Africa with a sizable industrial sector, accounting for 25 percent of the value of national output. In addition, South Africa is well endowed with mineral resources, producing 40 percent of the world's gold supply and a high proportion of its diamonds. The next most highly developed area is the Federation of Rhodesia and Nyasaland. Unlike South Africa, the Federation has no industry of any consequence other than a relatively small industrial complex in Southern Rhodesia. Copper from Northern Rhodesia and tobacco from Southern Rhodesia are the mainstays of the economy. Average per capita income in the Federation is estimated to be around $140 per year. The economy of East Africa is almost wholly dependent on agriculture: coffee, cotton, sisal, and livestock are the important commodities produced. Average per capita incomes are low; they average around $100 and are as low as $56 in Tanganyika.[2] No estimates exist for the national income of the protectorates in South Africa, but undoubtedly Basutoland and Bechuanaland are among the least developed and poorest areas in the region as a whole. Swaziland, with its growing mining industry and high agricultural potential, is probably wealthier than the other two protectorates.

All of these countries depend heavily on exports for their economic well-being. In 1956 the value of exports as a part of the total domestic product was estimated to be 31 percent for South Africa, 41.3 percent for the Federation of Rhodesia and Nyasaland, and 26 percent for East Africa.[3] On a per capita basis, the value was £35.8 for South Africa, £25.5 for the Federation, and £20.5 for East Africa. A narrow range of primary products dominates the exports: gold, diamonds, and wool from South Africa; copper and tobacco from the Federation; coffee, cotton, and sisal from East Africa.

Table 1. Estimated African and non-African population of Southern, Central, and East Africa, 1960

Country	Population (in thousands)				Percent of total		
	Total	African	European	Other	African	European	Other
Republic of South Africa	15,841	10,808	3,068	1,966	68.2	19.4	12.4
Basutoland	802	800	2	a	99.7	0.3	a
Bechuanaland	298	295	3	a	99.0	1.0	a
Swaziland	252	243	7	2	96.4	2.8	0.8
Southern Rhodesia	3,070[b]	2,830[b]	218	16	92.2	7.1	0.5
Northern Rhodesia	2,420	2,340	73	9	96.7	3.0	0.4
Nyasaland	2,830	2,810	8	12	99.3	0.3	0.4
Kenya	6,587	6,300	68	219	95.6	1.0	3.3
Uganda[c]	6,524	6,437	11	76	98.7	0.2	1.2
Tanganyika	9,232	9,123[d]	22	87	98.8	0.2	0.9
Total	47,856	41,986	3,480	2,387	87.7	7.3	5.0

Note: Because of rounding, population figures will not necessarily add horizontally to the exact total in the first column, and percentages will not necessarily add horizontally to 100.0.

a Negligible.

b For Southern Rhodesia the estimates of the African and total population must be viewed with special caution in the light of the 1962 census of African population, which produced a figure of 3,616,600 Africans (see our Table 3).

c Census of 1959.

d Includes a small number of Arabs.

Sources: For the Rhodesias and Nyasaland, *Monthly Digest of Statistics* (Salisbury: Central Statistical Office), December 1962. For Basutoland, Bechuanaland, and Swaziland, *Report of an Economic Survey Mission* to those three protectorates (London: H.M.S.O., 1960). For the other countries, *The Statesman's Year-book, 1961* (London: Macmillan, 1961), pp. 259, 332, 336, 341.

As Table 1 shows, nearly 90 percent of the population of this region is African. Moreover, in all but two of the countries the African percentage runs higher than 95 percent. The European population of the region, whose distribution has profound social and economic implications, is heavily concentrated in the Republic of South Africa, and to a lesser extent in Southern Rhodesia.

Despite the different levels of development and the rural character of society, occupations, and incomes throughout the area tend to be differentiated along racial lines. Generally, the non-Africans — Europeans, Asians, and the "colored" population, or persons of mixed parentage — form an economic elite and have much higher incomes than the Africans. In the Federation of Rhodesia and Nyasaland, the average personal income of Europeans is estimated to be more than twenty times greater than that of Africans, while in East Africa average European wages are twenty-five times greater than those of Africans.[4]

Europeans and non-Africans are entrepreneurs, large-scale farmers, plantation operators, bankers, traders, industrialists, administrators, and skilled technicians. The Republic of South Africa is the only country which has a substantial unskilled European proletariat, but European workers are protected from African competition by laws that reserve special categories of employment for Europeans. Generally, though, the Europeans and other non-Africans are the medium through which the elements of the market and of modern technology have been brought into the area. Most Africans, on the other hand, are either unskilled laborers or small-scale agricultural producers, though a small number are becoming skilled workers and traders and are entering the professions. There are probably less than 200 trained African doctors in the entire region, and an even smaller number of trained engineers.[5] An increasing number of Africans are assuming administrative posts in several of the countries. This is most notable in Tanganyika, but even there, after a year of independence, less than one third of the senior posts in the administration are held by Africans, the rest are filled by non-African officials.

Throughout the region as a whole a relatively small portion of the African population is in the wage economy.[6] In 1956, for example, only 25 percent of the Africans in the Republic of South Africa, 15 percent in the Federation of Rhodesia and Nyasaland,

and 7 percent in East Africa worked for wages. (The comparable figure for the population of the United Kingdom is 40 percent.) One of the salient characteristics of the labor system is the widespread prevalence of migratory labor. Many Africans, mostly males, remain uncommitted to wage employment but ebb and flow between their agricultural holdings and the wage economy, leaving their families to subsist on their holdings while they work for wages. The men move not only within the various countries but between the countries as well. In 1956 one fifth of those working for wages in the Republic of South Africa and one third of those in the Federation of Rhodesia and Nyasaland were migrants from outside the borders of these two countries. At the same time more than half the indigenous young adult males in Southern Rhodesia and the Republic of South Africa were absent from their rural homes but were not part of a stabilized wage-earning population. The migratory labor system, which, as is explained in later chapters, is an outgrowth of economic and political forces, has an important bearing on the problems of raising African agricultural productivity.

An overwhelming proportion of the Africans reside in rural areas and are associated with agricultural production. The proportion of rural dwellers is correlated with the level of economic development. Thus, more than 90 percent of the Africans of East Africa, more than 80 percent of those in the Federation of Rhodesia and Nyasaland, and more than 70 percent in Southern Africa are rural dwellers.[7] As a corollary, there are few urban agglomerates in this region. In all of Southern Africa, which is twice the size of France and has a population in excess of 14 million, only five cities have more than 500,000 inhabitants. The Federation of Rhodesia and Nyasaland, also twice the size of France, but with a population of close to 8 million, has no city with more than 310,000 inhabitants and only two with more than 200,000. East Africa, three times the size of France and with a population of 21 million, has only three cities with a population in excess of 130,000 and none with more than 250,000. Despite the overwhelming preponderance of the rural population, there is little pressure on the land except in limited areas of South Africa, Nyasaland, and Uganda. The over-all average population density is 2.5 persons per square mile, a man-land ratio twelve times more favorable than that of India and twice as favorable as that of the United States of America.[8]

The density of the rural population means little, however, without consideration of the physical resources of the area, which are in no way equal to that of the great agricultural-producing areas in the temperate zones of the United States or Canada, or in the tropical rice-producing areas in Southeast Asia. With the exception of the Republic of South Africa and the protectorates in Southern Africa, all of the countries under review are in the tropics. Although there are pockets of fertile land, much of the area is arid, swampy, mountainous, and often beset by disease. One estimate has classified approximately one quarter of the land in Southern Africa, one half in Central Africa, and two thirds of that in East Africa as land which is not usable for any form of agricultural production.[9] Furthermore, in many areas where land is usable, the soils are poor — deficient in calcium and phosphorus. Rainfall throughout the area is generally irregular.[10] Many of the deficiencies in natural resources can be offset only by investments in irrigation, disease control, drainage, and soil improvement, and as yet, little has been done in this direction.

Even though the resource endowment is not as favorable as in some parts of the world, there is still considerable scope in many parts of the region for increasing agricultural output through an expansion of cultivated acreage. In this respect these countries differ greatly from the heavily populated areas of Bengal or Holland — lack of land is not necessarily a limiting factor in expanding production. Rather, in many areas, lack of knowledge, poor techniques of production, limited markets, and tribal traditions are among the more important factors restricting output.

Most of the output of African producers does not reach the market but is consumed directly. The crops grown by Africans are largely food crops that can either be sold or consumed directly. The major exceptions are cotton and coffee in East Africa, tobacco in Central Africa, and many minor specialty crops. Livestock, mostly cattle and goats, is produced widely, and can also be consumed directly, though cattle are still widely viewed as symbols of prestige. All figures on production must be treated with caution, but it is estimated that 95 percent of the crops and 60 percent of the livestock produced by Africans in the Republic of South Africa does not enter the market.[11] There are no estimates for the three protectorates in Southern Africa, but one report characterizes the African producers in this area as basically subsistence producers.[12] More than 85 percent of the value of African produce in the Federation of Rhodesia and Nyasaland is for subsistence, and in East Africa at least 80 percent does not enter the exchange economy.[13]

With so large a share of the total output being used to maintain the farm population, there is little surplus for the market. Consequently, cash incomes earned from African agriculture are low — probably less than $10 per person per year in Tanganyika, a little more than $10 per person in the Republic of South Africa and Southern Rhodesia, and around $15 per person in Northern Rhodesia. In Uganda, where there is the most widespread peasant production for market, cash income from agriculture is around $30 per capita.[14]

Output for subsistence and low levels of income are characteristic of all African agriculture in the region. Much of African agriculture is not integrated into the market economy and contributes little to national money income and little to economic growth aside from the sustenance of the rural population. The resources that are now locked into a subsistence economy must be used more productively if they are to provide the surplus and savings needed to finance growing demands for higher expenditures on social overhead — more schools, more hospitals, and better roads. One of the essential preconditions for the more productive use of resources is to expand the exchange economy and thereby commercialize or "monetize" African agriculture. It is only through a spread of the exchange economy and the extension of concepts of cost-price rationalization that there will be increased output for market, specialization of production, and division of labor, and so a more productive use of resources. However, these concepts are still alien to many African producers; much of this area was only exposed to the exchange economy in the second half of the nineteenth century, and many facets of the pre-money economy have persisted to the present time.

AFRICANS AND THE LAND

As a population group, the Africans in Southern, Central, and East Africa are now denoted as the Bantu. With the exception of a few tribes, notably those in Northern Kenya and Eastern Tanganyika who are Nilo-Hamitic, the people of this linguistic grouping inhabit most of Africa south of the Sudan.

The most important units in the traditional social fabric of the Bantu were, and still are, the tribe and the extended family or kin group. The kin system is based on either the paternal or maternal line, and the kin group is a body of males tracing their descent from a common ancestor for several generations in either line. In Southern Africa it is usually through the male line, while in the northern areas it is frequently through the female line. Many of the relationships within kin groups and between kin groups are closely knit, and almost all of the actions of the group are dictated by the requirements of the community. Individualism and enterprise are not necessarily in keeping with these requirements.

Most of the obligations incurred in tribal society are social rather than the type of obligation incurred in an exchange economy. These tribal obligations include offers of gifts and labor among kin and friends, both as a matter of course and during ceremonial occasions. Transactions between members of a kin group do not involve "payment" for services, and exchanges need not be related to the "value" of the gift given or received. Opportunities and power within the group depend on status, and status does not depend on control over material wealth but rather on the claims that are held against persons.[15]

The tribe's development can be traced back through a central group of families to a common ancestor or ancestors who assimilated other groups or tribes. The central group provides the traditional councillors of the tribe in accordance with inherited status. The unifying factor in the tribe is usually the chief who is considered to have some mystical association with his ancestors and with the land.

The first Europeans to encounter Africans found their level of material achievement to be low, though there were some exceptions. An example of one view of the backwardness of the Africans of East Africa is that given by Sir Phillip Mitchell, a former governor of Kenya. He described the Africans in East and Central Africa at the turn of the present century, when the first Europeans moved into the area, as follows:

> Inland of the narrow coastal strip they had no units of government of any size or stability; indeed, with a few exceptions such as Buganda, nothing beyond local chiefs or patriarchs. They had no wheeled transport and, apart from the camels and donkeys of the pastoral nomads, no animal transport either; they had no roads nor towns; no tools except small hand hoes, axes, wooden digging sticks, and the like; no manufactures and no commerce as we understand it, and no currency, although in some places barter of produce was facilitated by the use of small shells; they had never heard of working for wages. They went stark naked or clad in the bark of trees or the skins of animals, and they had no means of writing, even by hieroglyphics, notches on a stick or knots in a piece of grass or fibre; they had no weights and measures of general use . . . They were pagan spirit or ancestor proprietors, in the grip of magic or witchcraft, their minds cribbed and confined by superstition.[16]

The early tribal economy was a simple and noncommercial one based almost entirely on subsistence production and a plentiful supply of land. This applied to both pastoral and agricultural producers and was most pronounced in areas of uncertain and sparse rainfall. The pastoralists who required land for extensive grazing, moved their livestock as the occasion demanded, that is, whenever their land was overgrazed or their water supplies diminished. The agriculturalists — and in the southern regions of Africa many of these were also cattle owners — required extensive supplies of land to practice shifting cultivation and bush fallow.

Generally, this system of agriculture involved a form of land rotation that is still widely practiced. Land was used as long as it was fertile, possibly up to three or four years; then, when the fertility of the land was diminished, it was left to revert to bush until fertility was restored. The producers in the interim moved to another patch of land. On some occasions and in some areas as long as twenty years would elapse from the initial abandonment of land to its regeneration. Frequently, too, entire African villages would move as the need arose for new land.

The system of shifting cultivation whereby tribes moved from area to area had important effects on the organization of government. It has been suggested that the Ganda of Buganda were able to develop the complex forms of government that surprised the early Europeans because they were able to practice sedentary agriculture, and so did not have to shift around. They were able to have a fixed locus because of the fertility of their soils, the reliability of the rainfall, and the ability to grow plantains without depleting the soil.

In some of the high forest areas, such as those found in Northern Rhodesia, the ash of burned branches was (and still is) used to prepare the soil for planting. This form of cultivation known as *chitemene* involves cutting branches off of trees, piling them on the ground, and burning them for ash. The chemical ingredients in the ash improve the productivity of the soil, though the benefits are not long-lasting. As soon as the benefits wear off, the cultivator moves to another area and repeats the procedure. This process has undoubtedly led to the diminution of the woodlands of Africa, for burned areas have proved to be the most suitable for growing the small grains that are the staple food in many parts of Southern and Central Africa. In the absence of changed systems of production, it is likely that this custom will continue to be widely practiced.[17]

The agricultural implements used by the early Africans were the digging stick, the hoe, and the axe; today these are supplemented in some areas by the plow, harrow, and by the planter, but seldom by the tractor. In 1961 there were fewer than ten privately owned tractors in Uganda, where African peasants are relatively wealthy.[18] The methods of cultivation used at the time Europeans moved into the area were remote from those evolved by Jethro Tull, the father of the European agricultural revolution. Because there was no need for intensive land use, low-yielding extensive means of production were employed. Techniques were primitive: manure was not used, nor was there any selection of seeds. There was no straight-line planting, nor much of the simplest form of crop rotation; fertility was maintained by rotating the land. The major crops produced were maize, small grains, groundnuts, beans, peas (in northern areas), cassava, and yams. In addition, Africans lived off game insects and wild fruits.[19]

There was some division of labor based on sex: men usually tended cattle and did the heavier work that might be construed as capital formation, bush clearance and building huts, for example. Women performed the day-to-day work of agricultural production and the preparation of food: hoeing, weeding, threshing, and making beer. Often, though, work was carried out communally with mutual-help parties exchanging their labor for a later call on the labor of their kinfolk. Frequently, the limits of cultivation were — and still are — imposed by the sheer limit of physical endurance.

The prevailing system of shifting cultivation made both agronomic and economic sense. Agronomically, it was a concession to the nature of the soil. As has been pointed out, the soil is poor in many parts of this region of Africa, particularly in the arid and semiarid regions of East Africa. The tropical soils of Africa do not appear to be well suited for intensive cultivation. At one time most European scientists believed that the system of shifting cultivation was destructive and seriously depleted the soil; they suggested that it should be replaced by continuous cropping. It now appears to be appreciated that, in fact, under the system of shifting cultivation, a relatively sparse population was in ecological balance with its environment. The problem today is that the environment has changed. Population has increased, and, in some instances, European occupation has limited the land supply available for shifting cultivation by African producers. Nevertheless, many of the traditional methods of production have persisted, taking a very heavy toll of the soil.

Economically, within the limit of his horizons, the African producer was rational in his production methods. Land was plentiful, labor was relatively scarce, and capital virtually nonexistent. The plentiful and free land supply was substituted for any intensive labor effort that might have required extra energy-inputs (which undoubtedly had a cost). Thus land was used extensively to produce a limited output. And since this was a noncapitalistic society where there was no "waiting and wanting," everything was produced for consumption within the span of the season before the new crops were reaped. There was no diversion of effort for "round-about" production, no irrigation, and no capital formation other than some land clearance, and the building of primitive storage facilities to satisfy short-term needs. Economically it was a backward society for the range of choice was very limited, both for producers and consumers. There was no surplus so that producers had no choice other than to produce to live or else to take

from others what they had produced; consumers had no option
but to consume what they themselves produced.

Though some of the institutions governing individual land use
and land tenure in the region occupied by Africans have been
modified by external forces, many of these institutions are still
governed by ancient custom rather than by European-introduced
concepts of rights to land. Customary rights to land vary considerably in detail, but three cardinal principles appear in all African
tribal societies:

(a) There shall be no private ownership of land. The land occupied by a tribal community shall belong to that community and
cannot be alienated without its consent.

(b) Every individual shall have security of tenure.

(c) No member of the community shall be without land.[20]

Under customary tenure, land is allocated to tribal members
according to an individual's need. The allocation is made through
a system of interpersonal relations. There is no market for land
and no impersonal method of fixing its value (though in some
areas where high-value cash crops are grown, land improvements
are negotiable). Grazing land is communal.

The variations in customary tenure are of interest in themselves,
but here we are concerned with the effect of the persistence of customary tenure on the commercialization of African agriculture,
the expansion of the market, and the division of labor. One aspect
of these problems is discussed in a government report on the economic development of Nyasaland.[21] The report points out that
under the prevailing traditions in Nyasaland there is no land ownership. There is only the right to cultivate. This right, which is
inheritable, passes through the female line. Often the result is the
fragmentation of land holdings among several women. The report
goes on to say that the male cultivator has little interest in the
future of the land; as he has no control, he has no incentive to
improve the land. Furthermore, even if he did improve the land,
the enterprising cultivator could not realize a capitalized value
from his improvement because the land is not salable. In the
view of the authors of this report, there is no incentive to increase
investment in land; land is not a negotiable asset so that producers
cannot derive any capital gains from their investments in improve-

ments. This, in turn, prevents the best use of resources and the raising of productivity in African agriculture.

The importance of modifying and changing prevailing tenurial systems was also stressed in the report of the *East Africa Royal Commission, 1953–1955*. The commission's view was that the system of customary tenure restricted enterprise, and that the introduction of a market for land would permit a more rational use of resources and an expansion of specialized production:

> Individual tenure [as opposed to communal tenure] has great advantages in giving to the individual a sense of security in possession, and in enabling, by purchase and sale of land, an adjustment to be made by the community from the present unsatisfactory fragmented usage to units of an economic agricultural size. The ability of individuals to buy and sell land by a process of territorial law, instead of a process of custom, opens the door to that mobility and private initiative on which a great sector of economic progress tends to depend . . . The specialist farmer is relieved of the liability of providing a place for the subsistence of his clan relations. Moreover individual tenure should lead to the release and encouragement of new genius and to new experiment in finding the most productive use of land.[22]

Social customs and the absence of an impersonal market for land are important factors in inhibiting the commercialization of African agriculture. In Northern Uganda, for example, land is plentiful, but progressive producers cannot expand their holdings, employ labor, and possibly mechanize production because such actions would be contrary to customary obligations.

One customary obligation is that there be mutual help in providing labor. Occupiers of land rotate their labor among kinsmen to help with harvesting and other work. The ambitious producer who might wish to break out of this pattern of joint production, to expand his holding, hire labor, mechanize, and concentrate on expanding his own production would incur the displeasure of his kinsmen. In a situation where land is distributed on an interpersonal basis rather than by any impersonal market mechanism, the disturbance of customs is considered to be antisocial. Thus it is very difficult for "progressive" producers to secure permission from tribal authorities to take up extra land, even though a considerable amount of unused land is available in the area. The absence of a land market thus retards one of the first shifts in the direction of commercialization of production — the division of labor.

The customary tenure systems have undoubtedly been adequate to meet the needs of a society that was not concerned with expansion of production but rather with providing security at a low level of equilibrium. However, there can be no gainsaying the importance of reorganizing tenure arrangements and establishing a land market as part of the process of commercializing African agriculture. As is pointed out in Part III of this book, there are many human and other costs involved in any program of change of this kind. In this regard the experiments in Southern Rhodesia and in parts of Kenya are of special interest, for they are aimed at converting large areas of communally held land into individually held tracts and changing customary rights in the land to negotiable rights. The fact that there is such a program in Southern Rhodesia — a move away from the customary distribution according to need toward distribution according to ability to pay — is one of the reasons why Southern Rhodesia has been selected for special study.

Land and land rights are of special importance because the fabric of African society is so closely linked to the land by custom. Yet land is only one of the factors of production and its significance in tribal society should not be allowed to override the importance of other factors. A major characteristic of African agriculture at present is the low level of technical competence of most producers. In many areas the methods of production used are similar to those of the premoney economy. There have been changes but these lag far behind what could be accomplished if levels of managerial ability were to be raised. Indeed, as is stressed in later parts of this book, the major problem in raising productivity in African agriculture is that of improving the technical competence of the producers.

There is also a great shortage of capital in African agriculture. In the past the major investments in much of Southern, Central, and East Africa have been made to facilitate European production, and levels of investment in African agriculture have been low. In addition, there has been little private capital formation other than through "direct" application of labor to improve land. African agriculture needs an infusion of operating capital, particularly as small increments of this type of capital can yield large returns. Up to the present, however, there have been few effective programs for providing credit or subsidies to African producers.

In general, there is a great deal of underemployment in African agriculture. In some areas land and labor are underutilized because of the immobility of labor and a shortage of capital. In other areas producers have the factors to increase output but not the incentive to expand production beyond their immediate requirements. The lack of incentive may be due to purely economic considerations (marginal cost of added input exceeding marginal revenue) or to sociological or cultural factors (traditional preference for noneconomic activities over higher income). Throughout the area economic and pecuniary considerations are assuming increasing importance in decision-making about increasing inputs, but cultural or sociological factors still have a strong influence on resource use — particularly on labor inputs. This may be a transitional phenomenon, but it is one that no consideration of present problems in the use of African agricultural resources can ignore.

EUROPEANS AND THE LAND

The advent of European settlement in much of this region disturbed the equilibrium between the Africans and the land. In this respect the colonization of parts of this region was dissimilar to the colonization of West Africa, where the Europeans were interested in trade and were content to leave the production of tropical products in the hands of indigenous producers. Any desire to take up land and settle was dampened by the threat of tropical disease and by the subsequent policies of the British government in protecting African rights to land.[23]

The Europeans who colonized Southern Africa were interested in land, not trade. The first of these frontiersmen or trekkers left the Cape of Good Hope in the early half of the nineteenth century to escape British dominion and to seek new lands in the uncharted hinterland.[24] They were cattle grazers and farmers, not traders, and their primary interest was in acquiring land in the temperate areas of Southern Africa. In some respects their quest for land was not unlike that of the Western frontiersmen of the United States of America. There was, however, one fundamental difference between the South African and American movements. Unlike the American pioneer of the Far West, the South African frontiersman encountered a numerically superior indigenous population that was seeking land for itself.

Conflict was inevitable, and the arbitration of land rights was settled by the force of arms. The movement of European settlers subsequently extended to Bechuanaland and Swaziland. By 1890 they were established in Southern Rhodesia. Later there was limited settlement in what is now Northern Rhodesia, Nyasaland, Kenya, Uganda, and Tanganyika. These settlements, many of which were small, were not part of a general northward extension of settlers from South Africa and Southern Rhodesia. They came about, rather, as a consequence of the extension of British sovereignty over these areas in order to destroy slave trade, promote missionary activity, search for minerals, and, in the instance of Tanganyika, to defeat Germany in World War I.[25]

In the process of settlement, the Europeans established an unusual pattern of relations between agricultural producers and the land. The relations among Europeans, Africans, and the land were so arranged that they operated at two levels. At one level were the legal and other institutions introduced by the Europeans to implement a public policy of apportioning land between Africans and non-Africans. Many of these institutions still persist so that in large areas there is an over-all allocative framework that demarcates rights to land as "European" and as "African." At the other level, within the over-all framework of land apportionment, much of the land allocated for African use is still governed by the customary systems of tenure and traditional rights to land that are part of the premoney economy. Rights to European land, on the other hand, are based on property rights similar to those found in Europe.

The amount of land allocated for European occupation in each country is shown in Table 2. The wide range in the proportions of land held by Europeans results from the interaction of climatic, political, and economic factors.[26] The three countries where Europeans hold the most land — the Republic of South Africa, Southern Rhodesia, and Swaziland — all have agreeable climates. They are temperate and subtropical and are comparable to the areas of the New World that have attracted so many European immigrants in the twentieth century. Favorable climatic conditions are

*Table 2. European land and European population in
Southern, Central, and East Africa*

Country	Percentage of land alienated or reserved for Europeans (1958)[a]	European percentage of population (1960)[b]
Republic of South Africa	89.0[c]	19.4
Basutoland	0.0	0.3
Bechuanaland	6.0	1.0
Swaziland	49.0	2.8
Southern Rhodesia	49.0	7.1
Northern Rhodesia	3.0	3.0
Nyasaland	5.0	0.3
Kenya	7.0	1.0
Uganda	[d]	0.2
Tanganyika	0.9	0.2

[a] 1958 estimates derived from a number of government reports. See also map facing p. 686 in Lord Hailey, *An African Survey*, revised 1956 (London: Oxford University Press, 1957). Between 1958 and 1960 some of the proportions changed, but not significantly.
[b] From our Table 1.
[c] Includes a very small portion of land set aside for Indians and persons of mixed parentage.
[d] Less than 0.5 percent.

conducive to European settlement and colonists have established themselves permanently in these countries. As permanent inhabitants, they do not regard all the land as an African heritage but rather as an important element in a sociopolitical framework designed to protect European levels of living.

In 1910 and 1923 respectively, South Africa and Southern Rhodesia assumed control over their internal affairs. The governments in these two countries were able to introduce policies more in keeping with their own philosophies than were those of the earlier colonial administration in London. These "national" philosophies were essentially European, for the policy-making bodies in the two countries were chosen by an electorate composed almost entirely of Europeans. Such governments were concerned, naturally enough, with preserving European standards. This was to be accomplished by dividing the countries into noncompeting racial groups with a dual standard for each major group. Europeans were to retain political control through a restricted franchise and European standards were to be preserved by preventing interracial competition that might lower European levels of consumption and raise African levels of consumption at the expense of the Europeans.[27]

Land policy was an important element in implementing this general philosophy of noncompeting groups and in maintaining European standards. In the course of settlement large areas had been proclaimed as African areas for the sole use of African tribes. If Africans so wished, they could, however, farm or purchase land in much of the rest of these countries. After independence, however, South Africa and Southern Rhodesia were divided into ethnic areas that were to be European or African; there was to be no right of indiscriminate, interracial sale or purchase of land.[28] The amount of land apportioned to each group was based on a dual standard of need, premised on the vastly superior needs of "civilized" Europeans compared with "primitive" Africans. The allocation of land for African use was also influenced by the need to ensure an adequate supply of African labor for the mines, industries, and farms in the European areas.[29]

The dual standards applied at the time when these two countries became independent have since been modified but they still reflect the idea that European standards must be protected and that European needs are much greater than those of Africans. In the Republic of South Africa the European 20 percent of the population can take up land in close to 89 percent of the country, and conversely, the African 66 percent of the population can farm in only 11 percent of the land. A high proportion of the African area is well-watered, fertile country, but one outcome of this policy is that some of these areas are among the most densely populated rural areas in sub-Saharan Africa; e.g., the Transkei, the largest of the African areas, has a population density of close to 20 acres per family. The African areas on a whole have a population density one hundred times greater than the average for Southern, Central, and East Africa as a whole.[30] The pressure of population on land resources has contributed a great deal to forcing Africans to enter employment in the wage economy and become migrant laborers. In Southern Rhodesia, at the time of writing, the land is almost equally divided between the Europeans and Africans, even though only 8 percent of the population is European. However, in Southern Rhodesia, there is approximately 100 acres of land per African family, although the quality of much of the land is poor.

The three protectorates in Southern Africa, Basutoland, Bechuanaland, and Swaziland, have climates suitable for European settlement. However, much of Bechuanaland is arid, which limits the opportunities for settlement. The British government has followed a policy of prohibiting any European settlement in the small mountainous country of Basutoland. Swaziland is well watered and parts of it are fertile; the small number of European settlers in these areas holds close to half the land in the country. And these holdings stem from large concessions obtained from local chiefs around the turn of the century. The pattern of land allocation is similar to that in South Africa and Southern Rhodesia in that there are large blocs of European and African land, but unlike these countries, interracial sales of land are not prohibited. There is no need to raise European standards at the expense of the Africans, as land is still plentiful in Swaziland.

The amount of land alienated (i.e., already sold to Europeans) or reserved for European use in Northern Rhodesia, Nyasaland, and East Africa is relatively limited. In general, the climate and resources of these countries are not conducive to permanent European settlement. Even if large areas had been reserved for European occupation it is unlikely that large numbers of settlers would have been attracted to them. Apart from health hazards, few would-be immigrants have the capital or skills needed for tropical agriculture. In addition, unskilled immigrants from Europe were deterred by the prospect of competing with low-paid African labor. To those Europeans who sought a haven or a home in a new country in the first half of the twentieth century, the opportunities in the temperate areas of the United States, Canada, or Australia, or even South Africa and Southern Rhodesia, must have been far more appealing than the uncertainties of taking up land in tropical Africa.

There were exceptions, however. The healthy and fertile highlands of Kenya were reserved for European use, and immigrants and pioneers settled in the "White Highlands." The initial purpose of reserving the highlands for European occupation was to exclude the Indians rather than the Africans.[31] Europeans also took up land in healthy parts of Northern Rhodesia and Nyasaland and forms of *de facto* segregation of land holdings came into effect. But generally it was colonial policy — and all these territories were colonies or protectorates — to treat most of the land in these countries as part of an African patrimony. An attempt was made to balance the need to encourage European enterprise with that of reserving land traditionally held by Africans for use by Africans. European enterprise was deemed necessary to develop export crops to provide revenues toward local costs of administration and to provide raw materials for the metropole. European individuals, companies, and syndicates were encouraged to take up land under concessions or grants from African chiefs. Frequently, these rights to land were secured through the direct intervention of colonial authorities and frequently, too, they led to the displacement of Africans. Except in the "White Highlands" of Kenya, however, European settlement is not widespread, though holdings are large and most of them are in fertile, well-watered areas. The areas that are considered to be European in Northern Rhodesia, for example, are relatively small but include most of the 16 percent of the total area that is free from the tsetse fly. The Europeans in Tanganyika occupy some of the most fertile and well-watered land, as do the tea estates in Nyasaland. Similarly, the European-held land in Bechuanaland and Swaziland is in the best farming areas. But in these countries, unlike South Africa and Southern Rhodesia, European farms and plantations are enclaves of commercial production in what are otherwise vast areas of production devoted mainly to subsistence.

The significance of European-controlled enterprises varies considerably from country to country, but except in Uganda, the Europeans, whether few or many, are the mainstay of the market economy. In South Africa and Southern Rhodesia they provide not only for the export market but also for the internal market. Almost all of the export crops of South Africa are produced on European farms, while the entire tobacco crop and much of the corn exported from Rhodesia are produced by Europeans. Non-African farms in Northern Rhodesia are major corn exporters and produce dairy products for the mining areas; all the tea from Nyasaland, the country's major export, and almost all the sisal from Tanganyika are produced on non-African estates. Almost all the major export crops now produced in East Africa are not indigenous to that area but were introduced by Europeans. In Southern Rhodesia the 6,000 European production units marketed £41 million worth of agricultural products compared with £4.1 million marketed by the more than 300,000 African producers; in Northern Rhodesia the less than 2,000 European producers marketed £4.5 million while 400,000 Africans marketed less than £1 million. In Nyasaland the few European farms and estates marketed slightly more than the large number of African holdings. European production in the Federation as a whole accounted for more than 80 percent of the value of all sales in 1958.[32] In Kenya, 90 percent of all marketed output and 76 percent of all exports are produced on the 7 percent of the land held by the small European farming community,[33] while in Tanganyika 45 percent of the value of all exports comes off the 2 percent of the land held by non-Africans.[34] In Uganda, however, where peasant production for export is widespread, only 10 percent of the value of exports comes from the 1 percent of the land held by non-Africans.[35]

At present, in the early 1960's, the over-all pattern of land holding is one where Europeans occupy land — frequently the most fertile land — under the same conditions as they might hold land in Europe. Land is owned outright or held under long-term leaseholds. Land and rights to land are negotiable and are traded among Europeans and in some instances among all non-Africans, but seldom between non-Africans and Africans. This is either because of restrictions that prohibit interracial sales or else because of the maintenance of *de facto* segregation. Except in Uganda, and in one or two limited areas elsewhere, Africans do not own land outright and there is no market for land. The Uganda agreement of 1890 recognized the rights of an established monarch, and this recognition was confirmed by allocating title of the vacant land to members of the ruling hierarchy.[36] Generally, African-held land is still held under the customary tenure that precludes the concept of land as a negotiable factor of production.

THE CASE OF SOUTHERN RHODESIA

No two countries in the area under review have identical problems of agricultural development. Southern Rhodesia has been selected as an area for intensive study, not only because of interest in the problems of development in Rhodesia itself, but also because many of its problems encompass those found in different parts of Southern, Central, and East Africa.

Southern Rhodesia is similar to the Republic of South Africa in that a relatively large amount of land has been apportioned for the European population. The Europeans in Rhodesia consider their roots to be in that country; they do not view themselves as expatriates nor do they consider all land in Southern Rhodesia to be part of an African heritage. In this respect Southern Rhodesia provides an example of the interaction of politics, economics, and land apportionment which, up until recently, was not too dissimilar from that in South Africa.

The chief European industry in Southern Rhodesia is agriculture and the contributions of the Europeans to the economy of Southern Rhodesia are not dissimilar to that of non-Africans in other parts of Central and East Africa. They are the major employers of African labor, they are almost the only producers who make substantial investments in agriculture, and they provide valuable tax revenues. In some respects their operations represent enclaves of commercial production in areas where the greater part of the agricultural resources is used for subsistence. However, in Southern Rhodesia this area of modern production is relatively large and so provides an opportunity to examine the structure of a well-defined dual economy. The different rates of growth for European and African agriculture can be examined and the reasons for the differences identified.

Southern Rhodesia is similar to many other countries in the region in that the migratory labor system is an important factor in the total economy of the country. However, since the movements of indigenous males are almost wholly confined to movements within the country there is a close relation between the expansion of the Southern Rhodesian economy as a whole and the opportunities for migrants to find wage employment. In this, the example of Southern Rhodesia provides an opportunity to examine the link between Africans on the land and migratory labor and the possible consequences of changing the existing system of migratory labor — a matter of interest throughout the region.

Although the land apportionment system in Southern Rhodesia discriminates against Africans (as in South Africa), there is no absolute shortage of land for Africans. The situation is somewhat similar to that in East Africa and other parts of Central Africa, and raises many of the same questions of development policy.

What is the most appropriate role of land, labor, and capital in increasing output? What types of investment policy would be most effective in these circumstances? Should the emphasis be on raising productivity per man or per acre? Should there be more investment in infrastructure or greater expenditure on expanding services?

In addition, the problems of the development of African agriculture in Southern Rhodesia incorporate many of the problems of raising productivity among a people who are still strongly influenced by the customs and traditions that preceded the introduction of the exchange economy. There is still a widespread distrust of the marketing system and a high preference for noneconomic activity over higher income. In this respect, many of the problems of expanding production for the market and encouraging some cost-price rationalization are similar to those elsewhere in the region even though some tribal customs and traditions might be at variance with those elsewhere. Consequently, a study of the problems in Southern Rhodesia can indicate general guidelines of development for many other parts of Southern, Central, and East Africa.

Besides providing an opportunity to study these general problems, the case of Southern Rhodesia is of special interest because the government has recently embarked on an ambitious program for changing the relation between the Africans and the land. This program envisages a break with custom and tradition and the conversion of inalienable rights to land into negotiable assets. In this, Southern Rhodesia is atypical, but it makes the country all the more worthy of study, for the program highlights many of the institutional problems of development that are to be found in all of Southern, Central, and East Africa.

Part II: The Dual Economy of Southern Rhodesia

Chapter 2

The Economic and Social Background

Southern Rhodesia is an entirely landlocked country; at its closest point to the sea it is some 200 miles from the Indian Ocean. The country lies entirely within the tropics between the latitudes of 15°34'S and 22°25'S; it is 150,000 square miles in area, three times the size of England or approximately the same size as California. It is bounded on the north by the Zambezi River which divides the country from Northern Rhodesia and on the south by the Limpopo River which marks the border with the Republic of South Africa. Bechuanaland lies to the west and Portuguese East Africa to the east.[1]

The country is a relatively high region surrounded by lower land on all sides. The main elevation is the central plateau, known as the High Veld, which traverses Southern Rhodesia from southwest to northeast and joins the relatively narrow strip of mountainous country that runs north and south along the border with Portuguese East Africa. About one fifth of the country is high veld, 4,000 feet above sea level, sloping down to a considerable area which is between 3,000 and 4,000 feet above sea level. Altogether between one half and two thirds of the country is higher than 3,000 feet above sea level.

There are two major low-lying areas: the large, hot, dry southern plain which comprises about one third of the country and tapers to the Limpopo River on the southern border and the small, hot, malarial area of the Zambezi Valley in the north.

The soils of Southern Rhodesia are predominantly sandy, with scattered, relatively small areas of loamy and clayey soils. The sandy soils cover about 70 percent of the country and on them is grown Rhodesia's major export crop, Virginia flue-cured tobacco. Their inherent fertility is low, but high productivity can be maintained by good soil management and by heavy investments in chemical fertilizers. At present only the Europeans have the managerial ability and the capital to convert these infertile sandy tracts into lands yielding a rich tobacco harvest; consequently, no Africans grow this type of tobacco in Southern Rhodesia.

The Rhodesian climate is dominated by rain — or lack of it. A warm rainy season from October to March is followed by a dry season during which there is a wide range of temperature. Although the mean average rainfall is 28 inches, only a small percentage of the total falls in the months from April to October. The rains are erratic and inconsistent both in their onset and in the amounts that fall during the "rainy season." This has serious consequences for agricultural production.

The distribution of the erratic, seasonal rainfall is also uneven, generally being higher in the eastern part of the country and declining in the western and southern regions. The wettest areas receive an average of more than 40 inches of rain annually; the driest, less than 12 inches. The following figures[2] show what percentage of Southern Rhodesia's total area receives an average annual rainfall of less than 16 inches, what percentage receives 16 to 20 inches, and so on:

Less than 16 inches . . .	5.1%
16–20	8.3
20–24	17.6
24–28	31.6
28–32	19.8
32–36	12.5
36–40	3.0
40 or more	2.1

It can be seen that about 40 percent of the country has more than 28 inches of rain, which is considered to be the minimum annual rainfall required for most of the staple grains grown in Southern Rhodesia.

In the high areas along the eastern border, mean annual temperatures are below 60° F. The hottest parts of Southern Rhodesia are in the Zambezi Valley, where mean temperatures are around 80° F. and in the Limpopo Valley, where mean temperatures are 72.5° F. In general, temperature varies with altitude, and the High Veld, the area with the heaviest concentrations of Europeans, has a very salubrious climate with a mean annual temperature in the middle sixties. In the colder months of June and July temperatures drop considerably and frosts are not unusual.

The main drainage system of the country is formed by the Zambezi, Limpopo, and Sabi rivers. The smaller river courses are without water from April to October, but in the heavy rainy season they become roaring torrents. The Zambezi, which plunges over the Victoria Falls, and the Limpopo on the southern boundary are of little agricultural or navigational importance. The massive Kariba Dam built on the Zambezi is primarily for the generation of hydroelectric power. The Sabi River is the biggest river within Southern Rhodesia, flowing from the mountains of the eastern region to the Indian Ocean fairly close to the eastern border. The Sabi and some of its tributaries are used to irrigate an estimated 46,000 acres of land. A new irrigation program, now under way, will bring an additional 30,000 acres under cultivation, primarily for production of sugar and citrus.

The vegetation of Southern Rhodesia is tropical savannah and can be classified into four major formations governed by climatic factors.[3] These formations are forest, grassland, woodland, and bushland. The forest formations are not significant. Grasslands occur on the central plateau in isolated, though often extensive, areas with open, rolling topography. Woodland vegetation occupies the major portion of Southern Rhodesia and consists of many types, characterized by trees spaced closely or widely apart and by medium and tall perennial grasses in the drier areas. As rainfall decreases and temperature increases, woodland gives way to bushland, which is made up of closely spaced shrubs and small trees, with taller trees scattered throughout and a generally sparse cover of annual grasses. The prevalence of shrubs, often forming areas of impenetrable thicket, is the most important feature of this formation. This widespread woodland and bushland must be cleared wherever agricultural cultivation is to be extended. Most Africans have used family labor for land clearance, so that there has been a considerable amount of "nonmoney" capital formation in the process of extending production.

At one time almost half of Southern Rhodesia was afflicted by human and animal tryponosomiasis, or sleeping sickness, but an intensive campaign against the tsetse fly, which transmits the

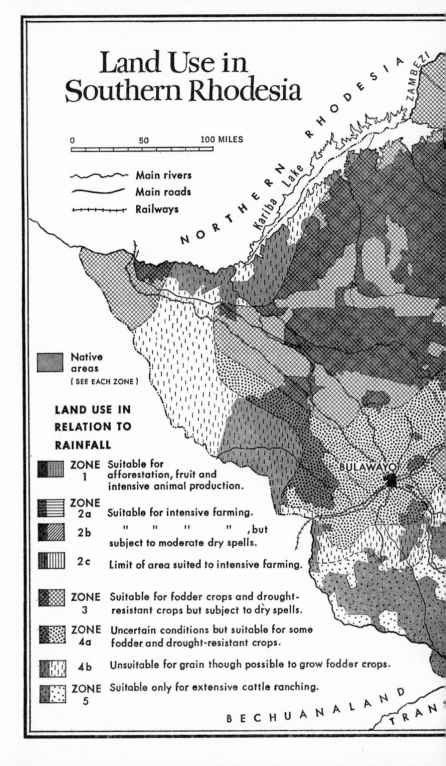

Land Use in Southern Rhodesia

0   50   100 MILES

~~ Main rivers
— Main roads
+++++ Railways

NORTHERN RHODESIA

ZAMBEZI

Kariba Lake

Native areas
(SEE EACH ZONE)

LAND USE IN RELATION TO RAINFALL

ZONE 1 Suitable for afforestation, fruit and intensive animal production.

ZONE 2a Suitable for intensive farming.

2b " " " " , but subject to moderate dry spells.

2c Limit of area suited to intensive farming.

ZONE 3 Suitable for fodder crops and drought-resistant crops but subject to dry spells.

ZONE 4a Uncertain conditions but suitable for some fodder and drought-resistant crops.

4b Unsuitable for grain though possible to grow fodder crops.

ZONE 5 Suitable only for extensive cattle ranching.

BULAWAYO

BECHUANALAND

TRAN

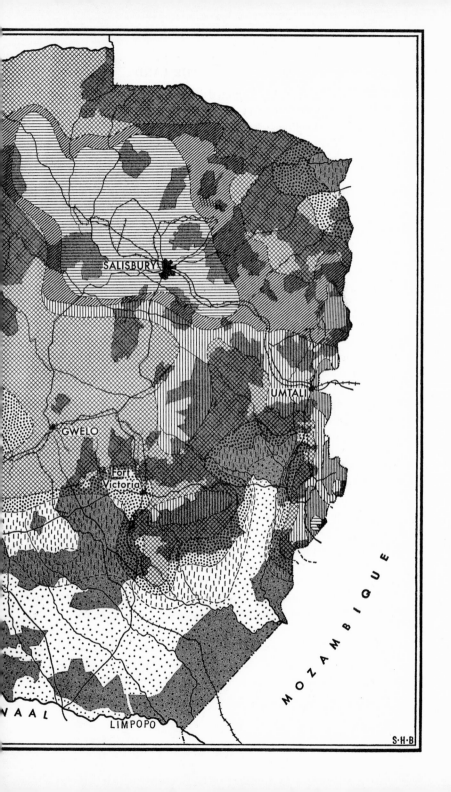

SALISBURY

UMTALI

GWELO

Fort
Victoria

MOZAMBIQUE

VAAL

LIMPOPO

S·H·B

disease, has successfully confined it to about 18,000 square miles or 12 percent of the country mostly along the border of Portuguese East Africa. Sleeping sickness among human beings is now negligible. The effect of the disease on cattle, however, has made some areas unusable for cattle raising, the economic activity most in keeping with natural conditions and traditional customs.

The topography, soils, and climate of Southern Rhodesia are not favorable for intensive production. The potential productive capacity of the land is indicated by the map on the preceding pages that divides the country into five production or land-use zones.

The map indicates that only about one fifth of the country's land, mostly in the High Veld and eastern mountain areas, is suitable for intensive crop cultivation. At the other extreme, 15 percent of the land is suitable only for extensive cattle ranching, with as much as 30 acres of range land needed to sustain one large animal. The remaining two thirds is subject to uncertain weather conditions that govern its suitability for producing grain, fodder, drought-resistant crops, and livestock. In much of this area at least 10 to 20 acres of range land are required to maintain one large animal. All in all, it is clear that, in common with many other parts of Southern, Central, and East Africa, Southern Rhodesia does not have a well-endowed agricultural resource base. More than 75 percent of the country is subject to conditions that make crop production a risky venture.

The extent of Southern Rhodesia's mineral resources is still undetermined, but enough is known to indicate that the country is fairly well endowed with minerals. The central feature of the mineral distribution system is the 350-mile "Great Dyke" that runs north and south through the country. The "Great Dyke" contains large reserves of chrome and asbestos, platinum and nickel, but no economical process has yet been devised to extract these metals from their containing ore. Other base metals are scattered throughout Southern Rhodesia. Copper, mica, lithium, tin, and copper phosphate are found in varying quantities. There is also a large coal field at Wankie in the northwest and a very large deposit of high-grade iron ore in the eastern section.

An optimistic estimate of mineral wealth was given by Sir Edgar Whitehead, former prime minister of Southern Rhodesia, in 1960:

We possess probably the widest ranges of mineral resources of any country in the world. Without going outside our own frontiers, we have not only almost unlimited resources of extremely high-grade iron-ore and extremely cheap coking coal of suitable quality but also most of the commercial alloys that are used in building up a steel industry. We have more chrome than we shall ever know what to do with, proved nickel in substantial quantities, and over the border in Northern Rhodesia ample supplies of manganese. Tungsten has been worked for many years, and I do not think there is any commercial alloy of steel which cannot be found in payable quantities within the Federation.[4]

Unfortunately the economics of mining are such that many of these resources have not been fully exploited.

POPULATION

In the spring of 1962, for the first time, Southern Rhodesia took a census of its African population. The result was a surprisingly high figure, 3,616,600, about 20 percent above the official estimate then current.[5] On June 30 of the same year there were 223,000 Europeans, 11,000 Coloreds, and 7,600 Asians.[6] Thus, the total population of Southern Rhodesia around mid-1962 was 3,858,200.

Before 1962 the only figures issued on the African population were estimates based on sample counts, tax returns, and employment censuses. These estimates, and therefore the published statistics on Southern Rhodesia's total population, were not very reliable; for example, the mid-1961 estimates of 2,910,000 Africans and 3,150,000 total population were clearly too low. Nevertheless, the available figures for the sixty years ending 1961 (at five-year intervals) are presented in Table 3 for what they are worth in indicating population growth.

According to the table, the total population at the turn of the century, when Europeans were first pushing the settlers' frontier into Southern Rhodesia, was about half a million, of whom 11,000 were Europeans. The figures suggest that it took more than twenty-five years for the population to reach one million, and that the rate of growth was much higher in the 1940's and 1950's than in earlier decades.

A good part of the increase in the rate of growth of the African population can be attributed to a decline in mortality rates. Improved food distribution, extension of administrative services, and

Table 3. Estimated population in Southern Rhodesia, 1901–1961
(in thousands of inhabitants)

Year	Total population	African	European	Other
1901	510	500	11.1	n.a.
1906	660	650	13.5	n.a.
1911	780	750	23.7	2.9
1916	870	840	28.3	3.1
1921	910	870	33.8	3.3
1926	980	940	39.5	3.7
1931	1,130	1,080	50.1	4.1
1936	1,320	1.260	55.6	5.4
1941	1,510	1,430	69.3	6.6
1946	1,870	1,780	83.5	7.5
1951	2,230	2,080	138.0	10.4
1956	2,740	2,550	180.0	13.3
1961	3,150	2,910	221.0	17.5

n.a. = not available.

Notes: For all dates, the African estimates (and hence the estimates of total population) have not been revised in the light of the first census of the African population in April–May 1962, which showed an African population of 3,616,600. Detail will not add exactly to totals, which are rounded to the nearest ten thousand.

Sources: For 1956 and 1961, *Monthly Digest of Statistics* (Salisbury: Central Statistical Office), December 1962; for earlier years, issue of May 1961.

acceptance of European medical practices have all contributed toward reducing the mortality rate of the indigenous population. At the same time there has been no apparent reduction in the fertility rate. According to a sample survey, life expectancy for both sexes is 48 years and the infant mortality rate is about 125 per 1000. The result has been a net reproduction rate of 2.1 percent per year, and a rate of natural increase of African population estimated to be more than 3 percent.[7]

The major factor in the growth of the European population has been an accelerated rate of immigration. European immigration increased from around 4,000 a year in the late 1930's to close to 14,000 a year in the late 1940's and early 1950's. Since 1953, migration statistics have been reported on a federal basis, and so there is no accurate record of immigration into Southern Rhodesia; but immigration into the Federation of Rhodesia and Nyasaland increased for several years after 1953 and there is no reason to doubt that most of the newcomers settled in Southern Rhodesia. The effect of the immigrants on population increase was such that in the two-year period 1955–1956, when the European natural increase (excess of births over deaths) in Southern Rhodesia was only about 6,600, the European population increased by about 25,000.[8] Largely as a result of immigration the European population more than doubled from 1946 and 1960, increasing from 83,500 to 218,000. The rate of increase in the European population, however, has slowed since 1959 as political uncertainty has increased. The number of non-African immigrants into the Federation has declined sharply, and at the same time there appears to be an increase in emigrants. In 1961, for the first time, there was a net emigration of non-Africans from the Federation; the number leaving exceeded the number arriving by 1,241.[9]

HISTORY

Little is known of the early history of Southern Rhodesia, the unexplained Zimbabwe ruins in the southern part of the country are still an enigma but the weight of available evidence indicates that they are the remnants of a higher "culture" than existed at the time the Europeans entered Southern Rhodesia.[10] The level of social and political organization was such that a surplus was available to maintain the workmen who constructed the buildings and to feed a royal court practicing an elaborate ritual. Archaeological evidence derived from the ruins indicates that at some time prior to the tenth century A.D. there was trade between this area and the Orient. The nature of this trade is a matter of speculation though it is fairly well established that Arab traders, who plied their dhows between Arabia and the East Coast of Africa, exchanged merchandise from Persia, India, and Arabia for slaves, ivory, and spices.

The first modern Europeans to penetrate the hinterland of Central Africa were the Portuguese, whose quest for a sea route to India led them to establish outposts on the east and west coasts of Southern and Central Africa. In 1505 the Portuguese established a small settlement at Sofala, near the present-day city of Beira, on the Indian Ocean. Portuguese writers of the sixteenth century described Central Africa as being part of the kingdom of Monomotapa or Benomotopa where there appeared to be a fairly well-developed governmental system and where gold, fruit, cattle, and elephants were plentiful.[11]

The Portuguese made several attempts to exploit the goldfields but had little success. They did not settle in Central Africa but confined their activities to exploration, trade, and the exploitation of one or two small gold and silver mines near Tete, close to the present border of Portuguese East Africa and Rhodesia.

In the course of time the African civilization described by the Portuguese as the kingdom of Monomotapa waned, and the cohesion and social organization of the earlier era disintegrated. Tribal warfare, disease, and depredation depopulated the area, and it was in this sparsely settled region that the powerful Matabele tribe established themselves in the early part of the nineteenth century. The Matabele, after breaking away from the main body of the warlike Zulus in Southern Africa, recoiled from their initial contact with the Europeans in South Africa and moved northward to present-day Rhodesia. They soon extended their demesne throughout the area north of the Limpopo, displacing the original inhabitants, the Barotse, and subjugating the Mashona to the north. The Matabele remained concentrated in the southwestern part of the country (Matabeleland), with their royal household at Bulawayo, while the Mashonas remained in the northeastern section (Mashonaland).[12]

The Matabele were not isolated from the Europeans for long; as South Africa became settled, a European vanguard moved north of the Limpopo. The first to come were explorers, hunters, and missionaries. In 1855, Dr. Livingstone discovered the Victoria Falls on the Zambezi and in 1859 the first mission station was established in Southern Rhodesia. As South Africa began to yield its vast mineral wealth, prospectors entered Matabeleland to search for minerals. They were followed by the settlers.

The king of the Matabele, Lobengula, granted several concessions to European fortune seekers. The most important of these was granted to a partner of Cecil Rhodes, the great English financier and imperialist after whom Rhodesia is now named. Though the concession was primarily for mineral rights, it opened the way for European conquest and settlement of Southern Rhodesia. Rhodes used the concession to obtain a royal charter from the British government authorizing his company, the British South Africa Company, to exploit the mineral wealth of the vast areas north of the Limpopo. The royal charter was gazetted in 1889. It was to run for twenty-five years and be subject to review and renewal at ten-year intervals thereafter. The charter, which was in effect until 1923, permitted the British South Africa Company to

carry into effect divers concessions and agreements which have been made by certain of the chiefs and tribes inhabiting the said region, and such other concessions, agreements, grants, and treaties as [they] may hereafter obtain within the said region or elsewhere in Africa, with the view to promoting trade, commerce, civilization, and good government . . .[13]

The company was also given the right to settle and administer an area of "unspecified northward extent beginning immediately to the north of British Bechuanaland and to the northwest of the South African Republics and to the west of the Portuguese dominion." The company also obtained several concessions beyond the Zambezi, and during the 1890's much of present-day Northern Rhodesia was gradually brought under company control. For thirty-five years the company ruled the two Rhodesias, an area greater than the combined areas of Germany and France.

The company was granted wide powers relating to government and commerce. It had authority to preserve law and order and was entitled to make ordinances, subject to the approval of the secretary of state for the colonies, and to establish and maintain a police force. It was also to discourage slavery, regulate traffic in spirits, and to appoint such officers and courts as were necessary for the administration of justice. In the commercial sphere the company was to "carry on any lawful commerce, trade, pursuit, business operations, or dealings whatsoever in connection with the object of the Company."

Having obtained the charter, Rhodes was eager to fulfill its mandate and anxious to exploit any mineral potential of the area covered by his concession. He organized a pioneer column of 187 Europeans and 150 Africans in South Africa. Accompanied by two troops of police from British Bechuanaland, the column moved into the sparsely settled areas of Mashonaland, bypassing Lobengula's immediate center of power at Bulawayo. The column established the town of Salisbury in 1890. Farms and prospecting rights were allocated to the pioneers, and large blocks of land were set aside for companies and syndicates. By 1893 there were some 3000 Europeans in what is now Southern Rhodesia. Inevitably there was conflict between the Europeans and the African inhab-

itants, each having different concepts of the rights granted under
the king's concessions. In 1893 there was an incident and war
broke out with the Matabele. Following the death of their king,
Lobengula, and heavy losses due to a smallpox epidemic among
the Matabele, the country returned to an uneasy state of peace.
Shortly thereafter, in 1895, there was an uprising of both the
Matabele and Mashona tribes but by 1898 the country was completely subjugated and under European domination. The British
South Africa Company, which had incurred heavy costs in paci-
fying the country, was ready to reap its dividends by bringing
Southern Rhodesia into the world market.

The first requirement for development and exploitation was to
improve communication with the outside world and to achieve
access to the sea. The company constructed a railroad from Kim-
berley in South Africa to Bulawayo in the southwestern part of
the country. This line was completed in 1897. In 1899 Salisbury
was linked to Beira, the nearest ocean port, and the line from
Bulawayo to Salisbury was completed in 1902. The completion of
the railroad was a great economic boon, for it reduced a hazardous
and costly journey of 35 days from South Africa to Salisbury to
one of as many hours. In addition, as in so many other parts of
Africa, the railroad was a vital factor in reducing the cost of imports and opening the way for the export of bulky, low-unit-value
commodities such as corn — the first major agricultural export
from Southern Rhodesia.

The company's expectations of obtaining rich returns from
mining were not realized. The extent of their disappointment can
be gauged by the fact that in 1910 the ten leading Rhodesian gold
mines produced a profit of £614,000, while eleven leading Johannesburg mines were yielding a profit of close to £7 million.[14] Silver
production was disappointing, as was the production of base
metals. The chrome and asbestos and copper produced between
1906 and 1923 was valued at less than £10 million. Coal showed
promise but between 1904 and 1923 the total value of coal production was only £2.5 million.

In the face of rising costs and low revenues from mining the
company decided to capitalize on what appeared to be its greatest
asset — land. Restless shareholders in the United Kingdom and
on the continent of Europe were assured that their investments

were well secured by the millions of acres of unalienated or unsold land in Southern Rhodesia. In 1907 there were only 1,731 surveyed farms in Southern Rhodesia covering close to 16.1 million acres out of the 100 million acres in the country. Of the 16.1 million acres of surveyed farm land, well below one million acres had been sold, but the granting of large farms to syndicates established the present pattern of large-scale holdings in Southern Rhodesia. Eighty-two companies held 824,000 acres given in exchange for certain rights and interests acquired by the British South Africa Company; 162 farms totalling 5.07 million acres were given or to be given to companies and syndicates who introduced capital for the general development of the territory. For services rendered to the company 1,124 farms were given to individuals (pioneers, police, and others), and 38 farms had been given to clubs, societies, municipalities and so forth — a total of 28,390 acres alienated without cash sales. Sixty farms of 316,304 acres had been sold for £18,838 and 163 farms of 86,525 acres had been alienated on permits of occupation for £41,679.[15] Unoccupied land was to be offered to companies and syndicates to encourage these groups to invest in agricultural development, settlers were to be encouraged to take up land, and, in addition, the British South Africa Company was to exploit its own land holdings for productive purposes. The company stocked and equipped its own farms for breeding dairy and beef herds. Company land was also used for growing citrus under irrigation, producing corn (or maize) and other crops, experimenting with the production and processing of tobacco, and indeed investigating every branch of agriculture that might hold promise. These company estates suffered all the vicissitudes of experimental agriculture, but they achieved some commercial success. In addition they provided much of the information that has aided agricultural development in Southern Rhodesia.

To recruit settlers for immigration to Southern Rhodesia, offices were opened in the United Kingdom, and arrangements were made for company farms in Rhodesia to be used to train the settlers in farming under African condition. Despite the company's efforts, however, the immigrant population of the territory increased slowly, rising from 14,000 in 1907 to 33,620 in 1921. By that year, 24.5 percent of the European population was engaged in agriculture, 12.5 percent in mining; commerce provided employment for

16.8 percent, public services for 14.5 percent, and the railways for 11.08 percent. Total employment in industry accounted for only 3,395 persons, or 10.10 percent of the European population.[16]

Those Europeans who were farming were primarily maize or corn producers, and in 1909 corn was first exported to Europe. Some tobacco was also grown but marketing problems retarded the early development of that crop. Attempts were made to introduce cotton into the territory, but cotton production was negligible. The number of cattle, which had been severely depleted by rinderpest in 1896 and East Coast fever in 1902, rose rapidly, however, from 341,000 head in 1914 to close to a million in 1923.

The bulk of the population — the Africans — were either altogether out of or merely on the periphery of the European-controlled exchange economy. Most Africans continued to produce in their customary manner and subsisted off the land. Land was plentiful, and there was little pressure on Africans to earn a livelihood from other sources. Some, to pay taxes or to purchase consumer goods, made forays into the money economy, selling produce or seeking short-term wage employment, but only a small proportion of the Africans were committed to the exchange sector.

With so much of the population outside the exchange economy, the size of the internal market must have been small and tempo of economic activity slow. There were no industries of any consequence. Internal roads were poor, many of them being well-nigh impassable in the rainy season. High freight rates and the long haul to South Africa or the coast hampered the limited export and import trade. The major source of external capital was the British South Africa Company, which was finding its investments to be disappointing.

It was eventually the dual role of the company — as administrator and profit-making concern — and the issue of land rights that led to the company's withdrawal as the governing body of Southern Rhodesia.[17] The company had assumed that it was the "owner" of the land of Southern Rhodesia. However, this assumption was implicit rather than explicit, and in 1918 the question of ownership of unalienated lands in Southern Rhodesia was contested before the Privy Council in the United Kingdom. The claimants were the British South Africa Company, the Crown, representatives of the European settlers, and the Africans. Judgment was given in favor of the Crown, and all unalienated lands were vested in the Crown. Henceforth the company could sell land only to defray costs of administration, in its capacity as an agent of the Crown, but not to make a profit for its shareholders. This decision, in conjunction with a strong drive by the small numbers of European settlers to have local self-government, reduced the company's desire to retain its role as administrator of the colony. The company's chief interest turned to gaining as favorable a settlement as possible for its shareholders at the time when it relinquished its administration.[18]

In 1923 Southern Rhodesia acquired the status of a self-governing colony, though certain powers — most notably the right to veto legislation considered to be discriminatory against Africans — were reserved to the Crown. Official estimates in 1926 indicated a population of fewer than 1,000,000 persons — 39,500 Europeans, 940,000 Africans, and 3,700 others — in a country of nearly 100,-000,000 acres. Only 180,000 or about one fifth of the Africans worked for wages. Mining and agriculture were the major employers: 70 percent of the Africans and 35 percent of the Europeans in employment were engaged in these industries. There was as yet no secondary industry of any consequence — as late as 1932 the official yearbook of the colony did not even mention manufacturing as a factor in the Southern Rhodesian economy — and the total population of the two major urban centers, Bulawayo and Salisbury, was less than 50,000.

During the 1920's the tempo of economic growth was slow. Exports of primary products climbed gradually and government expenditures increased slightly. This slow development was severely disturbed by the world-wide depression of the thirties and the sharp break in commodity prices. The value of gross output of agriculture, which reached a peak in 1927, fell sharply. Not until 1937 did the value of agricultural output again exceed that of 1927. Mining suffered from the decline in base metal prices. The increased price of gold, resulting from the devaluation of sterling in September 1931, led to a rise in output, but this could not offset the heavy fall in the output of asbestos, coal, and chrome. It was well into the thirties before the production of these commodities recovered sufficiently to equal 1929 levels.

There are no estimates of the national income or national output in these years; but the levels of living must have been low in this sparsely populated country where so many were engaged in subsistence production. In 1930, Professor Henry Clay described the economy as one that had four branches of economic activity: (1) trade between European merchants and those African producers who "produce certain commodities in excess of their own needs . . . and who have acquired a taste for commodities of European manufacture which they can obtain in exchange for their surplus"; (2) mining, "most exclusively export in the direction of its activities, but an important employer and purchaser of domestically produced foodstuffs"; (3) European agriculture; and, finally (4) transportation, the "work of the railway." These four sectors were the major employers and mainstays of the economy; all were linked to the export market. Professor Clay concluded his report with a strong plea that steps be taken to develop African agriculture so as to enlarge the size of the small domestic market that existed at the time and thereby lessen the country's dependence on a depressed export market. In his view the combined purchasing power of the 800,000 Africans was no greater than that of the 80,000 Europeans then living in the colony.[19]

The rapid economic growth that occurred after World War II did not come from the development of African agriculture; rather, it was a direct result of a rapid acceleration of European immigration into Southern Rhodesia and a large inflow of capital from South Africa and the United Kingdom. European skills, enterprise, and capital combined with a plentiful supply of land and labor to expand agricultural production, to raise mining output, and to establish industry. Between 1938 and 1956 the net income produced in the money sector rose from £20.7 million to £177 million.[20] During this eighteen-year period there was an 800 percent increase in net income, while the total population rose by 76 percent. Sketchy evidence (based on retail price indices for European consumers in Salisbury) indicates that the retail price level rose by about 140 percent in these years. Based on these estimates, the average annual increase in real incomes amounted to 30 percent. In contrast to the exchange economy, however, there was little change during these years in the productivity of African agriculture or in the income of those engaged in it. Increasing numbers of Africans entered the wage economy as migrant laborers.[21]

The European immigrants brought skills and capital with them. Before the war the capital of new immigrants had never amounted to more than £400,000 a year but the immigrants entering Rhodesia between 1946 and 1953 were estimated to "own" £31.4 million.[22] The influx of Europeans created a demand for goods and services, particularly housing. Salisbury and Bulawayo enjoyed a great construction boom and mushroomed in size; by 1959 these two cities — Salisbury with 82,000 persons, Bulawayo with 49,000 — accounted for close to 65 percent of the total European population.

Funds from abroad flowed into the country to supplement domestic savings and to sustain a very high rate of investment. Between 1949 and 1953 an estimated £233.7 million was invested in Southern Rhodesia, and of this 70 percent came from outside the country. The annual rate of investment in these years was never less than 35 percent of the country's net income and rose as high as 62 percent in 1952. Since 1953, when Southern Rhodesia joined Nyasaland and Northern Rhodesia to form the Federation of Rhodesia and Nyasaland, there has been no territorial breakdown of investments nor are there comparable figures for foreign investment. It appears, however, that more than £600 million were invested in the Federation between 1954 and 1958 and that about one third of this amount came from abroad.[23] There is no reason to doubt that Southern Rhodesia enjoyed its share of these investments.

The formation of the Federation, with Salisbury as its capital, was helpful to the development of Southern Rhodesia in at least two ways. In the initial years of the Federation, when the copper revenue from Northern Rhodesia was high, the country received benefits from the distribution of that income. Secondly, as the most advanced of the three territories, it gained from the creation of a common market that incorporated a tariff structure to encourage and protect the local manufacture of certain goods — for example, textiles — even though the increase in prices fell on consumers in territories which formerly had unhampered access to world markets.[24] The most spectacular single event in the postwar years has been the construction of the Kariba Dam for generating hydroelectric power on the Limpopo River. This dam, which is one of the largest in the world, has been financed in part by one of the largest single loans ever made by the International Bank for Reconstruction and Development. Initial investment in the dam and ancillary developments is expected to exceed £80 million of which the IBRD has contributed £28.6 million. Total investment by 1971 is expected to be £113 million. The dam is primarily a single-purpose dam; to provide power for the copper industry in Northern Rhodesia and to replace power generated by the rapidly aging thermal-power stations in Southern Rhodesia. It is also anticipated that the ready availability of low-cost power will encourage industrial growth in Southern Rhodesia.[25]

During the 1950's all sectors of the exchange economy expanded, and at the same time the structure of the economy changed. The amount of tobacco produced tripled between 1945 and 1958, its value rising fourfold, as Southern Rhodesian exports of Virginia flue-cured tobacco were substituted for tobaccos formerly imported to the United Kingdom from the dollar areas. Corn production doubled and livestock increased rapidly. European agricultural output increased at a rate of more than 12 percent per year, one of the highest growth rates in the world. Mining declined in importance but total output increased. The industrial sector expanded very rapidly and the value of gross output from industry rose by almost 17 percent per year. Light industry and secondary industry augmented food processing, tobacco manufacture, and other industries usually found in preindustrial economies. By 1958 manufacturing replaced agriculture as the largest single contributor to the country's gross domestic output.[26]

The expansion and change in the structure of the economy was accompanied by a high level of external trade as imports and exports increased. At the same time the expanding economy led to an increase in the number of persons who worked for wages. The number of Africans in wage employment rose from 500,000 in the postwar years to 642,000 in 1960, though close to half of these wage earners were migrant laborers who came from outside the country. By 1960, 37 percent of the employed Africans were working in agriculture, 15 percent in domestic service, and 11 percent in manufacturing. The remainder were employed in a wide range of other categories. Average earnings of Africans in the wage sector rose from £56 in 1954 to £84 in 1960 — a 50 percent increase — while the European Consumer Index rose by 30 percent. The average earnings of Europeans in wage employment rose from £875 to £1,117 in the same period.[27]

In the relatively short space of fifteen years, the poor and backward economy of Southern Rhodesia was transformed into an economy that gave every appearance of being vigorous, dynamic, and expanding. Although the rate of expansion has diminished since 1958 as a result of political uncertainty and the threat of the breakup of the Federation, and investment and immigration have declined, the over-all growth rate has been impressive. Gross domestic product increased by more than 60 percent between 1954 and 1960, gross domestic product per head rising from £65 to £91. But, this impressive growth rate has been confined almost entirely to the money sector of the economy, and almost all of the increase in output has been generated by European-controlled enterprises, especially in manufacturing, commerce, and agriculture. The large African agricultural sector, which still embraces 70 percent of the population and 44 percent of the land resources in the country, has demonstrated little growth. Output has barely exceeded the rate of increase of population in African agriculture, and the relative contribution to gross domestic output has fallen from around 11 percent in 1954 to 5 percent in 1960. So long as so high a proportion of the country's population is engaged in feeding itself and produces so little surplus, over-all rates of growth will be unbalanced and the disparity in incomes between the wage sector and African agriculture will widen. This may not be detrimental in itself, for the opportunity to subsist does provide a means of sustaining persons who might not have alternative employment. Nevertheless, if there is to be sustained economic growth and a more even distribution of income, the national resources locked in the subsistence sector must be used to produce more than they do at present. No country can afford to have so high a proportion of its resources producing so small a proportion of its output. In this respect the problem of development in Southern Rhodesia is similar to that in many other parts of Southern, Central, and East Africa.

When the first settlers entered Southern Rhodesia, the gulf between the newcomers and the "natives" could not have been wider, culturally, socially, or economically. To the early settlers this gulf must have seemed unbridgeable in almost every respect, and the idea of social and economic integration, if it occurred to them at all, must have seemed unrealistic in the extreme. The Africans were living under conditions so primitive that they could be compared only with those of the Stone Age. Their tools and implements were of the crudest sort. The wheel was completely outside their experience. They lived off the land, producing to subsist, and were perpetually at the mercy of drought, famine, wild beasts, and hostile neighbors. Their numbers were limited by constant tribal wars, starvation, disease, and infant mortality. They neither read nor wrote, nor did they practice any commerce or trade.

It is scarcely remarkable that the settlers, judging by their own standards, should have regarded the "natives" as their inferiors. They judged by what they found and their attitude set the pattern for interracial relations over the following years. This pattern divided the population into noncompeting groups and established a master-servant relation between the Europeans and the Africans. Only now, in the early 1960's, is this pattern crumbling under the pressures that come from within and from without, including those from the United Nations.[28] Nevertheless, in 1963 still, the major issue in the general election held in that year was that of the rate of progress of change in legislation governing race relations. The party opposing rapid change won the election — a faction that has hastened the dissolution of the Federation of Rhodesia and Nyasaland.

One of the earliest actions of the British South Africa Company was to establish a separate department to handle African affairs. A cadre of European officials were appointed as native commissioners to oversee many and diverse matters, ranging from the maintenance of law and order to the building of rural roads. The legacy of the company's policy, which was based on the system in use in the Cape Colony in South Africa, remains to the present and is incorporated in the constitution of Southern Rhodesia. The constitution provides for a Native Affairs Department to be headed by a chief native commissioner. The Native Affairs Act of 1927, "an Act to make provisions for control of natives and the conduct of native affairs," confirmed the policy. Though the act has been amended in many respects, it still remains on the statute books.

The creation of separate administrative units for Europeans and Africans was part of the formal mechanism for dividing Europeans and Africans into noncompeting groups. There were separate agencies for European agriculture and African agriculture, European education and African education, European housing and African housing. For each racial group there were separate taxes, separate medical and social facilities, separate rights and privileges. One ostensible exception to this is in the franchise which is color blind although the qualifications for the vote have been such that most Africans have been excluded from the voter rolls.[29] Different standards were applied to each group. There was a "vertical dualism" in the country and in every sphere the Europeans were to be "masters" and the Africans "servants," with no direct competition between the two racial groups.[30]

At the outset there was little need for the settlers to fear competition from the Africans except in regard to land, and land was plentiful. European technology and education secured European superiority (backed by European arms). As the economy developed and some Africans acquired skills and education, however, they posed a threat as potential competitors to some Europeans.

The Europeans determined to safeguard their "inherited superiority" and their high levels of consumption. The amorphous policy of paternalism was replaced by more positive efforts to divide the country and the economy into noncompeting racial groups. A lucid exposition of this policy, which is not unlike that of *apartheid* in the Republic of South Africa, is to be found in the following statement of Sir Godfrey Huggins (later Lord Malvern). Speaking as prime minister of Southern Rhodesia, in 1938, he said:

Because of the presence of the white man the Bantu is, with accelerating speed, lifting himself out of his primitive conditions. His inter-tribal wars have been prohibited, and his once frequently-recurring epidemics have been checked. His numbers are increasing. Tribes once separated by traditional animosities are developing the idea of racial unity . . . The

Bantu is resolved to learn, and within as yet undetermined limits is capable of learning. To forbid him opportunities is contrary to natural justice, but are we to allow him to develop and in the course of time, because his requirements are so small, to oust the European? . . . .

While there is yet time and space, the country should be divided into separate areas for black and white. In the Native area the black man must be allowed to rise to any position to which he is capable of climbing. Every step in the industrial and social pyramid must be open to him, excepting only—and always—the very top . . . The Native may be his own lawyer, doctor, builder, journalist or priest, and he must be protected from white competition in his own area. In the European area the black man will be welcomed, when, tempted by wages, he offers his services as a labourer, but it will be on the understanding that there he shall merely assist, *and not compete with*, the white man . . . The interest of each race will be paramount in its own sphere.[31]

The noncompetitive group approach did not favor equal treatment for each group, and the allocation of national resources by the all-European legislature was premised on a much higher level of needs for Europeans than for Africans. Separate administration and budget control for African and non-African affairs provided a means whereby more funds could be channeled into European development. In addition, land policy — discussed in the next chapter — and wage policies not only prevented direct competition between black and white but were also designed to maintain the different standards of each racial group.

In the field of wage legislation, the Industrial Conciliation Act of 1934 ensured the scarcity value of skilled workers by preventing Africans from acquiring certain skills. The terms of the act restricted Africans from qualifying for apprenticeships, joining recognized trade unions, and being classified as skilled workers. Skilled workers, being both scarce and organized, were able to negotiate for relatively high wages. However, under the Industrial Conciliation Act, the control over unskilled (African) wages was largely in the hands of the government. The result was that there was a wide gap between European and African wages, with European wages being much higher than comparable wages in Britain, Canada, Australia, and New Zealand. One student of the subject declared that this policy had made European workers in Rhodesia "aristocrats" as compared with similar workers in Britain, even though they were no more efficient than the British workers. Furthermore, their high wages "were part of the product of the labor they supervised" and "white incomes were high only because there was an extreme inequality of income between white and native workers in the same industry or workshop." [32]

Incomes of other Europeans were also protected. Special tax measures benefited European farmers and miners. Land apportionment and marketing arrangements discriminated against Africans and favored Europeans. The whole system of economic and social control was geared to protecting European incomes and maintaining high levels of living among the European minority at the expense of the African majority.

The exploitation of Africans for the benefit of Europeans and the establishment of different standards for Europeans and Africans were deemed necessary not only to maintain the privileged position of the Europeans in the country but also to attract European immigrants. Increased numbers of immigrants were essential to maintain European hegemony. The Europeans were aware that sooner or later there would be a social and economic challenge from the African majority, and that their best safeguard was to reduce the disparity in numbers between themselves and the Africans.[33]

This policy did help to attract immigrants in the postwar years but it also led to increasing economic and political discontent, especially among the growing number of urbanized Africans. There were strikes for higher wages and for the repeal of some of the more onerous conditions of the Industrial Conciliation Act. At the same time an upsurge in African nationalistic sentiment led to increasing demands among the Africans for greater political representation.

In 1953 the creation of the Federation of Rhodesia and Nyasaland provided an opportunity for an ostensible change in political and social policy within Southern Rhodesia. The earlier policy of noncompeting groups or parallel development was to be replaced by one of "partnership." This concept of "partnership" is best described in the words of Sir Godfrey Huggins the main architect of the Federation:

> We are anxious to build up this country on the basis of a partnership between the various races, not to use colour as a test of a man's ability and culture. We can only develop and hold this country as partners. In the present stage of development it is difficult for some people to

realise this, and because of the stage of development of the backward people it is not easy for outside observers to realize that we believe in such a policy and are attempting to carry it out.[34]

The formation of the Federation brought about some fundamental changes. A federal parliament came into being with a minority of Africans among its members (12 out of 59 in 1958). For the first time Africans were to be directly represented by Africans in a parliament in Southern Rhodesia. In addition there were three European members to represent African interests. The federal government was charged with the exclusive responsibility for most of the matters of common concern in the three territories: external affairs, defense, immigration, citizenship, customs, excise and income taxes, posts, and transport. The one notable exception to this principle was that the federal government was to have no jurisdiction over "native affairs" — that is, African affairs. The conduct of African affairs was reserved to the three governments. The Southern Rhodesian government was therefore able to follow its own distinctive policy regarding African affairs, and as there were no Africans in Southern Rhodesia's legislative assembly, this policy continued to be formulated by an all-white legislature.

Since 1953 internal and external pressures have forced some modifications in the policy of noncompeting groups. The most significant of these pressures was the very rapid growth of African nationalism both within Southern Rhodesia and in other countries of sub-Saharan Africa. Increasing pressure has developed for changes in both the economic and political realms. In the latter there have been significant changes that now make it possible for a few Africans to be selected to the legislative assembly through a modest expansion of the franchise among the Africans. But the government of 1963 has resisted making further sweeping political changes that would enfranchise the bulk of the African population. The political changes that were significant in the 1963 election led to the first direct representation of Africans by African representatives in the legislative assembly in Southern Rhodesia, but they still fall far short of the aspirations of the African nationalists. The present franchise still reflects the policy of dividing the electorate into noncompeting groups by having a constitution that limits the right of most African voters to share a common roll with Europeans. In the economic realm, however, the government has made significant changes in some of the economic arrangements that formerly differentiated between Europeans and Africans.

Emphasis has been placed on the need for over-all "economic development" as a requirement to raise levels of living in the country, and this requires the best utilization of all human resources within the country, rather than any reliance on immigrants. In the words of the prime minister of Southern Rhodesia in 1960:

> Our belief is that, with the natural resources with which Nature has endowed our country, there is absolutely no reason why we should not become a very great industrial nation. Probably the most important consideration is not just the existence of those resources, *nor the importation of know-how for their exploitation, but the proper education and training of our own people* so that we are able to do the work ourselves. This is the basis on which we are working at present.[35]

The first of the major changes in policy concerned the development of African farming through the Native Land Husbandry Act. The implementation of this act, the economics of which will be discussed later, entailed an increased rate of investment in African agriculture even though, in some instances, such development would compete with European agriculture. This was an important shift in economic policy, undoubtedly motivated by the hope that if levels of living could be raised in African agriculture then African peasantry would be "contented" and would turn away from political demands. This sentiment is expressed in the *Report of the Chief Native Commissioner for the Year 1954,* in which the commissioner stated that the "rapid implementation of government policy by application of the Native Land Husbandry Act right throughout all the Native reserves and rural areas is vital to establish and ensure a contented and progressive Native peasant . . . Inevitably he will disregard the political sirens of the urban areas, who themselves are making no headway with their self-aggrandisement schemes." [36]

A further indication of the new policy is to be seen in the expansion of educational facilities for Africans. Expenditure on African education was increased and by 1961 had risen to 19 percent of the Southern Rhodesian budget. Enrollment of Africans in schools rose from less than 270,000 in 1953 to 534,000 in 1961, and by 1964 or 1965 it is expected that there will be adequate facilities for all African children to receive lower education.[37] Secondary school facilities are being expanded, though there are no prospects as yet for accommodating all those who wish to go through secondary school. (In 1961 only 5,069 Africans attended secondary schools.)

Steps have been taken to relax some of the more onerous restrictions on Africans that have been in force since the period of company rule. "Qualified Africans" have been given greater freedom of movement within the country; they no longer need to have special authorization every time they wish to move about the country and shift their residences. A multiracial university has been established; restrictions on liquor consumption have been relaxed; segregation in federal offices and in the federal government has been abolished, and several Africans have been appointed to senior positions in the federal government. In addition the migration of foreign Africans into Southern Rhodesia is now restricted, which reduces the over-all supply of African labor in the country, thus protecting the local Africans. This could well lead to an increase in African wages.

A further major change has been the removal of some of the restrictions that excluded Africans from competing directly with Europeans in skilled occupations. A new Industrial Conciliation Act and the Apprenticeship Act that came into effect in 1960 have removed the legal barriers to Africans becoming apprentices. This change has enabled them to gain the status of skilled workers and obtain the right to "equal pay for equal work" on a basis which does not tend to favor Europeans. The new legislation permits Africans to join trade unions and prohibits the formation of parallel unions based on race or color. Indeed, the law specifically defines the industrial interests without any regard whatsoever to race or color, so that trade unions are to be based on functional rather than racial lines — a major departure from earlier policies.

The shift in policy is also seen in the amendment of the Workmen's Compensation Act. The original act of 1922 and the Native Labourers' Compensation Act set the minimum compensation for "incapacitated" European labor at £750, plus up to £100 for hospital expenses. In the case of death the European worker's dependent was entitled to a sum equal to three years' wages. An

African, however, would be compensated to the extent of £15 to £50 in the case of permanent total incapacitation, and £20 in the event of death. New legislation, in the 1959 Workmen's Compensation Act, embodies a nonracial principle and has introduced a single formula for the purposes of computing compensation. Compensation is based on the workmen's rate of pay without regard to color.

In the final analysis, the composition of the legislature is probably the most important of all the factors that govern the pace of integrating the economy. In this regard the European minority has consistently refused to reduce the property and educational qualifications for voting to the point where Africans will be widely represented. The consequence has been that every action by the all-white legislature in regard to African advancement is taken with an eye to the wishes of the European electorate. This electorate has had no wish to yield its privileged political position nor has it wished to diminish economic advantages that have accrued under the earlier system of noncompeting groups. Yet at the same time there is a growing realization that if the economic privilege of a high level of living is to be maintained, the size of the national income must be increased and that an increase in national income depends, in the first instance, on the development of African abilities and a rise in African incomes.

At one time the European minority might have shared the view that an increased rate of economic development and higher levels of living for Africans would allay political demands. Today, however, there are few Europeans and Africans who believe that economic advancement can be a substitute for political advancement. The dramatic developments elsewhere in Africa have made Africans in Southern Rhodesia impatient with slow political changes and have impressed the European minority with the need for some alterations in the political sphere. Consequently, at the time of this writing, constitutional amendments have been introduced in Southern Rhodesia whereby in 1963 Africans, for the first time, have direct representation in the Southern Rhodesia legislative assembly. These constitutional changes have extended the vote to the Africans in such a manner that the African legislators are in a minority. But it is an open question whether these changes will satisfy the aspirations of Africans. In a situation where policies are still guided by racial considerations, even though to a lesser extent than before, it seems unlikely to this writer that the Africans will be satisfied with anything less than a majority in the legislative assembly. This is conjecture, however. The answer lies in the future.

An extension of the franchise may foster a redistribution of resources, particularly of land. No matter who has the vote, however, many of the problems of economic development will persist, especially those relating to African agriculture. Political change in itself provides no panacea — the problem of raising productivity applies to independent African countries such as Tanganyika and Uganda as well as to countries with multiracial populations. Political change may aid in the process of liberalizing the economy as a whole and in removing the restrictions that prevent the optimum use of resources. But political changes of the kind that result in an exodus of Europeans and a flight of capital from European agriculture (as has happened in Kenya), would leave Southern Rhodesia even more heavily dependent on indigenous resources than before. In that event, the development of African agriculture will be all the more urgent, if over-all levels of living are to be maintained.

Chapter 3

Land Apportionment

Over the years land has been an important element in the evolution of economic theories and ideas. The Physiocrats, the fathers of modern economics, believed that land was the source of all wealth. A shortage of land was one of the principal features of Malthus's dismal theories of overpopulation; Ricardo applied the law of diminishing returns to land and made it the basis of distribution theory. Henry George's theories and arguments on taxation of unearned increments centered around rising land values. More recently, many economists have come to view land merely as one of the factors that go into the production of a given output.

In a world of *real politik,* however, land is not just a factor of production. Land and rights to land are enveloped in a host of political, institutional, and sociological implications that give it a meaning far beyond its market value. This is not to say that many of the attitudes that engender revolutionary slogans, such as "Land, Liberty, and Bread" in Russia or "Land and Liberty" in Mexico, do not stem from economic causes. Nor does it mean that the social and political revolutions that have led to land distribution programs in Bolivia, Egypt, and Iraq have not been based in economic as well as in social causes. The peasant in Iraq or Iran who gives half his crop in rent to the landlord, or the Bolivian peasant who cannot produce a surplus with which to pay his rent, must feel that the ownership of the land he tills would remove an onerous burden and redistribute incomes in his favor. His meager income might well be doubled if he were to own the land rather than rent it.

It is no coincidence that rights to land have played a prominent part in social, political, and economic upheavals in countries with large peasant societies. Peasants rarely have anything other than land and labor whereby to sustain themselves. Without capital, with limited mobility and few alternative opportunities for making a livelihood, they are tied to the land; threats to their position vis-à-vis the land are threats to their security. This concept of

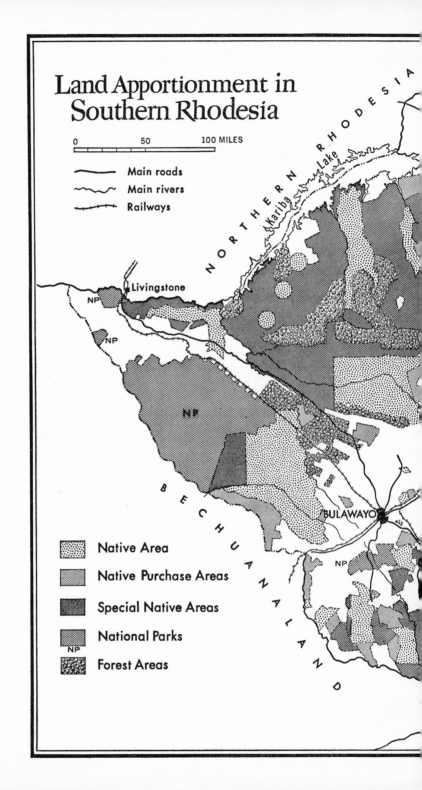

Land Apportionment in Southern Rhodesia

0   50   100 MILES

—— Main roads
~~~ Main rivers
+++ Railways

NORTHERN RHODESIA

Kariba Lake

Livingstone

NP

NP

NP

BECHUANALAND

BULAWAYO

NP

▦ Native Area
▦ Native Purchase Areas
▦ Special Native Areas
▦ National Parks
NP
▦ Forest Areas

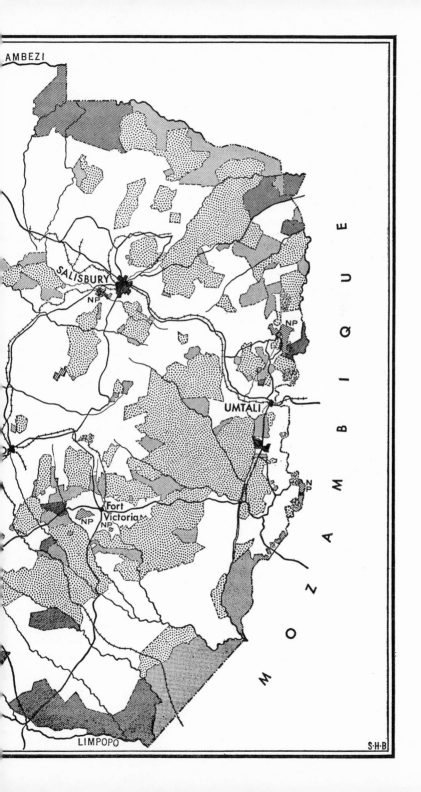

security may be a self-defeating one, in that clinging to the land restricts specialization of production, extension of markets, and division of labor, and so economic growth, yet it is nevertheless a potent force in peasant societies. For most peasants, the land is, or appears to be, the only visible and tangible basis for sustenance and subsistence, and therefore it has an importance that transcends purely economic considerations.

In many societies reorganization of land ownership and land rights has been a basic element in implementing state policy. The communes in China and the collectives in Russia are means whereby the state has abolished private land ownership and promoted its social and economic ideology. In South Africa the ideology of *apartheid,* or separate development, is built around territorial segregation; in Kenya, the reserving of the White Highlands for European occupation has been part of a policy of white exclusiveness in these areas, while in Southern Rhodesia, as has been pointed out, land apportionment by race gives effect to the policy of dividing Europeans and Africans into noncompeting groups and of maintaining high levels of consumption for the Europeans.

In Southern Rhodesia, many social, economic, and legislative changes affecting the relation between the 223,000 Europeans and 2,870,000 Africans have taken place in recent years. Viewed against the absence of change in prewar years, the postwar changes have been great indeed. As of early 1963, race is not necessarily the overriding factor in determining opportunities for advancement in many spheres, though it would be naïve in the extreme to believe that it is not an important one. There is one issue, however, in which race is still a primary consideration, and that is the ownership of land. To all intents and purposes, the 97 million acres in Rhodesia are divided along ethnic lines, with 42 million acres — the "native areas" — allocated for African use, 48 million for European use, and 6 million acres for parks, game reserves, and the like (see pp. 58–59). Africans and Europeans live and till the soil in their respective areas, and the many Africans who work on European farms, until recently, have been considered to be "temporary visitors."

The land apportionment system, originally intended to protect African rights, is now referred to by many as the "White

Man's Magna Carta." [1] In the view of most of the European minority, land apportionment is justified by more than purely economic considerations, though undoubtedly these are most important. Land apportionment has been, and still is, considered to be the essence of preserving a "way of life" which still has many feudal overtones. It is one of the major features in a system geared to maintain high consumption levels for Europeans. It is also considered to be a bulwark against the interracial social intercourse that many Europeans consider undesirable. Furthermore, the system of apportionment affords comfort (albeit mythical) as an obstruction against the nationalistic pressures of the African majority. The white minority believes it provides a safeguard for them against being engulfed by a vast majority of Africans whose civilization, levels of living, and aspirations are considered to be much inferior to those of the Europeans. Conversely, articulate Africans have seen land apportionment as proof of European intransigence in extending to Africans the right to move freely, to own land, and to trade where they wish.

The issue of land and race could hardly have been of concern to the handful of European pioneers and tribal Africans when the Europeans first entered the sparsely populated country. In 1890 land was abundant for all. The primitive tribal African, concentrating on subsistence production, needed only a small amount of land at any one time to feed himself and his family, and there appeared to be little to prevent the British South Africa Company from selling large acreages to settlers. The royal charter authorized the company to "improve, develop, clear, plant, irrigate, and cultivate any lands included within the territories of the Company and to settle any such territories and lands as aforesaid, and to aid and promote irrigation and to grant lands for terms of years or in perpetuity and either absolutely or by way of mortgage or otherwise." Article 14 of the charter, however, enjoined the company "that careful regard shall always be had to the customs and laws of the clan or tribe or nation to which the parties respectively belong especially with respect to the holding possession, transfer, and disposition of lands and testate or intestate succession." [2]

Although primarily interested in a search for mineral wealth, the company also set aside large-sized holdings for pioneers, companies, and syndicates. There appeared to be no limit to the amount of land it could alienate, and no clear definition of the rights of Africans to hold or dispose of land. As has been pointed out, these rights were all the more obscure because tribal traditions included no concept of property rights as they are understood by Western law. Land was the "property" of the chief in that he had the right to allocate it among his tribesmen, but neither tribesmen nor chiefs had the right to sell or dispose of land outside the tribe.

Even though there was an abundance of land for Africans and Europeans, there was competition over limited areas of Matabeleland. Most of the settlers selected holdings in the relatively small area of heavy red and black loamy soils, not in the granite, thin-soiled sandveld which the Africans could work with their primitive implements and which was suited for production of their traditional crops. By the middle of 1894, nearly all of the limited area of these soils had been alienated, and while a large portion was not immediately occupied, it was "held" by Europeans. As European settlement continued to encroach on "African" lands, the company thought it desirable to allocate lands to Africans for their exclusive use. These lands were to be reserved *from* European occupation and were to be areas where the natives could live according to their tribal custom. In 1894 a Lands Commission was appointed and was specifically charged with the duty of assigning to the Africans of Matabeleland "land sufficient for their occupation whether as tribes or portions of tribes and suitable for the agricultural and pastoral requirements including in all cases a fair and equitable proportion of springs and permanent water." All questions of the settlement of Africans on the land were to be decided by the Administrator-in-Council subject to review by the British High Commissioner in South Africa.

The Land Commission found that the many grants of land to Europeans in areas where the Africans had formerly resided, or were still residing, made it necessary to go out of the immediate area of European occupation to provide alternative lands for tribal use. After some consideration, the commission's recommendations, which were accepted by the secretary of state in 1895, led to the assignation of two large tracts, the Shangani and Gwaai reserves, for African use. In addition to these areas, which included 2.12 million acres, they also recommended the creation of a small reserve of 12,000 acres for the use of the wives and sons of Lobengula, the deposed king of the Matabele. Some measure of the Matabele view of the suitability of these reserves is evident from the *Report of the Southern Rhodesian Native Reserve Commission of 1915,* which commented that the Africans refused to move to Shangani and Gwaai, "the former which they declared was unhealthy and the latter waterless." [3]

Nevertheless, an important principle was established. Reserves had been established on a tribal basis. Land was set aside for the exclusive use of the Africans, though they were free to acquire land elsewhere if they had the means to do so. The motives behind this first apportionment undoubtedly included a desire to make it easier to alienate land to Europeans. That is only half the story, however, for while the lands assigned to the Africans were poor in quality, there was also a recognition of the need to protect African tribesmen by assigning lands to them *en bloc.* In the normal course of events, these lands might well have passed into the hands of the Europeans by virtue of their superior political and purchasing power.

In 1896 the Matabele revolted, and after a short war, they were partially subdued. A condition of their final surrender from well-nigh impregnable positions was a promise that they would be given lands in open country where they would be free from interference. Many of the Matabele did not wish to return to their former lands, now under white aegis. Formerly, many of them had exchanged their labor for the right to graze on European farms or had merely squatted on unused portions of European farms. Now, however, many of the settlers wanted these lands to graze their own cattle.

In 1898, after Mashonaland was joined to Matabeleland to form Southern Rhodesia, an order-in-council introduced into Southern Rhodesia as a whole the so-called "Cape Clause" which had hitherto been confined to Mashonaland. This clause specified that an African could hold or dispose of land on the same conditions as a non-African, but no contract for encumbering or alienating land would be valid unless it was made in the presence of a magistrate who was to ensure that the African concerned understood the contract and that the consideration for the contract was fair and reasonable. The order-in-council also extended to the whole country the admonition, formerly confined to Mashonaland, that, as the need arose, the company should apportion additional lands for African occupation.[4]

In complying with the order, the company invited their native commissioners to recommend additional land for tribal occupation. The commissioners were given no uniform criteria for the selection of reserved areas, and there was a wide divergence in their conception of what constituted an adequate and suitable area for African occupation. Yet these men, acting largely on their own, laid the foundation of the existing reserve system. In subsequent years the areas originally designated for African use were enlarged as a result of investigations made by various commissions and committees, but the initial allocations were largely based on the recommendations of individual commissioners.

In reviewing the situation some twenty years later, the Native Reserve Commission of 1915 reported that the commissioners had acted on a variety of different assumptions. In some areas commissioners assumed that, because there was no European settlement, the whole or greater part of the unoccupied land should be reserved for Africans. In other instances districts were wholly alienated to Europeans and no land was set aside for African use. Some commissioners demarcated small areas for occupation by petty clans or tribes wherever they were settled, so that certain districts were covered with a patchwork of small reserves; other commissioners made the boundaries of administrative divisions the boundaries of reserved areas regardless of tribal arrangements. As a result of the various actions of the commissioners, some 104 reserves were designated ranging in size from a scant 5,000 acres to the Sabi Reserve of 1.5 million acres. In making their recommendations, all of the commissioners followed the principle of leaving undisturbed the land already occupied by or alienated to Europeans. As a result the land reserved for Africans excluded the healthy and relatively fertile highlands, where the Europeans had settled after finding the land virtually unoccupied. It was through these highlands that the railroad was soon to pass. As a result, no reserve at all was within 25 miles of the railway — the main artery of trade in the country. This is still the situation today.

In 1902 most of the recommended areas were formally proclaimed as reserves. In most instances this merely involved a *de jure* recognition of a *de facto* situation, for the Africans were already settled in these areas. In some cases, however, the size and location of the proposed reserves had to be modified because of the vast discrepancies between the commissioners' estimates and the actual acreage that was available. These discrepancies were not surprising, for no land survey had been made when the commissioners selected the areas suitable for reserves. Guesswork had to substitute for knowledge, and on some occasions it was found that reserved areas existed only on paper.

In 1902 the total population of the country was estimated to be around 510,000 people, of whom close to 11,000 were Europeans. The area of the reserves was in the neighborhood of 21 million acres. The remaining territory, something under 80 million acres, was open to purchase by Europeans and, under the terms of the Cape Clause, by Africans. However, unfamiliar with the workings of an exchange economy, Africans seldom found themselves in a position to exercise their nominal right to purchase land, even if they could locate a seller, whether it was the company or a European. In 1925, when white settlers were pressing for repeal of the Cape Clause, only about 45,000 acres were privately owned by Africans. By that time, however, 31,000,000 acres had been acquired by Europeans.

As population and livestock increased, pressure grew for modification of the reserves. Africans using land-extensive production systems spilled over into unalienated areas and unoccupied European farms. In 1913 a drought intensified competition for well-watered land. In addition, many European farm owners, to free their land for grazing cattle, forced squatters to move. They also evicted "labor tenants," persons who exchanged labor for the right to graze their cattle on European land, so that the lands formerly used for grazing African cattle could be used for European-owned cattle. The Africans forced off moved to nearby reserves, adding to the existing congestion in certain areas. At the same time other reserves were almost unoccupied.

It was against this background that the imperial government of the United Kingdom established a commission in 1913 to make a "final" apportionment of land on a racial basis and to decide whether the reserves should be extended in size. The commission was to consider not only the immediate requirements of the Africans but also their probable future needs arising from the natural increase in population. The commission was also to take into account the African population outside of the reserved areas. The Land Commission issued an interim report in 1914 and a final report in 1915.

The interim report was the first to consider some of the implications of the impact of European influences on African development. The commission also examined the question of whether larger reserves for use on a traditional tribal basis was the best means of accommodating a growing African population. It recognized that the Africans were no longer a homogeneous group of backward tribesmen and that some of them were becoming sophisticated. The increasing population could not be accommodated solely by allocations of land. The commission held that a policy of extending tribal subsistence farming would be self-defeating, as it would merely lead to an extension of a backward system of production. In keeping with the spirit of the time, the commission placed great faith in the efficacy of education and of association with Europeans as a means of breaking down the less desirable elements of tribalism. In line with the view that the Africans should not be isolated from European influences, the commission recommended an end to extending the areas reserved for African use. The report stressed the need to safeguard the rights of tribal producers on the acreage already reserved for them, but it also conveyed the sense that Europeans should not be denied the right to purchase land throughout much of Southern Rhodesia.

In their final report the commissioners made clear their feeling that 21 million acres were adequate for an estimated 700,000 Africans, and they concerned themselves more with changes in the size and shape of individual reserves than with extending their acreage. Generally, they aimed to have moderately sized reserves evenly distributed throughout the territory, a policy that foreclosed any notion of partition of the country along racial lines. The apparent logic behind the commission's policy was that very small reserves were undesirable, as they would have no capacity for expanded population. At the same time, despite the view that proximity to civilizing influences was important, there were objections to some reserves being situated near towns and mining camps where "they become a resort for persons of low character." Large reserves in remote districts were frowned upon because their occupants would be distant from adequate administrative control and from those centers of education and progress which, in the commission's opinion, were important in the development of their inhabitants. Evenly distributed reserves of moderate size would be most desirable, not only for ease of control but also because they would facilitate the spread of education and presumably would aid in the breakdown of tribalism by a process of osmosis. In this respect the commission's goal of breaking down tribalism was probably the first expression of the idea of nation-building. In the view of one prominent African nationalist the breakdown of tribalism and the subsequent process of nation building has been the greatest legacy of the colonial administration in Southern Rhodesia.[5]

The commission could not attain its ideal of moderately sized reserves throughout the country, but recommended the abolition of the smallest reserves, an enlargement in the size of some, and a reduction in the size of others. The recommendations were ultimately embodied in an order-in-council of 1920 which made a "final disposition" by allocating a total of 21,600,000 acres for tribal reserves, or an average of 30 acres per African in the country. These lands were vested in the British High Commissioner and were to be "set apart for the sole and exclusive use of the native inhabitants of Southern Rhodesia." Africans could still exercise their privileges under the Cape Clause and purchase land elsewhere in the territory.

The right of Africans to purchase land was debated at length during the early twenties, particularly in the constitutional discussions preceding the expiration of the charter of the British South Africa Company and the granting of internal self-government to Southern Rhodesia. Among the settlers there was considerable sentiment for removing the Cape Clause and denying Africans the right to purchase land indiscriminately. A 1920 resolution from the all-white Agricultural Union Congress, for example, requested legislation making it impossible for individual landowners to sell land to Asiatics or Africans in a European community. This view was buttressed by the chief native commissioner's report for 1920, in which he wrote that "in the interests of all alike it is not desirable that natives should acquire land indiscriminately owing to the inevitable friction which will arise with their European neighbors." [6] This view was stressed despite the fact that so small an acreage had been purchased by Africans. The British government, however, was unwilling to modify the Cape Clause and the long-accepted principle of equal rights for all in the purchasing of land outside the reserves.

Southern Rhodesia was granted self-government in 1923. The constitution enshrined the principle that the reserves were set apart for the sole and exclusive use of the African people. A schedule of the 21,600,000 acres that constituted the reserves was appended to the constitution itself. When the government of Southern Rhodesia came into being, the state took title to all of the unalienated land in the colony, but the reserves continued to be vested in the person of a British High Commissioner for "the sole and exclusive use of the Africans." In 1937 control of the reserves passed to a newly established board of trustees consisting of a chairman nominated and approved by the secretary of state (though in practice this has been done by the governor), the chief justice of the colony, and the chief native commissioner of the colony. The approval of the secretary of state was also required if any portion of the reserves was to be alienated. The size of the reserves has remained virtually unchanged from 1923 to the present, although since then additional land has been allocated to Africans as "special areas" and "purchase areas."

With the achievement of self-government, pressure continued to grow from the settlers for the restriction of rights under the Cape Clause. In 1925 the government of Rhodesia appointed a commission under the chairmanship of Sir Morris Carter, a former chief justice of Uganda and Tanganyika, to examine the possibilities of introducing a land policy that was more in keeping with the views of the local settlers than those that had prevailed in the Colonial Office. The Carter Commission was to determine whether the country should not be divided into European and African areas with the rights to hold land in each area being confined to the respective racial groups; that is, whether the Cape Clause should be abolished.

The commission report in 1926 [6] stated that separation of Africans and Europeans was both expedient and practicable. The expressed view, which still pervades much of Southern and Central Africa, was that "however desirable it may be that members of the two races should live together side by side with equal rights as regards the holding of land, we are convinced that in practice, probably for generations to come, such a policy is not practicable nor in the best interests of the two races, and that until the native has advanced much farther on the paths of civilization, it is better that points of contact between the two races should be reduced." [7]

The commission advanced many social, economic, and psychological reasons for the segregation of land holdings. They cited the fears of European farmers that proximity to native lands would spread livestock disease; that stock thefts would increase; that land values would depreciate if African farmers were interspersed with European farms. The commission also took the view that interspersed farms would create an atmosphere of insecurity which would tend to slow down the rate of European immigration into the country. There can be little doubt that this aspect of the problem carried considerable weight in the commission's deliberations. The commission maintained that Africans would prefer "to live among their own people," but also held that if Africans desired to purchase land outside the tribal areas, then they should have the opportunity to do so, though only in segregated areas designated for that purpose.

The commission's recommendations represented an extension of the principle of segregation by race. The Cape Clause was to be repealed. The country was to be divided into European and African areas and there would be no further right of indiscriminate purchase of land by members of either race. The commission considered the possibility of dividing the country into separate, consolidated areas by race, but, whatever views they may have held as to the desirability of partition or territorial *apartheid,* there was never any serious question of the implementation of such a policy. The complete separation of European and African areas would have involved so much social upheaval and cost that it was deemed wholly impractical. The commission did, however, recommend that the European areas be consolidated by setting aside lands abutting the existing European farms and ranches for later European settlement. These lands, adjacent to the choice areas already settled by Europeans, were deemed suitable for European occupation even though in some instances Africans were squatting on them. The criteria for European occupation were those of location and fertility — the capacity of the land as a means of providing a fairly high level of living for its owners. This was essentially a European "needs test," that is, the land had to be capable of providing an adequate income that would be attractive to potential immigrants and sufficient to maintain European standards of consumption.

The commissioners considered the existing reserves of 21,000,000 acres to be adequate for the needs of some 700,000 Africans residing in them. They felt, however, that some provision had to be made for a further 250,000 Africans residing, squatting, or farming on rented land in the European areas and in those areas that were to be declared to be European. In addition, further acreage should be made available for an estimated 50,000 African families already in the reserves who "may wish to take up land on individual tenure or will remain on land allocated to Natives outside the Reserves." The commissioners added up these needs and recommended that enough additional lands be apportioned for African use to provide between 96 and 103 acres per family (estimated at 3.5 persons). The exact acreage to be made available was to depend on the extent of mission, forest, and national park land available for redistribution, but they calculated that the implementation of their main recommendations would provide grazing for 5 to 6 head of livestock, as well as 20 acres of arable land per African family.

In the commission's view the needs of Africans would be met by making enough land available to sustain each family at subsistence level. Average acreage per family, rather than income off that acreage, was the criterion for gauging African requirements. This criterion set a pattern that has been followed ever since. It is a pattern based on a static concept, that is, land is the only factor of production, and the aim of land policy is to provide land enough for each African family to subsist. This emphasis on land as an end in itself rather than a means of raising average incomes has persisted to the present.

The principles recommended by the Morris Carter Commission are the basis of the present system of land apportionment. Under pressure from local white settlers, the government abandoned the earlier admonition of the British government to the British South Africa Company that Africans must have the same rights as non-Africans in land transactions, and moved toward the South African model of complete area segregation. The government did recommend that certain areas be set aside in which Africans could purchase land and farm on an individual basis. In the minds of many settlers in Rhodesia, however, this was a *quid pro quo* for the dropping of the right of indiscriminate purchase of land by Africans.

The commission also recognized the emergence of an urbanized "detribalized" African — even though their numbers were very few in 1925. Excepting those Africans needed for work in the European urban areas, the commission recommended that detribalized Africans should live in townships in the native areas, and provision should be made for these townships. The fact that there was no economic reason for townships to exist in these areas appeared to have been overlooked.[8] In this respect the commission's recommendations confirmed a pattern of thought that, backed by subsequent legislation, made every African who worked in a European area a temporary visitor. This line of reasoning, which is still part of the philosophy of the apportionment acts, has exacerbated many of the difficulties arising from the present migratory labor system.

The government accepted the principles of the Carter Commission's report and incorporated them into the Land Apportionment Act of 1930. This act, which had been amended several times in the ensuing years and replaced by the act of 1941, has been the cornerstone of land policy in Southern Rhodesia. It has constituted one of the most contentious issues affecting race relations in the colony. There have been modifications of it to meet special situations — the law was modified, for example, to permit African students to reside at the multiracial university in Salisbury and to enable an African barrister to open up chambers in the city.[9] At the time of writing further modifications have been proposed such as the desegregation of certain recreational facilities.[10] By and large, however, the system of land apportionment in the act has been one of the major institutions used to divide the economy into noncompeting racial groups and to differentiate the opportunities open to the members of each group.

The 1930 act led to the formal establishment of a European Area, a Native Area, an Undetermined Area, a Forest Area, and an Unassigned Area. (The reserves were already formally established.) All but the European area were described in schedules attached to the act; in other words, the European area consisted of all land not in the schedules or special government notices that placed the land in another of the categories mentioned above. The native area was in effect the native purchase area as recommended by the Carter Commission. The native areas, like the reserves, were areas in which "no person other than an indigenous native may hold or occupy land." The total area apportioned for Africans was 28.5 million acres — 21 million acres of reserves and 7.5 million acres in which those Africans who wished to farm on an individual basis, rather than communally, could purchase land. The European areas were slightly more than 49 million acres in all.

The act also established a Native Land Board which could recommend the sale of land in purchase areas to indigenous Africans on "payment of such purchase price as the Minister of Agriculture and Land may determine." The Land Board could prescribe conditions prior to the granting of land, and the land could be forfeited on failure of "beneficial occupation." [11] However, though the Land Board was entitled to sell some 7.5 million acres to individual owners, not much more than one million acres, occupied by some 6,500 farmers, has been disposed of up to the present time. Purchase areas require surveying, many of them lack water and roads, and there has been no capital available for their development. In addition, large portions are infested by the tsetse fly. The biggest obstacle, however, has been that many of the areas have been occupied by African squatters who had moved on to them before they were classified as purchase areas.

In the area declared to be "undetermined," Europeans could sell their lands to Africans, and once this was done the land would become part of the "native area." The undetermined area was less than 90,000 acres in extent. The forest area, which was to be preserved for afforestation, was composed of 590,000 acres. The unassigned area of 17,793,000 acres was to remain unassigned to Europeans or Africans. Pending such assignation, there could be no alienation of this land, most of which was in remote and dry areas, and a portion of which was infested by tsetse fly. In the following years, as is shown below, this unassigned land was to provide a cushion for expanding acreage to meet the subsistence requirements of an increasing African population without diminishing European acreage.

No African was entitled to hold or occupy land in the European areas except under certain special provisions of the Land Apportionment Act. One of these was that an African could be a "labor tenant." The owner or occupier of alienated land could enter an agreement "whereunder a native or his family shall be permitted to occupy a portion of such land under condition that he supply labor to such owner or occupier." Provision was also made for municipal and other local authorities to provide land for the use and occupation of Africans. Africans could not purchase such land. Similarly, no Europeans, other than educators, missionaries, or traders, could occupy land in the African areas.

In 1941 a new consolidated Land Apportionment Act was passed. It retained the principal features of the 1930 act but tightened up the conditions under which an African could occupy land in a European area. This was partially aimed at preventing European farmers from leasing lands to Africans in return for their labor or for rent. This system of "Kaffir farming," as it is known in Southern Africa, was widely resented by many Europeans who found that despite the Land Apportionment Act their neighbors were still Africans. The act also tightened the provisions whereby non-Africans could occupy land in native areas; this was done to curb the Europeans' practice of renting purchase areas for the grazing of stock. Other clauses permitted the establishment of native townships in the native areas, as recommended by the Carter Commission. In addition, the governor was also given the power, requested by local authorities, to approve the establishment near European towns of native urban areas where it would be lawful for Africans to occupy, though not to own, land. (The local authorities did not respond to this invitation, and in 1945 an amendment was introduced to the act compelling municipalities and town management boards to establish native urban areas.)

The notion, as expressed in the apportionment acts of 1930 and 1941, that population should conform to an ethnic control map, ran counter to economic forces operating at the peasant level. African producers were wasteful in their use of land, but in the absence of capital and technical assistance, and without alternative forms of employment, land was essential to their security, just as it is in most peasant societies. As population increased or their lands became eroded, they merely moved on to unoccupied areas, regardless of whether the control map decreed these areas were to be European, unassigned, or for individual tenure. There were few fences in the colony. Furthermore, though some areas were supposed to be reserved for Europeans or for African purchase, many of these areas were supporting large African populations at the time the apportionment was put into effect. Consequently, despite the legislative division of the country into different zones of racial occupation, the actual situation was quite different.

During the war years, little was done to disturb the Africans living or farming in unauthorized areas. By 1948, however, the problem of implementing the division of land between Europeans and Africans assumed some urgency. The African population had increased by more than 700,000 persons between 1941 and 1948, while the area apportioned for their use had remained almost unchanged. Close to 300,000 Africans were either residing on European-owned land or were occupying land within the areas marked for European use. The demand for European land was increased by returning servicemen and growing numbers of immigrants. In addition, land was needed for African servicemen who were returning to Southern Rhodesia. At the time, 17 million acres of land were still officially designated as unassigned and 15 million acres within the European area had not been alienated, though much of it was occupied by African squatters.

The government embarked on a policy of clearing Africans from European areas. Africans were evicted even though they had occupied some of these areas for generations. Frequently there was no place for these people to go, and in some instances, the government attempted to resettle the illegal land-occupiers in reserves. Unrest and violence followed, and in 1948 the government set up a committee "to inquire into the question of additional land for native occupation." [12] This committee and subsequent committees embarked on a series of exercises whereby the African areas were gradually expanded at the expense of the unassigned areas, which were largely infertile and disease-ridden. Some of the additional areas apportioned for African use were communally held; others were "purchase areas" where individual Africans could purchase land. The new communal areas were designated as "Special Native Areas" to distinguish them from the reserves already provided for in the constitution, but to all intents and purposes the rights to land and methods of production within the special areas were no different. (To have expanded the reserves would have required a change in the constitution and this would have required an exchange of views with the British government about the issue of discrimination in land allocation. This might well have been embarrassing to the government of Southern Rhodesia.)

As is shown in Table 4, the European area has remained almost unchanged in extent from 1930 to 1959; during that time, though,

Table 4. Distribution of Southern Rhodesia's land into "areas," 1930, 1953, and 1959 (in acres)

	1930	1953	1959
European Area	49,149,174	47,407,792	48,062,000
Native Reserves	21,600,000	20,859,350	21,020,000
Native Purchase Areas	7,464,566	5,657,135	8,052,000
Special Native Areas	—	4,135,427	12,878,000
Unassigned	17,793,300	14,207,918	—
Wankie Game Reserve	—	2,989,000	4,000,000
Forest Area	590,500	987,745	3,190,000
Undetermined	88,540	59,755	57,000
Total	96,686,080	96,304,122	97,259,000

Source: Southern Rhodesia Legislative Assembly, *Second Report of the Select Committee on Resettlement of Natives*, Presented to the House on Tuesday, August 16, 1960 (Salisbury: Government Printer, 1960), p. 15. The document contains the following note: "The above figures are approximate, Apparent discrepancies in the totals are due to surveys which from time to time have fixed accurately natural boundaries such as rivers and mountain ranges." I have reproduced the figures exactly as given in the source document, though it would be possible to make small revisions in some of them in view of information contained in the annual reports of the chief native commissioner. There were no substantial changes in land distribution in 1960, 1961, 1962 or 1963.

the total area available for African occupation was expanded by 13 million acres, from about 29 million to close to 42 million acres, the new land being taken almost entirely from the 18 million unassigned acres. By 1961, however, all of the land in Southern Rhodesia had been assigned, and some 37,000 African families were still squatting or farming in unauthorized areas. Once again, a select committee was grappling with the problem. They recommended some purchase of European land for African use, the conversion of purchase areas into special native areas so as to leave African squatters undisturbed and the establishment of small unreserved areas where farmers of any race could buy land. However, these recommendations have not been accepted; they were undeniably one of the factors that contributed to the defeat of the government in 1963 and at present the situation remains as before. Now that there is no more unassigned land available any extension of African acreage will have to be at the expense of the European area or there will have to be a move away from the present policy of separation toward one of integration.

SIZE AND QUALITY OF THE NATIVE AREAS

Between about 1930 and 1960 the population of Rhodesia increased from around 1.1 million to 3 million. The number of Europeans grew from approximately 50,000 to 220,000, while the African population increased from about one million to about 2.9 million. Since 1930 the European areas have been close to 48 million acres while the African areas expanded from 21 million to 42 million acres. In 1961 there were less than 7,000 European farms and ranches in the country. Their average size was close to 5,000 acres, but 895 of these farms were more than 10,000 acres in size and accounted for 19 million acres. In 1960 there were nearly 350,000 holdings in the "Native Areas."

The native areas of Southern Rhodesia are almost wholly agricultural. They consist of native reserves and special native areas, where farming is still on a communal basis governed by tribal tradition, and the native purchase areas, where farms are individually owned. As shown on the map, these areas are not homogeneous nor are they contiguous. Communal farming is carried on in 157 different areas scattered throughout the country, about one third of the total area being in arid regions of Matabeleland. The blocs vary considerably in size, the six largest accounting for 812 million acres, the six smallest for only 63,000 acres or 2 percent of the total area. The average size, arithmetically, is 20,000 acres. There are 185 native purchase areas ranging from 732,000 acres to less than 3000 acres, the average size being 95,000 acres.

The primary limitations on the agricultural output of African farms are imposed by natural conditions, the dominant factors being the extent and distribution of rainfall and the fertility of the soil. Annual rainfall exceeds 32 inches in 17.6 percent of the country, but only 8.4 percent of the African areas — or 3.15 million acres — lie in these regions, compared with more than 12 million acres of European land. Half of the country and half of the African areas are in the zone receiving 24 to 32 inches of rainfall. Though 31 percent of the country has a rainfall of less than 24 inches, close to 39 percent of the African areas is in this low rainfall area.

As was pointed out in the preceding chapter, Southern Rhodesia is not a well-endowed country agriculturally. The following table shows how the various land-use zones discussed in Chapter 1 are divided between European and non-European areas. It is clear that the process of land apportionment has favored European producers. Not only does the total area allocated for the small number of non-Africans exceed that allocated for African use, but non-African producers hold the bulk of the land suited for intensive use. They occupy 98 percent of the region suited for dairying and fruit-farming, and 82 percent, 67 percent, and 60 percent re-

Table 5. *African and non-African shares of various land-use zones in Southern Rhodesia*

Zone	Land in square miles			Percent of total land		
	Total	African	Non-African	Total	African	Non-African
All zones	153,740	66,430	87,310	100	43	57
1	1,740	30	1,710	100	2	98
2a	13,620	2,400	11,130	100	18	82
2b	9,880	3,240	6,639	100	33	67
2c	7,740	3,070	4,670	100	40	60
3	58,760	29,500	29,260	100	50	50
4a	15,979	4,970	11,000	100	31	69
4b	23,120	11,040	12,070	100	48	52
5	22,910	12,180	10,730	100	53	47

Description of zones
Zone 1: Suitable for afforestation, fruit, and intensive animal production.
Zone 2a: Suitable for intensive farming.
Zone 2b: Suitable for intensive farming, but subject to moderate dry spells.
Zone 2c: Limit of area suited to intensive farming.
Zone 3: Suitable for fodder crops and drought-resistant crops, but subject to dry spells.
Zone 4a: Uncertain conditions but suitable for some fodder and drought-resistant crops.
Zone 4b: Unsuitable for grain though possible to grow fodder crops.
Zone 5: Suitable only for extensive cattle ranching.
  Source: The information upon which this table is based is derived from the Minister of Agriculture and Lands, *Farming Systems in Southern Rhodesia*, Bulletin no. 1599 (Salisbury: Government Printer, September–October 1951).

spectively of the three other zones suited for intensive production. In short, 70 percent of the 32,900 square miles that comprise the area suitable for intensive production have been earmarked for European use. For the rest, the country appears to be divided fairly equally between non-Africans and Africans, except that the small region in Zone 4a is primarily European by virtue of its location close to the main railroad from Salisbury to Bulawayo.

The African areas include 30 percent of the land that is suitable for intensive farming. They also include half of the largest land-use region in the country that is suitable for some fodder and drought-resistant crops and half of the land suitable for extensive cattle grazing. Although the Africans do not have an equitable share of the most favorable farming areas, this in itself cannot fully account for the differences in rates of output between the European and African sectors, nor for the low productivity of African agriculture. In this respect, the problems of raising African agricultural productivity can be separated from the problems of inequitable land distribution, and can be identified with the problems of raising African agricultural productivity in other parts of Southern, Central, and East Africa.

LAND APPORTIONMENT AND URBANIZATION

The sudden postwar spurt in Southern Rhodesia's economic development gave rise to problems of urbanization. Such social and economic problems would have arisen in most societies, but they were compounded in Southern Rhodesia by the continued prevalence of the philosophy that governed the land apportionment acts. According to the Urban Affairs Commission, 37 percent of the African labor force in 1956 — 244,905 out of a total of 609,953 wage-earners — were employed in non-rural occupations in towns, suburbs, mining camps, or other places where the European population exceeded 1,200. Yet the commission reported that despite this growth in nonrural labor "up to the present European thought and action has tended to regard the African as being essentially a member of a rural society with urban activities regarded as a temporary deviation from the norm." [13]

The major centers of economic activity in Southern Rhodesia are in the European areas, but the essence of the apportionment acts is that "no native shall acquire, lease, or occupy land in European areas," a theme in keeping with the philosophy of noncompeting racial groups, but not with the creation of a stable, urban community and labor force.[14] From the outset control measures such as the pass system and the registration of employment contracts were instituted to regulate the flow of labor to the urban areas; but as the demand for urban labor increased the custom developed, without legal foundation, of allowing Africans to reside in locations on the outskirts of European towns, though their numbers were subject to control.

The Land Apportionment Act of 1941 permitted the governor to approve the establishment of native urban areas by local authorities, making it lawful for Africans to occupy land in the vicinity of European centers of activity. The local authorities did not respond to this invitation, however, and another act (Act No. 14 of 1945) made the establishment of such areas obligatory. Still later, the Native Accommodation and Registration Act (Act No. 6 of 1946), obliged the local authorities to provide adequate housing for urban Africans. At present there are three types of residential areas for Africans: Native Urban Areas, Native Locations, and Native Village Settlements. The administrative and legal aspects of control over these areas are so complex and confused that the Urban Affairs Commission of 1958 was constrained to comment: "If this overlap of powers is confusing to officials of the government, how much more so must it be to others and particularly to those who are expected to settle and make their homes on the land so set apart for them." [15]

Until 1963, in all these urban settlements, the philosophy that Africans are temporary visitors has been expressed in the denial of the right to purchase land, although Africans could lease land for 99 years in the native village settlements, provided the lessees agreed to erect a house to meet certain requirements. Since 1963 it has been possible for Africans to purchase land in certain townships and to borrow funds for building homes. (Land purchases and settlements are designed to meet the needs of the small group of middle-class Africans who are now emerging.) For the remainder, accommodation is provided primarily by the local authorities. The relation between housing and the migratory labor system is important. The act of 1946 obliged local authorities to charge the same rental for single quarters as for married quarters.

Since single quarters are cheaper to erect (in the form of hostels) and cheaper to maintain than married quarters, the ratio of single to married quarters is very high. The result is that housing for wives and families is very scarce, and this has militated against the movement of whole families to urban areas. The effect has been to reinforce the migratory labor system by encouraging men to leave their families in the rural areas while taking up wage employment in the towns.

The Urban African Affairs Commission of 1958 made many far-reaching recommendations. It did not forego the policy of residential segregation but urged the government to recognize the existence of permanently urbanized African communities. It also urged modification of the Land Apportionment Act to give security of tenure to these communities stressing the improved efficiency to be gained by reducing labor turnover and stabilizing the labor force. The commissioners recommended that Africans be given the right to purchase land in these urban areas, that local authorities change their methods of financing housing, and that a greater number of married quarters be constructed. They also suggested that rents for married persons be subsidized and that the laws of supply and demand be recognized as better regulators of the labor supply than were past laws. Despite the recommendations of this report the policy of considering Africans in urban areas as temporary visitors has continued. This has added to the pressures on rural Africans to become migratory laborers and, as will be shown later, has contributed to the problems of agricultural development in the African areas.

CONCLUSION

The role of land as a factor of production and the effects of changing tenurial arrangements in the African areas are discussed in the next part of this book. However, before concluding this chapter on the general policy of apportionment, there are several related economic and political aspects of the apportionment policy that deserve consideration. The evolution of the system of apportionment supports the view that national resources have been so allocated as to maintain high consumption levels for Europeans even though the system of allocation penalizes the Africans. Nothing could show this more clearly than the ratio of land distribution by race and the quality of the land so distributed and farmed by each group.

About 15 percent of the European areas are suitable for cultivation; 3 percent are used for cultivation; in 1961, 10 million acres of European land were still unalienated. Thus a great deal of cultivable land is left unused largely through lack of capital and a lack of skilled manpower. These land resources are idle resources contributing little to the economy, though they may be considered "excess capacity" lands held in reserve to meet any sudden demand for products. (This type of excess capacity was an important factor in enabling the European producers to respond to high tobacco prices and so raise the level of exports to a point that could provide for the imports needed for development purposes.) Nevertheless, idle resources do not contribute to economic growth, especially when there are underemployed or unemployed human resources that could combine with the land and add to national output. (In addition, the use of relatively large amounts of scarce capital to "shift" subsistence producers from one area to another has resulted in no net increase in African output.)

It is also plain that any policy premised on providing land enough for subsistence production for all the African people is a self-defeating policy. Such a policy can only perpetuate low levels of productivity and economic stagnation. One of the important processes in economic development is to reduce the number of people engaged in food production, so as to release labor for other types of gainful employment. In this regard a major issue in Southern Rhodesia is whether the economy as a whole can expand rapidly enough to absorb whatever population comes off the land. Part of this process of economic expansion depends on higher-yielding use of human and other resources. For this to happen there has to be a reorganization of existing institutional arrangements.

The dilemma and conflict of racial division of land and economic growth is well illustrated by a simple example. There are in the African areas some lands that are suited for tea production. The capital required to establish a moderate-sized tea plantation ranges from £150 to £500 per acre. Private European enterprise is prepared to provide both the capital and the skill to develop tea estates in the African areas. This would convert low-yielding subsistence areas into high-yielding tea areas. But the estate operators want security of tenure before they will make any substantial investments. However, because of the obsession over land and race, it is impossible to give any guarantee of tenure; as a result the economy as a whole loses.

There are possible arrangements that could be made within the existing framework of land apportionment, such as joint European-African cooperative ventures or joint estate and "outgrower" schemes. However, it is unlikely that private capital would be attracted by these arrangements so that if any such arrangements were made, public funds would have to be used for these developments. This would require a diversion of funds that might have been used for other productive purposes. Thus, policies that place racial considerations above others are either preventing the introduction of capital and skills in the African areas or are limiting the total amount of investment in agricultural development. Ironically, a similar situation exists in Uganda where there is a national policy of the paramountcy of African interests. There the Europeans who produce tea have the capital and skills, but cannot acquire more land because the Africans are fearful of any extension of European control over land. In both instances, because of racial considerations, the potential of the land is not being fully exploited. In Southern Rhodesia, land in the European areas is left idle because of lack of capital, while Africans are underemployed because of lack of land.

The system of apportionment in Southern Rhodesia was evolved at a time when most Africans required protection from the superior purchasing power of the Europeans. Today it is still true that many Africans are so unsophisticated that they require protection from speculators. However, the division of land along racial lines is immobilizing resources and as such has little to commend it on economic grounds. There are various means whereby this situation can be changed. One such means would be to repeal much of the Land Apportionment Act and reinstate the Cape Clause whereby interracial sales or exchanges of land have to be approved by a magistrate. Another would be to establish land boards, with European and African representation, to oversee any sale or exchange of land.

Up to the present, however, the policy of land apportionment has been a positive expression of the philosophy that Europeans and Africans should form noncompeting groups and that there should be differential standards for each group. There is no "competition" for land between these groups within the framework of a market economy. In the absence of market "competition" between groups legislative apportionment creates a direct link between the franchise and land. At present the policy on land apportionment is made by a government elected as the representatives of the qualified voters and these voters represent a minority with a vested interest in maintaining the present system. This can only be changed within the present system by the legislators' abandoning their present positions — an unlikely event, as they represent those who fear they have much to lose by change. The other method of change within the parliamentary system would be to extend the franchise to more Africans so that their interests would be more fully represented. This has been resisted.

Land hunger is a potent force in a peasant society, however, and the countervailing force to parliamentary action may well be extralegal. The implications of the following remarks, the first by an African nationalist and the other by a Royal Commission, require no comment: "The problem of the African, the cause behind this story of a people's agony is LANDLESSNESS: LANDLESSNESS, so that the people will be forced out into the labour market, to the mines and farms where they will be herded together in camps, compounds and locations, where each white industrialist, farmer and housewife will be allotted his or her fair share of hands. In the towns only their labour is wanted — themselves not . . . Even prejudiced experts on the causes of the Mau Mau movement admit that land of which the Kikuya tribesmen had been deprived was among the major causes of the Mau Mau revolt." [16]

The Royal Commission that examined land problems in East Africa stated:

Two facts stand out resulting from the policy of the exclusive tenure of land in the Highlands by Europeans. Firstly, the bitterness which has persisted over the extinguishing of African right in the area, and secondly the sense of injustice caused in African eyes by broad areas reserved for a few individuals alongside an African reserve in which land hunger exists. Even those loyal Kikuya who have been risking their all in the fight against Mau Mau have, in giving evidence before us, questioned the grounds for maintaining unused land for the exclusive use of Europeans when the needs of their people are so great. It was seldom that any African suggested to us that any European who was using his land fully should be deprived of that land, but our attention was constantly being directed to the fact of unused or partially used land in the Highlands.[17]

It is not for us to comment on the moral or social aspects of land apportionment; however, from an economic viewpoint, it militates against economic growth through a distortion of resource allocation. Whether the economic costs of this system will ever weigh enough to change it within the present legislative framework is a moot question. If not, other forces may bring about changes despite the will of the minority.

Chapter 4

The Dual Agricultural Economy

STRUCTURAL DUALISM

Most of the countries in Southern, Central, and East Africa contain two distinct agricultural economies, a "modern" sector organized primarily by nonindigenous entrepreneurs, settlers, and farmers, and a "traditional" sector that is exclusively indigenous. The modern sector takes various forms. In some countries, such as Tanganyika, it is essentially a limited enclave producing primary products for export. In other areas, such as South Africa and Southern Rhodesia, the modern sector is diversified and produces both for internal consumption and for export. The indigenous sector, however, never produces solely for export, though it may produce both for export and for internal consumption.

The economy of Southern Rhodesia encompasses both modern and traditional agriculture. The apportionment of land by race provides a ready geographic basis for distinguishing the two sectors, since the European areas can be equated with modern agriculture and the African areas with the traditional agriculture.

A major distinction between the two agricultural systems lies in the size of the holdings in each; European agriculture is large-scale, African agriculture is small-scale. In this the pattern is not dissimilar from the pattern of some Latin American countries, such as Colombia. In Rhodesia, however, the prevailing concepts of tenure and property rights enhance the divergent structure of production units much more than does the system in Colombia. The farms in the European areas have been surveyed and are clearly identifiable. They include both crop land and grazing land within their boundaries. African holdings, on the other hand, are not clearly identified nor do they include grazing land. Grazing land is communal and at best the size of holdings "associated" with a family can only be estimated.

A survey of European holdings in 1956–1957 indicated that there were less than 7,000 production units on 33 million acres of land. Half the farms were in the 1,000–5,000 acre range, but approximately 42 percent of the European land was in farms or ranches that exceeded 25,000 acres in size.[1] In 1959 the mean size was slightly below 5,000 acres, of which 122 acres were cultivated. If the 895 ranches of more than 10,000 acres each are excluded, the average size of holding in 1959 was close to 2,500 acres, of which 140 acres were cultivated.[2] Most of the cultivated acreage is in the areas of higher rainfall where production units range from 2,000 to 3,000 acres. In the fertile Mazoe Valley, for example, 248 farms occupy 787,000 acres, of which 15 percent are cultivated.

There is no information on the average size of African holdings. In 1960 close to 350,000 African families lived in the African areas. In the purchase areas, where approximately 6,500 families held land, holdings ranged in size from 50 acres to 1,000 acres in the driest regions. It is estimated that the remainder of the African areas provided 83 acres of land per family and that of these slightly more than 8 acres were cultivated.[3] The distribution of the population is not even, however, and in some areas the average holding is small, being less than 6 acres of cultivated land per family, while in the drier areas the average size is more than 15 acres.[4] The size varies over a wide range within the different African areas; one sample of 473 holdings in all rainfall areas indicated that 5 percent were smaller than 5 acres, 53 percent were between 6 and 10 acres, and 5 percent more than 40 acres in size.[5]

The differences in size of holdings extends also to livestock herds. The principal livestock in Southern Rhodesia are cattle, and in 1958 Europeans owned 1.5 million head while Africans held 2 million.[6] European herds averaged close to 300 head per production unit. The size of herd varied; in the principal live-stock-raising areas, the average size of a herd is close to 480 head, while in the principal crop-raising areas it is close to 280 head.[7] In 1960 there were 231,000 African livestock owners with an average of slightly more than 5 adult cattle per owner.[8] The range in size of individual herds is not known, but a sample of 486 cultivators indicated that 12 percent had no cattle, 21 percent had between 1 and 5 head, and less than 1 percent had more than 40 head.[9]

Another major difference between European and African agriculture concerns regional and crop specialization. In Colombia both large-scale and small-scale producers grow coffee in the coffee-producing areas. This is not the case in Southern Rhodesia. The European producers specialize by area and product. For example, more than 70 percent of the corn grown by Europeans is produced in the corn belt.[10] The principal tobacco-producing areas are located in the region best suited for profitable tobacco production. Dairying is carried on in the most economic areas for the production of dairy products. In contrast, there is little regional specialization of production in the African areas. The same principal crops are grown throughout the country, regardless of climatic conditions. The incomplete 1948–1949 sample survey indicated that the average acreage under individual crops was much the same in different regions.[11] Since then there has been a tendency to increase production of corn rather than drought-resistant crops in the drier areas.[12]

The differences in specialization are also apparent in livestock production. Mixed livestock-crop farming is practiced in all parts of the country outside the regions that are infested by the tsetse fly. European production, however, is concentrated most heavily in the areas where the marginal returns from raising livestock are highest relative to other forms of production. African livestock, on the other hand, are concentrated most heavily in the areas of good rainfall where land could be used to greater economic advantage under crops, since such land under cultivation yields an average return three or four times greater than when it is used for grazing. Differences in product specialization apply to livestock too. European producers raise livestock for breeding purposes, or for slaughter, or for dairying as distinct from other forms of production. African producers do not differentiate in the end products of their herds.

The difference in techniques of production is pronounced. European producers have adapted Western technology to African conditions and have combined resources to meet changing economic conditions. The raising of tobacco and corn illustrates this. As the demand for these crops increased and land prices rose, production was intensified in the areas best suited for these crops. Between 1951 and 1957 acreage under tobacco cultivation in the six major tobacco-producing areas declined by 10 percent but yield per acre rose by 50 percent; in the major corn-producing areas acreage under cultivation expanded by 17 percent and aver-

age yields rose by more than 40 percent.[13] These higher yields
through intensification of land-use involved heavier expenditures
in yield-increasing products, principally fertilizer, and improved
techniques of production. The consumption of fertilizer has risen
very rapidly in Southern Rhodesia, representing close to 10 percent of total current expenditures in European agriculture in
1958.[14] Expenditures on hybrid corn were increased, and between
1950 and 1958 the acreage planted to hybrid corn was doubled,
to cover more than 80 percent of all the corn-producing areas.
(The average yield from an acre of hybrid corn is 11.3 bags compared with 5.9 bags from an acre planted to ordinary corn.)[15] At
the same time rapid mechanization took place, while the labor
force increased only slightly. Capital was also being substituted
for labor.[16]

Techniques of production in the African areas are as different
from those in the European areas as day is from night. The family
is the labor unit. There has been very little application of Western
technology. Resources are not flexibly allocated to meet changing
demand. Farming is still based on principles of shifting cultivation, and despite the limited acreage land is used extensively.
Yields per acre are low, averaging between a quarter and a fifth
of those of comparable crops grown in the European area. Some
70 percent of the producers are using soil-depleting techniques of
production. Fewer than 2 percent use fertilizers or select seed and
many do not use organic matter to build up the humus in the
soil.[17] Aside from equipment, there is very little investment in
African agriculture. No precise figures are available but a sample
of 46 holdings indicates that investment in equipment ranges from
£15 to £81, the average for a 12-acre holding being around £30.[18]
The major pieces of equipment in the African areas are carts and
plows. There are few fences, storage bins, or other forms of investment.

Techniques of livestock production also differ markedly. In
European dairying both capital and skill are intensively employed.
There is very little dairy production in the African areas; though
cows are milked indiscriminately, official statistics indicate no
milk produced for sale by Africans. In general, European livestock
is extensively grazed with supplemental feeding in the dry, cold
winter. Grazing lands are maintained through rotation or by

regulating numbers of livestock on the range. The level of disease control is high, and herds are improved through artificial insemination. African production is largely a matter of the exploitation of the range cover. Heavy losses occur in the seasons when the range land cannot maintain livestock. There is almost no rotational grazing and outbreaks of disease are frequent.[19] As a result, while European producers of livestock receive an estimated 14 percent return on their capital, Africans receive only a 6 percent return.[20]

In Southern Rhodesia, as in most parts of Southern, Central, and East Africa, Europeans produce primarily for the market, and Africans do not. The principal crops produced by Europeans are Virginia flue-cured tobacco, corn, potatoes, tea, and a variety of lesser cash crops. They also produce fodder and green manure crops for maintaining soil fertility. The Africans grow corn, small grains, groundnuts, and a host of minor food crops. The only crops produced solely for the market are extremely small quantities of Turkish tobacco and cotton. (See Appendix B.)

The official estimates of agricultural production in the European and African sectors in 1958, which may be taken as a typical year, indicate that the gross value of output in the European sector was £42 million while that in the African sector was £25 million.[21] These figures and other estimates of output should not be accepted uncritically. The valuation of production and the adequacy of quantitative data are open to question. The amount of subsistence production in the African sector, for example, appears to be seriously underestimated. Yet this and other available estimates, even though subject to wide margins of error, do indicate the major differences between the two sectors in the value of output and in the proportions of total output marketed. They show that in 1958 the African sector produced well over one third of the total agricultural output in Southern Rhodesia but marketed around one tenth of the total *marketed* agricultural output. Africans marketed only 18 percent of their corn output, 11 percent of their small grains, and 10 percent of their groundnut production.[22] In contrast to this the Europeans marketed all their tobacco output and 75 percent of their corn output.

Even though a large part of the European areas are farmed extensively, average output per acre is higher than in the African areas and the value of output per *cultivated* acre three times as great as that in the African areas.[23] It is very difficult to compare labor inputs in the European and African areas because of the differences in composition of the labor force. (See Chapter 7.) However, in 1958 the 230,000 employees in European agriculture produced 40 percent more than was produced by the more than 300,000 families associated with African agriculture. The average gross value of output per European production unit was close to £6,000 and from fragmentary data it appears that net returns to management must have been at least £1,000.[24] In the African areas the average gross value of output was less than £80 per holding, and average gross money incomes were less than £15 per year. Average money outlays for current expenses in African agriculture are unknown, but samples indicate an average of £3 per holding, leaving a net income of £12 per family holding. If an imputed cost is charged for labor, seed, compost, transport, and rent, then the average returns for management must be very close to zero if not negative.

The differences in productivity and income between European and African sectors are so great that they confirm the dichotomy in the agricultural economy. The cumulative contrast is demonstrated by the differences in rates of growth in the two ethnic areas. Between 1937 and 1958 the total value of output in the European areas rose by more than one thousand percent; the total volume of output increased by 259 percent — one of the highest agricultural growth rates in the world.[25] The growth rate of African agriculture, however, rose very slowly indeed. Decade after decade in this century the rate of increase in output has been less than 3 percent per annum, a rate that has somewhat approximated the rate of population growth in the African areas. (See Appendix B for data on native output.)

CULTURAL DUALISM

Many in Rhodesia and elsewhere would maintain that such a disparity in rates of growth is caused by cultural factors rather than by technical or economic factors. This view has been expounded by Dr. J. H. Boeke in *Economics and Economic Policy of Dual Societies as Exemplified by Indonesia* (1953). While most of his theory is based on Indonesian experience, Dr. Boeke has generalized it to the East as a whole and much of it has been applied to other areas of the world and is widely accepted in Africa.[26] He holds that in nonhomogeneous societies containing two population groups: "The most advanced [social system] will have been imported from abroad and have gained its existence in the new environment without being able to oust or to assimilate the divergent social system that has grown up there, with the result that neither of them becomes general and characteristic for that society as a whole." Furthermore, "most frequently the imported system is high capitalism," and because of the different nature of the two societies, "it is advisable to keep the term social dualism because this emphasizes the fact that the essence of social dualism is the clash between an imported and an indigenous social system of divergent character." [27]

Social or cultural dualism is based on divergent attitudes toward increasing productivity. Operators in the more advanced sector are, by definition, capitalistic and rational in their economic behavior. The indigenous sector of the economy, however, is either precapitalistic or noncapitalistic. Its patterns of behavior, attitudes, and value systems are the antithesis of the capitalistic ethic. Typically, the noncapitalistic sector is rural; producers are not materialistic; incentives to increase production, such as higher prices, have little effect; the indigenous population is not interested in production for profit but is concerned only with satisfying a limited range of wants that is almost static in character. There is almost no organization or rationalization of production to ensure continuity of output, nor much cost-price analysis, and little understanding of credit. Because of their nonacquisitive economic mentality, it is difficult if not impossible for indigenous producers to adapt to Western technology.

Indigenous society demonstrates little economic dynamism and is slow to change. So much so that, "social-economic dualism, far from being a passing phase, the termination of which may be hastened considerably by a Western policy of integration, must be accepted as a permanent characteristic of a large number of important countries, permanent at least within the measurable distance of time." Consequently there must be a "dichotomy of social-economic policy, which is fundamentally different according to the social groups at which it is aimed." [28]

In many respects the case of Southern Rhodesia fits the framework described by Dr. Boeke. There is an indigenous sector and a European sector largely imported from abroad. Each has a different culture, and neither has ousted or assimilated the other. Nevertheless, the notion that cultural factors explain the differences between European and African patterns of economic behavior, while widely held, is not universally accepted. Perhaps this can best be illustrated by extracts from a debate in 1960 in the legislative assembly of Southern Rhodesia where the general issue of African agricultural development was being discussed. During this debate the salient issues raised — knowingly or unknowingly — involved the validity of some of the short-run implications of the theory of cultural dualism.

On the one side speakers claimed that: "The African in general has no desire to produce more than he needs for subsistence level. That is the experience, I think, of all of us . . . who have lived here long enough . . . [and I think we] realize that [putting] silver in his pocket . . . is not the African's first aim and object. His first aim and object is to have enough food to eat and enough [home-made] beer to drink: he is not prepared to put enough effort into producing more. If I took up the time of the House I could give example after example where Africans have been shown by extension officers how to increase their yield per acre, but the moment the extension officer has been withdrawn their yield per acre has slumped to even lower than it was before the extension officer arrived." (2880)

The same speaker, discussing a decline in Turkish tobacco output during the incipient program for encouraging production of this crop, commented that "a large number of growers not only do not understand what they are doing but when they grow the crop they cannot be bothered to reap it." Commenting on the lack of interest of Africans in irrigation work, he went on to say that, in his opinion, this lack of interest was based on the "need for extra work" to produce two crops a year rather than one, and that while the Africans "may earn twice as much money — they are not interested in that, they are interested in having a subsistence level."

Another speaker expressed the view that "one of the biggest problems is the high leisure preference of the African — if he is offered the prospect of working twice as long for twice as much money he will prefer to work half as long for half as much." (2888) Still another suggested that a possible effect of raising prices to producers by removing a tax on African corn would be to reduce output by those producers. "By removing the levy and making it more profitable for the growers . . . it may result that the African may produce half as much as he did before, because the results are better." In the same vein was this comment on a suggestion that prices to some producers in remote areas be lowered by reducing a transport subsidy. "The result in the remote areas might again backfire because it is less profitable: . . . you might find all of a sudden twice as much maize is being grown . . . I think we must take the mentality of the people with whom we are dealing into account at the same time as the economics concerned. I think some [of the parliamentarians] who talked on this are probably submerged by too little knowledge of the attitudes and mental responses of the people with whom we are dealing. It is not purely a matter of economics. It is a matter of people and their reaction as people . . . There are vastly different reactions by Africans (as compared with Europeans) to certain financial and economic stimuli." (2889) A further comment in support of the notion of cultural dualism attributed the low level of productivity to "nothing more or less than bone idle laziness on the part of certain Africans." (2889) "This laziness is a result of innate forces," the speaker added.

A minority of legislators dissented. They insisted that African producers were, in the main, interested in raising output and that the "key to [increasing output] is the stimulation of incentive" by removing such things as the disputed tax on production which "is a serious handicap to output." (2884) These speakers held that it was important to base policy on the assumption that the indigenous producer had much the same aspirations as the European producer. In their view technical and economic factors were more important than cultural factors and the important requisite was to provide the means to assist Africans to increase output. They asked whether "there is too little money spent on extension services" and whether "the African farmer is getting the same type of advice and instruction as his European counterpart." (2884) In the same vein, one speaker stressed the fact that if "you want to get the right concept of the effect of a levy [on an African-produced crop] I would remind you of the occasion when the Finance Minister tried to impose a tobacco levy [on European producers]." He maintained that Africans and Europeans react in the same way to such a tax and that "given the right advantages [the African] will improve." [29]

The dichotomy of views is relevant because it influences economic policy. Some speakers were maintaining that the African producers have the characteristics ascribed to the indigenous sector in a dualistic economy — low aspirations and low income goals. Their preferences for leisure are such that they do not work harder in response to offers of higher cash returns. They would not increase the amount of produce marketed if the price were to rise; on the contrary, because of their limited and fixed income goals, a decline in price would lead to increased production so as to reach that income goal, low though it may be. If these views are correct, then there is a sound basis for dualistic policies. High taxes on production or low controlled prices for agricultural output would be justified from a supply response point of view — that is, the supply curve would be a backward sloping curve and low prices would encourage increased output. Other speakers, taking an opposite point of view, maintained that the economic behavior of African producers was much the same as might be expected from producers in the modern sector of the economy, and that there was no need for dualistic policies to encourage increased output.

These views on the economic behavior of the Africans are so far apart that it would appear difficult to reconcile them. They can be reconciled, however, if the changing nature of the traditional economy is recognized. Prior to the arrival of the Europeans in Rhodesia in 1890, there was limited exchange by barter (a practice that still exists in some indigenous societies) but no universally accepted medium of exchange and no exchange economy. The introduction of money and the goods and services it could purchase began the process of transforming the indigenous subsistence economy into a market economy. Production for revenue rather than for consumption and the sale of labor for wages began to assume importance.

In the early stages of Southern Rhodesian development there

was a well-defined dual economy. A money-oriented exchange economy existed side by side with a subsistence economy. There was little intermingling of the two except through the migration of African labor into the money sector. (Early reports speak of African labor entering the wage economy for as little as three months a year.) Today the use of money has become widespread and has permeated all but the most primitive and isolated tribal areas. Despite the spread of money and the concept of the value and purchasing power of money, however, there is still some economic behavioral dualism *within* the traditional sector. Perhaps the situation might best be characterized as one in which economic man coexists in the same economy with *traditional man in transition toward becoming economic man.*

Economic man is not necessarily the economic man of the textbooks; he is, however, generally motivated by the economic principles embodied in the capitalistic system. He tends to have identifiable, growing wants that are beyond his means, and his economic activity is concerned with satisfying as many of these wants as possible. He has an "eye to economic chance" and is "willing to stir [himself] to seize it." [30] He is concerned with raising his income and to do this he usually sells his labor or products in the market that gives him the highest net return. By and large, economic man tends to be rational about both ends and means, and frequently postpones immediate consumption so as to save and invest in productive goods that will give him a larger profit in the future.

Economic man's rewards of power, social status, and material satisfaction tend to be derived, in good part, from performance in the marketplace. In order to maximize returns, he concerns himself with expanding the market for his goods and services. To do this he has broken down the restrictive trading practices of the precapitalistic system and has developed specialization of labor and production. He has organized processes whereby continuous supplies are forthcoming to meet demand. Both the supply and demand for goods and services are somewhat responsive to price, and price changes tend to have an effect on his patterns of production and consumption.

Traditional man developed in a closed subsistence economy; he was nonacquisitive and his status was determined by factors other than material wealth. His restricted economy, which was based on a plentiful supply of land, was in internal and external equilibrium: a low level of production satisfied a low level of needs. There was a timelessness about society, and production was considered only in terms of immediate wants; no saving for the future and production for consumption was a seasonal exercise. Within the system agricultural production required relatively little sustained effort; there was scant division of labor and only a few household industries, basket-weaving, working on iron for spears and hoes, weaving of cloth. Clothes, where they were worn, were provided from hides and skins. Traditional man was not inventive nor was he one who stirred himself to innovate or introduce changes. His system was adequate to provide for his needs. Noneconomic activities (or nonproductive activities) occupied much of the time of the typical tribesman and were undeniably an important element in his system of value. The marketplace as understood by economic man was virtually nonexistent.

Traditional man had minimal subsistence goals, and low production targets in terms of physical output. Once there was an adequate food supply it became a matter of indifference to him whether output was increased or not, though it seems fair to assume that it was a matter of some concern if increased output could only be "bought" at a price of increased economic activity. In the words of Professor Myint, discussing a similar situation elsewhere, "while the people might have lived near the minimum subsistence level that standard, according to their own lights, did not appear too wretched or inadequate. Thus, in spite of low productivity and lack of economic progress, there was no problem of economic discontent and frustration: wants and activities are on the whole adapted to each other and the people were in equilibrium with their environment." [31]

The introduction of the exchange economy disturbed the internal equilibrium of this closed economy, for it raised the levels of wants of the producers. The appearance of new goods and services stimulated new desires through a demonstration effect. The spread of education and the influence of the church widened horizons. The indigenous producer found his earlier nonmoney system in conflict with a system that required him to produce for revenue or sell his labor to satisfy his needs.

It is this conflict in values which makes it difficult to assess the nature of dualism *within* the traditional sector and the extent of its significance. Where traditional nonmoney values predominate over economic values producers react differently than if the situation is reversed. If traditional values hold sway, transitional man, having very low aspirations, does not respond to opportunities to raise his income in the same way as he would if economic values were uppermost. A high preference for noneconomic activities can lead to perverse reactions to price increases — that is, when prices rise a producer with a fixed income goal will perhaps market less than when prices were low. In the same vein, migratory laborers react differently to economic stimuli depending on the strength of traditional or economic values. Those laborers who have low material aspirations and high preferences for leisure or noneconomic activities can work for shorter periods when wages are raised so as to have more leisure time. The supply curve for such workers will bend backward and high wages will attract them for a shorter time than if wages were low.

How significant is the traditional influence and how significant the economic influence? One important element in answering this question is whether the wants of indigenous producers are limited to those that can be satisfied by fixed, low incomes. At least one group of fifty Africans sampled by the author indicated that the aspirations and needs of African laborers and producers are not fixed and that their income goals are clearly related to the length of time they have been exposed to European consumption levels. The sample consisted of fifty casual laborers, who had salaries of £3 to £5 per month. As accurately as was possible the expressed wants of this group were ranked. Those who had been in the money economy longer than their "rawer" fellow workers ranked their wants at a much higher level. For example, they preferred suits to traditional clothing, shoes to boots, meat to corn meal. This suggests that as Africans are exposed to the money economy their wants become more sophisticated. It is not their wants that are limited, but rather their ability to satisfy them. Another sample of thirty better-paid hotel workers who had been in wage employment for an even longer period ranked their wants at a still higher level. Their aspirations included furniture, durable consumer goods, and automobiles.[32]

The matter of whether Africans prefer to maximize leisure once incomes reach a certain level was also examined. If Africans do have a higher preference for leisure than for additional income, it follows that most migratory workers will withdraw from the wage economy as soon as they reach their income targets and will return to the indigenous areas to engage in highly valued non-economic activities there. This hypothesis was tested on the same fifty low-paid casual migratory laborers, all of whom had left their families in the indigenous areas. All were asked their *opinion* as to what they would do if their wages were doubled. There were many qualifications, but 20 percent of the higher-paid group and 46 percent of the lower-paid group said they would return to the African areas sooner than they had anticipated. Obviously maximizing income was not their goal. Yet, 60 percent of the higher-paid group and 30 percent of the lower-paid group said they did not think a wage raise would influence their termination of wage employment, that is, they wished to secure as high an income as possible to satisfy as many wants as possible. In this they were behaving like economic men. The remaining 20 percent of the higher-paid group and 24 percent of the lower-paid group were undecided, though it was apparent that their thinking was in terms of time rather than income. Many of these undecided workers appeared to have a fixed time at which they proposed to return, regardless of income.

The test was too elementary and too one-dimensional to support firm conclusions, but the results tend to indicate that the fixed income or target income hypothesis is more applicable to lower-paid workers than to higher-paid workers. The results might well have been influenced by the nature of the work done, the prestige associated with it, fringe benefits, and other factors. Significantly, however, the lower-paid workers were all newcomers to the wage economy and so presumably were still strongly committed to traditional values.

The samples were limited in size and not necessarily representative. Each and every worker had his own psychological make-up, differences of upbringing, and personal traits. Nevertheless, the fragmentary evidence provides a basis for stating what would appear to be obvious. The degree of exposure to the money economy and the demonstration effect of urban life tends to alter the stated reaction of migratory laborers to wage increases. The opportunity costs of "leisure" become higher as traditional man becomes more immersed in the world of the economic man.[33]

This view is supported by the results of interviews with fifty African producers: twenty-five communal producers with an average of 7 acres of cultivated land apiece, and twenty-five producers from the purchase areas who had their own farms ranging from 50 to 100 acres. The evidence gathered from these inquiries substantiates the view that length of exposure to the money economy, through the migratory labor system, had a definite bearing on the behavior of producers. There was a wide range of sophistication among the producers in the sample, but *all* of them were concerned with producing their own food, and prices had relatively little influence on the first allocation of resources. They considered their food requirements in terms of numbers of bags needed to sustain themselves and their families, not the value of the crops. Their primary production goals were to grow the requisite *amount* of each staple commodity needed to feed their families rather than to maximize the value of their output. This general principle applied even when producers knew that land and labor used for food production could yield crops that would bring in a higher total income.

The traditional influence was strong. The first requirement was a defense against the threat of famine and hunger through the production and storage of *visible* food supplies. All of the producers interviewed expressed a distrust of the distribution system to meet their requirements; their concern was with security rather than with higher income. (Though, as is shown in the section on marketing, the present marketing system encourages retention of food crops.) This overriding traditional emphasis on security helps to explain the lack of specialized production, why all producers tended to grow the same staple crops regardless of agronomic conditions or comparative advantages. Opportunities for widespread specialization in high-value cash crops, such as Oriental tobacco, are limited, but even where the opportunity exists producers concentrate on producing the standard staple commodities. This emphasis on the security of food supplies and the accompanying distrust of the marketing system add some logic to the otherwise baffling phenomenon of unpicked cash crops. If labor is in short supply, the low-priced food crops will be attended to first and the cash crops may suffer.

Once producers have obtained adequate food supplies or planted a large enough acreage to meet their needs, then, in some instances, prices do play a role in resource allocation. Economic values may reassert themselves. Some producers use their excess land capacity in an economic manner by growing crops that will yield high returns. The number who are economic men in this respect is unknown, though from personal observation, they would appear to be a relatively small proportion of the total. Economic forces also tend to come into play to a much greater degree after harvesting than before planting. For example, from the interviews with producers it appears that when they grow crops which can be either sold or consumed, prices assume importance after the food supply has been secured. Apparently a sharp upward movement in prices encourages them to release more of their surplus food.

Other conflicts between traditional and economic attitudes are revealed in behavior in regard to cattle. Traditionally, cattle are viewed as status symbols and are held more for their symbolic value than for their economic value. The extension of the exchange system has modified the attitudes of some producers, though not all. A random sample was taken of fifty livestock owners who had between 4 and 26 cattle. Thirty of the producers would not consider a 25 percent increase in prices to be sufficient inducement to sell their "surplus" livestock — that is, those in excess of their plowing needs. The remaining twenty were prepared to sell should prices rise, but only half of them would sell if prices rose by 15 percent.

Such attitudes may provide some explanation of the peculiar response to a change in the cattle-marketing system introduced in 1958 when the free market replaced a fixed-weight and grade-pricing system. In the first year of the change prices rose sharply and there was a marked upsurge in sales of livestock; thereafter, though prices rose even further, there was little increase in sales. Presumably the sharp increase in price encouraged the minority — those interested in profit — to sell their cattle. Thereafter, even higher prices did not induce traditionally oriented producers to sell their cattle. The persistence of traditional values also tends to explain why producers utilize land to graze excessive numbers of livestock even though in some areas this land could yield a far greater income from crop production.

Most producers in the African areas appear to be in transition from being traditional men to being economic men. Food production is still a primary concern and production for the market is marginal, but there are indications that attitudes are changing and certainly as the next generation of producers becomes exposed to the modern economy they will be much more concerned with using resources to obtain higher incomes. A precondition for increased output to obtain higher income will be that they have the cooperant factors of production. In addition, there will have to be an adequate marketing system that can demonstrate that the holding of visible food supplies is not necessarily the best means of achieving security. The problem of developing these areas is one of hastening a change in attitudes and making sure that the means are available to increase output.

At present, however, the majority of the European minority accepts the concept of cultural dualism and assumes that most indigenous producers will be dominated for the foreseeable future by traditional values. This view is translated into policy actions that tend to retard rates of change and perpetuate low levels of output in the traditional sectors of the economy. Because it is assumed that African producers have low aspirations and limited needs, resources are allocated to provide Africans with only enough means to attain those limited ends. The limited amount of land, low level of investment in infrastructure, training, and credit, denies them the factors whereby they might raise their output. Their opportunities for attaining a surplus are restricted, and without a surplus they cannot increase their working capital and invest in higher-yielding methods of production. This, too, keeps yields low. Because their output remains low, the impression is reinforced that they have limited goals and aspirations. It is in this way that the acceptance of sociological dualism and a policy based on this concept tend to produce a self-defeating cycle of poverty.

There can be no doubt that traditional values are strong in the African sector but the boundary between traditional men and economic men in the country as a whole is not permanent or fixed, nor does it depend entirely on cultural heritage. The boundary is fluid. With the continued extension of the exchange economy, and all that it implies, there will be more rather than less identity among Europeans and Africans in regard to economic goals and aspirations and responses to economic incentives. Already a minority of Africans are economic men rather than traditional men. They are oriented toward the marketplace. Consequently if social and economic policies are to be differentiated by groups, it may be well to base the differentiation on economic criteria rather than on the social or cultural groupings as suggested by Boeke. Thus there could be dual marketing policies, one for subsistence producers and one for market-oriented producers or dual credit policies for credit-worthy and non-credit-worthy producers. European or modern producers, on the other hand, are believed to have different economic goals and much greater needs than the indigenous producer, and the government's allocation of resources for development provides them with a much higher level of assistance. The gap between the indigenous and modern producer therefore tends to widen.

Some indication of the dual standards applied can be gauged from the levels of assistance provided to each sector of the agricultural economy. Between 1949 and 1954, the last date for which comparable data are available, the government of Southern Rhodesia voted total expenditures of £210 million, of which £26 million or 12 percent was allocated for European agricultural services and works related to agriculture — irrigation, conservation, and the like — while £18 million or 3.9 percent went for African agriculture. The African allocation included funds for roads in the African areas, while roads that served the European areas were treated as a separate item distinct from the agricultural budget. Expenditures on research and veterinary services for European agriculture came to £3.4 million; there were no such expenditures for Africans, and only approximately £120,000 was for research and special services to African farmers. The modern sector has a well-established agricultural credit system which, in 1958, provided some £25 million to European producers, and the quasi-official Land Bank has made loans of close to £6 million to Europeans. A special credit system has recently been started for African producers but it has a lending capacity of less than

£100,000, less than 1 percent of that available for the European sector. It is true that in recent years expenditures for African agriculture have increased sharply but they are still far below the levels for other sectors of the economy.[34]

Development of a dual economy is not a problem unique to South Africa or Southern Rhodesia. Agricultural economies in other parts of the world present expanding "modern" sectors alongside near-stagnant peasant sectors. Though the dualism may not be as pronounced as in Southern Rhodesia, the presence of two sectors gives rise to similar problems of intersectorial development. There will, for example, be difficulty in establishing priorities for the allocation of scarce capital between the sectors. "Spread effects" from the expansion of the modern sector cannot be relied on to raise levels of production in the peasant sector in situations where, as in Southern Rhodesia, land is plentiful. An outflow of labor from the peasant sector may raise output per capita and the migratory labor system in itself may be beneficial in transferring techniques of production, but it also has drawbacks in raising productivity. Increased productivity has to be accomplished by programs of development within the peasant sector, but the widespread acceptance of the notion of cultural dualism has, at least until recently, restricted such programs. It has also tended to obscure the differences among producers within the traditional sector. There are enterprising and progressive producers who, given technical and other assistance, can continue to raise over-all levels of productivity in African agriculture. Throughout much of Southern, Central, and East Africa there is need for differentiated programs geared to a range of enterprise within the traditional sector.

Part III: African Agriculture in Southern Rhodesia

Chapter 5

Land Tenure

If African agriculture is to become more productive, close attention must be given to changing the role of land in African society. Some type of agrarian reform is required, though it need not necessarily be based on the usual concept of land reform. In many parts of the world land-reform programs are designed to redistribute returns to factors of production, particularly to land and labor. The share of agricultural output that goes to the landowner or *rentier* is often very high in relation to the share going to the renter, or the size of holdings is such that the returns both to land and labor are very low. Pressure for reform in these areas comes from a combination of land hunger, lack of alternative employment, and inequitable distribution of returns to factors of production.

Land hunger is a strong force in certain densely populated localities in Africa. It is also a strong force in much of Southern Rhodesia, even though there is an average of 100 acres per farm family in the African areas, for the Africans associate land hunger with the system of land apportionment described earlier. This issue of interracial equity will not be considered in the present chapter. Rather, the concern will be with the nature of land reform that might be required within the African areas to raise productivity. The problem in the African areas is not one of inequitable returns to different factors of production, for all land is communally held. The central issue concerns the type of land reform that is required. Would different tenurial arrangements encourage greater agricultural productivity? What effect would such changes have on the economy as a whole?

CUSTOMARY TENURE

Tribal land, as we have seen, did not, nor does it, "belong" to any individuals. Tribesmen in central and southern Africa "moved on from place to place, whether they were agriculturalists who moved slowly or pastoralists who moved more often. They did not own land as individuals; it had not occurred to them that land was something that could be owned as a spear was owned; it was something of which a man might have the use if the king agreed, but the right to use it was not something that could be exchanged for something else. It was the king's duty to see that his people were fed and so he gave them land; it was his duty to make the rain; but land was hardly more subject to ownership than rain." [1] The apportionment of land *en bloc* to tribal groups has enabled many of the tribes to continue their customary systems of tenure. Some changes and modifications have been made, but until recently ancient traditions have governed both the use to which land is put and its allocation to individuals. While only a few detailed studies have been made of the process of land allocation in the tribal societies of Southern Rhodesia, there is more information on the Mashona tribe than on the other tribes. [2] The Mashona constitute more than one half of the African population of Southern Rhodesia, and, though there are differences in customary rights to land between this tribal group and others, the Mashona system can be used as a basis for discussing land tenure.

The most important figure in the tribal setting is the chieftain. The chief is, by and large, a territorial ruler. In the Mashona system the tribal area is subdivided into semiautonomous wards, each under a hereditary headman. Each ward is a geographical and kinship unit containing a group of kraals. These kraals are the homesteads of a varied number of family units or householders. The kraal, or village, is essentially a temporary establishment, the members of which are related by family ties, the kraal-head being the head of the family. As the location of a kraal shifts, its members frequently have the opportunity to hive off and join other kraals where they have relatives, or to split off and form separate kraals. Thus each kraal community is ever changing, dividing, expanding, and splitting, and kinship ties stretch in all directions within and between kraals in the same ward.

Within the kraal, land is allocated to individuals by the kraal-heads. Typically, the father of a son about to marry obtains permission for the son to use a piece of land. The kraal-head indicates very roughly the area which can be used. Thereafter, a field, often about two acres in size, is cleared. Each year a little more virgin land adjacent to this field is prepared and planted, until after four seasons the whole area cleared may run to four acres. As more land is cleared, a portion of the land originally planted is abandoned and left to lie fallow. A new piece is planted each year, so that over a four-year period all the land is cultivated in between periods of reversion to grass and bush. The cultivator uses his judgment as to when the fallow land can be used again, knowing that poor soil takes longer to recover fertility than does good soil. His land-use pattern is to rotate his fields or to expand them further as the fertility of the planted fields declines. Alternatively, the whole kraal moves to a new area after four or five years. This is the more usual custom.

It is important to recognize that despite such a high degree of mobility under the customary system of land use, an individual's rights are always quite secure. Land is held by the community as a collective unit, but eligible members of the kraal have a vested right to use particular portions of the area. Individual rights to arable land are protected so long as the cultivator occupies the land or is presumed to have an interest in a particular holding. Clearly abandoned land is available for reallocation, but if a claim to this land conflicts with that of a previous occupier, the previous occupier has precedence. Grazing lands are communal. Unoccupied land is held for the benefit of the community as a whole for grazing, for collecting wood, gathering clay, collecting water, or to provide for other common needs. Moist areas — marshes or *vleis* — are used to grow vegetables.[3]

Individual holdings are not rigid in size nor are they clearly demarcated. The flexibility of the tenurial system has not been sufficiently studied to draw firm conclusions as to how important a factor this is, but the seasonal "elasticity" in the size of holdings is surely significant, particularly in connection with the ebb and flow of male labor in the migratory labor system. One thoughtful report concludes that a family's cultivated acreage varies in a concertinalike manner:

The family pattern of migrant labour is, however, not regular and the sizes of family holdings may well vary considerably from time to time. The indigenous system of tenure allowed these periodic adjustments to be made in a flexible manner. The degree of flexibility may be gauged from the fact that, at any time, up to an estimated 47% of able rural males is absent on migrant wage labour for periods ranging from a few months to several years, during which time their families at home are likely temporarily to restrict their cultivations, seeking to extend these again upon the return of the males.[4]

The importance of this phenomenon becomes apparent, too, when one considers the problem of establishing a system of clearly demarcated farming units of fixed size. Modern cadastral surveys, and property rights based on these surveys, do not permit the contraction and expansion of legal boundaries depending on the whereabouts of the male cultivators.

While neither individual holdings nor the traditional kraals have stable boundaries, the tribal ward, to which the kraal belongs, is a well-defined geographical unit set off by natural boundaries. The ward has much more social and economic significance than the kraal or village:

A village was not a home: it stayed for only a short while on the same spot. The tribal territory was not a home: it was too wide and vague for the mind of a man to [grasp]. But the dunhu [or ward] was home. It was big enough for a man's children and children's children to settle in; it was small enough to know everyone who lived in it. Within the *dunhu* boundaries a man could make use of the land for the purposes of his family unit. . . . within a dunhu the people felt they belonged so closely together that they would help each other cultivate their fields or build their villages as a matter of course. They thought of themselves as one big, old family; and as a matter of fact, this is what they really were, because in one *dunhu* most people are in one way or another related to the (*dunhu* headman). The dunhu, the land and its people, and the invisible spiritual bonds with the ancestors who lived and died there for generations, all these together made the intimacy of home. And even a man who leaves this place to settle elsewhere, will leave it in such a manner that the door . . . is never closed behind him. For he knows that there will come a day when he wants to come back to it, if only to die there and be buried in the soil that contains his ancestors.[5]

Within the ward each tribesman has a share in the land and the proceeds of the land, and the system of mutual obligations and reciprocal arrangements through which this is achieved provides the basis of his security. This traditional concept of security is at the heart of the problem to be faced in introducing tenurial changes in Southern Rhodesia.

The security of the African tribesman emanates from an entirely different set of relations than are found in Western society. It has little in common with security as conceived by economists. In tribal agriculture security is premised on the knowledge that one can always return to one's ward where one will always be accommodated as a member of the tribe. The tribesman has an inalienable right to share in tribal land according to his reasonable requirements. He belongs to a group, and as a member of that group he has the right to a piece of land, and so the right to a subsistence level of income. As a result he views land as much more than a mere factor of production or a negotiable asset. Land is, rather, a fundamental factor in guaranteeing the hereditary right to exist in one's preferred milieu. It is a means whereby one can cling to a way of life that is familiar and secure and is closely linked to an enduring past.

Such a relation to the land involves very little pressure for increased productivity, greater labor inputs, and higher levels of income. It is here that there is a basic conflict between the traditional concept of security and the Western idea that security arises from an expanding economy with rising levels of real income. Rising incomes and increased productivity in the economy as a whole enable more people to enjoy a higher level of living, with more education, more and better health services, and higher levels of consumption. These end products of expansion are precisely those that are desired by most of the people of Southern Rhodesia. However, it is patent that they cannot be obtained in a predominantly agricultural society where the factors of production, particularly land, are viewed as a means of providing security at a basic subsistence level rather than as a source of a marketable surplus.

If there is to be a surplus, then the traditional concepts have to be changed and attitudes toward land have to be changed. Emphasis has to be on the most productive *use* of land rather than on a pattern of use geared to provide security at a low level of production. The most productive use of land calls for land to be combined with other factors of production in a way that maximizes returns. This does not accord with a system where land is held merely to provide a subsistence income based on the need for each individual to have a minimum subsistence income from the land. To be freely accepted, however, any change from the traditional system must be one that provides greater security for all, and the benefits of change must be greater than the advantages that may be lost in the process of change.

THE ECONOMICS OF TENURIAL CHANGE

There is only limited experience in the type of change in African tenurial systems that will stimulate productivity and improve land use. All experience elsewhere in the world indicates that reform in tenurial arrangements alone cannot lead to increased productivity. Changes in rights to land have to be accompanied by the provision of complementary factors of production, such as credit facilities and the incentives to use them. Moreover, if land is to be used more in line with its potential, it must come to be viewed as but one of the factors in a production function and there must be a basis for distinguishing the economic value of different pieces of land. For this to happen land has to be negotiable, with its price regulated by a market mechanism that can place a value on land according to its potential.

Under the customary system of tenure, land in the African areas of Southern Rhodesia may be viewed as a rationed but free good. This is a paradoxical situation. Land is rationed because it is not unlimited in supply; the process of rationing is the tribal allocative process. Yet it is a "free good" in economic terms because it has no price or market value. All land is "free"; land in a good location with high fertility has the same zero price as poor land, even where different tracts yield widely different incomes. That is not to say that land has no intrinsic or psychic value. On the contrary, from the economic point of view the problem is that the psychic value of land tends to surpass the money value it would have if it were considered as a factor of production and had a market price related to its capitalized output.

If tribal land were to be converted into a negotiable asset, and if there existed a market for land that related its market value to its productive potential, the prices of different tracts might well differ sharply. Land that could provide a salable surplus would command higher prices than land that could not be used in this way. In these circumstances an efficient market for land would bring about a circular action: better land would be higher priced because it could produce more, but because it was high priced there would be pressure to use it to yield higher returns, and so better land would have to be put to more productive use than poorer land. It can also be argued that once land had a price, it would have to yield an income at least equal to that which could be realized from a comparable investment in fixed income-bearing securities. This would preclude emphasis on subsistence production and would ultimately lead to specialization of production and commercialization of agriculture, two of the essential goals of economic development in Southern Rhodesia, and indeed in all of Southern, Central, and East Africa.

So long as land remains a free good there will be no cost factor to encourage greater productivity. Reliance will have to be placed on the usual "pull" factors — the desire for higher incomes, for example — to encourage more productive use of land. Hitherto these pull factors have not been very effective in themselves. It is possible that a "push" factor could be introduced by having a variable land tax graduated on the basis of land potential, but such a tax cannot be implemented without a clear definition of the size and nature of holdings. In addition, experience has indicated that there are great difficulties in assessing the productive potential of land and in administering such a tax program.[6] By and large, it would seem that an effective "push" factor would come from the creation of an effective land market. Such a market would reinforce the concept that land is a valuable asset and might also lead to greater efforts to sustain its capitalized earning capacity. In other words, if land had a price and was not a free good, the rate of depletion of the soil might be diminished, for there would no longer be a zero interest rate of the land's use.

An additional and important argument in favor of converting land into a negotiable asset is that this would encourage the emergence of entrepreneurial and managerial ability among African people. Managerial ability is one of the scarcest factors in African agriculture, and where this ability does exist it may well be stifled because the able producer cannot acquire land. At present land is allocated on the basis of need and status. There is, however, a wide range in the size of holdings, and it appears that status does have a bearing on this distribution. An impersonal land market would help substitute ability for status and permit a progressive producer to expand his holdings to the limits of his competence and financial resources. Where necessary these resources could be supplemented by special credit programs for able producers. This could lead to the creation of units whose size would economize on the supply of managerial ability and help to maximize its use.

The creation of a market for land does not necessarily imply a system of private ownership of land. Land could be owned cooperatively or even collectively. All land could be nationalized, with the right to use land being marketed. In that case the market price would be for usufruct or the right to use the land rather than for possession. This is the system being adopted in Southern Rhodesia. Generally, though, the direct ownership of land and the rights that go with property are considered to be important elements in encouraging higher productivity through investment in land improvements. Direct ownership, in contrast to other forms of tenure, is believed to provide an important incentive to improve land. The assumption is that since the owner knows the capitalized value of improvements will accrue to him, he is encouraged to invest in improving his land.[7] (Though, as will be shown, this has not happened in some parts of Rhodesia.)

In considering changes in tenure, one has to bear in mind the type of society being created as well as the economic consequences of these changes. The creation of a market for land and the emergence of private ownership will surely mean that there will be renter and *rentier* classes. Adequate controls, however, can prevent the emergence of a large-scale land-holding hierarchy if this is desired. Though large-scale units, with a division of labor between managers and workers, may be much more productive than small-scale units, the prospect of large-scale production units arising in the African areas appears to be remote unless government farms are created. The shortage of suitable complementary factors of production and the problems of deriving technological returns to scale, particularly where management is in such short supply, make their appearance unlikely. Consequently, if one of the purposes of changing the tenure system is to encourage the rise of self-owned, self-operated family farms, the distribution of holdings must be arranged to meet this end, and in this event upper limits can be set on the size of holdings. If the system of interpersonal allocation of land is to be replaced by a land market, then holdings will have to be clearly defined and identifiable. Contracts will have to replace oral agreements, and contracts call for precise definitions of acreage. This will require surveys, allocations, and demarcations. It is this essential requirement that introduces rigidities completely alien to the customary system of land allocation, since once holdings have been surveyed and are clearly defined and distributed, each specific area belongs to some individual. This is in sharp conflict with the concept that every eligible member of a tribe is entitled to a share of the free land in a ward and that land should be distributed according to need (though there may well still be a right to share in the products of the land). The elasticity of the tribal system would no longer pertain and the inherent right to share land would have to give way. Land would no longer be a free good, villages would have to be stabilized, and techniques of production would have to change. This, in turn, would require the drastic reorganization of production techniques.

THE NATIVE LAND HUSBANDRY ACT

The first attempts to improve African land use in Southern Rhodesia operated within the framework of existing tenurial arrangements. A program based on simple land-use classifications was started in 1929. Land was classified either as arable or as grazing land. Attempts were made to encourage producers to locate, or relocate, their huts in such a way that communal grazing was confined to land classified as suitable for grazing, while cultivation was to take place on "arable" land. Producers were also urged to "centralize" fragmentary holdings and grazing land into consolidated blocks to permit more efficient use and to ease the burden of supervision on the fledgling extension service. Persuasion was the method used to encourage consolidation. In the absence of capital for fencing, the grazing lands and arable blocks were demarcated by locating "lines" of huts along the boundaries between the two types of land.

The first Agriculturist for Instruction of Natives, appointed in 1926, was able to claim some modest success for this program. By

1939 some 2,000,000 acres had been "centralized" and by 1955 it was claimed that approximately 40 percent of the land in the reserves had been consolidated. Some physical conservation work was undertaken during the process of consolidation: contouring was done, grass strips were planted, and other improvements were introduced to stabilize the soil. In general the major emphasis of this land-use program was on conservation and soil stabilization, not on increasing short-run productivity.[8]

Despite these efforts there was an increase in soil erosion, in both the African and the European areas, and the government created machinery to protect the natural resources of the country. In 1941 the passage of the Natural Resources Act led to the establishment of a Natural Resources Board, charged with overseeing the proper use of the Southern Rhodesian resources. The board was given sweeping powers regarding resource use in the African areas. If African lands were despoiled or deteriorating by reason of overgrazing or other misuse, the board, with the approval of the Trustees of the Native Reserves, could order the removal of stock and human inhabitants from these areas, provided suitable alternative arrangements were made for the people affected. The board could also recommend to the governor that he limit the stock in a given area if overgrazing was causing deterioration of the soil and its cover. Within the framework of the act, native commissioners were empowered to give orders to landusers to conserve natural resources and prevent their injury. This included orders relating to land use, methods of cultivation and the crops that could be grown, restriction or prohibition of cultivation, and control of water. Failure to comply with these orders was to be an offense but nothing contained in any order was to involve the user in any monetary contribution or financial responsibility.[9] Thus, for the first time, there was legal sanction for compulsion rather than persuasion as a means of improving production methods.

Despite these drastic powers and the accelerated expenditures on conservation works, however, the deterioration of resources continued, so much so that in 1954 the National Resources Board sounded a stern warning:

The time for plain speaking has now arrived, and it is no exaggeration to say that at the moment we are heading for disaster. We have on the one hand a rapid increase taking place in the African population and on the other a rapid deterioration of the very land on which these people depend for their existence and upon which so much of the future prosperity of the country depends . . .

The Board wishes to state as plainly as possible that no further time can be lost in providing money to meet this emergency and seeing to it that the status of the Native Agricultural Department is raised to the level required and in keeping with the responsibilities involved.[10]

The emphasis had been on conservation, but it was becoming clear that reducing livestock and conserving the soil might solve only part of the problem. As far back as 1947 the chief native commissioner had appreciated this; in his view the deterioration of conditions was linked to the migratory system and the need for a better division of labor:

I would like to accentuate that our difficulties are more those of over-population than overstocking. To reduce the carrying capacity of many reserves on the present population, will make the holdings quite uneconomical, so some solution will have to be found elsewhere. The estimated increase in population during 1946 is roughly 73,000. It is obvious we cannot go on setting aside extra land for Native occupation annually—it just won't last out. The solution appears to be to appoint a Royal Commission to examine the land problem from all its angles and make a final allocation of land. After that a Native will either become a peasant farmer only, adopting proper agricultural and soil conservation methods or become an industrialized worker with his tentacles [sic] pulled out of the soil. There is not enough land available for all Natives to be both wage earners and peasant farmers.[11]

After extensive hearings the government introduced the Native Land Husbandry Act in 1948. The act became law in 1951, but its implementation was delayed until 1955. The preamble to the act — one of the most far-reaching land-reform measures in Africa — states that its objective is "to provide for the control of the utilization and allocation of land occupied by natives and to insure its efficient use for agricultural purposes; [and] to require natives to perform labor for conserving natural resources and for promoting good husbandry."

The act has five parts, given here in the order of their importance:

(a) *a grant of farming rights* (part III of the act): This is the key to the whole act. Its final implementation would abolish the customary system of land holding. Individuals were to be granted farming rights on tracts with fixed boundaries. There was to be a land register and the rights to land were to be negotiable assets. Those who received them were to be cultivators of land at the time the act was being applied. Once farming rights had been granted they could be bought or sold but could not be "fragmented." Individuals could purchase up to three such rights.[12]

(b) *a grant of grazing rights* (part II): This section also introduced a revolutionary principle. Its aim was to correct some of the defects in earlier destocking programs. Formerly compulsory destocking could take place only after overgrazing had occurred. Under the act each communal grazing area was to have a rated carrying capacity, an upper limit on the number of animals permitted in the areas. The right to graze cattle was to be negotiable, however, so that cattle owners could expand their herds if they could find sellers of grazing rights.

(c) *good farming practices* (part I): This provision included the conditions of "good farming" in the Natural Resources Act. It stipulated certain good farming practices and provided regulations intended to prevent soil erosion, protect or conserve resources, and control livestock. Penalties for noncompliance were to be used only in the last resort; emphasis was to be placed on extension work to promote "better" farming. But the holder of a right might be forced to sell it after a third conviction for failure to safeguard the land or use it properly. This part of the act provided a means of breaking the migratory labor system and enforcing a division of labor, for "good farming practice" could require the sustained presence of a male cultivator. A cultivator who was also a migratory laborer could lose his right to farm if he absented himself from the land.

(d) *compulsory service* (part V): This section was introduced so that stockowners could be compelled to provide their labor to improve the communal grazing land in their area. It empowered the native commissioner or the local native council or chief to call out stockowners to perform special tasks, for which they were to be paid at the current rates applicable in that area for the class of work performed.

(e) *provision for villages and towns* (part IV): The act provided for land to be set aside for villages, towns, and business centers in which Africans could purchase land.

The purpose of the act was to slow down soil erosion, inhibit migratory labor, and provide greater security of tenure to producers. It continued much of the "conservation bias" of the Natural Resources Act but it also included a revolutionary approach to tribal tenurial systems. In one fell swoop, it proposed to replace the tribal-communistic system of allocating land according to need with a hybrid tribal-capitalistic system of individual holdings and communal grazing. The use of farmland and communal grazing areas was no longer to be "free." Once the act was fully implemented, price was to be a major factor in the transferring of rights between individuals. It was the intent of the act that the intricate network of social and tribal customs regarding land use and land transfer would give way to the marketplace. The use of land was to be regulated in accordance with the economic principles in practice elsewhere in the capitalistic world.

The security of tenure contemplated by the act was to be provided through the granting of farming rights to individuals. (This belief indicated a lack of appreciation of the nature of security in the tribal areas.) Outright grants of land were deemed to be impractical because of constitutional difficulties. The constitution vests the reserves in the Trustees of the Native Reserves and apparently the government did not wish to alter this by amending the constitution. Nevertheless, farming rights were to be inviolable and could be inherited. The initial grant of farming and grazing rights was to be a confirmation of one's holdings. Anyone who wished to sell his rights could do so and would acquire an initial windfall profit but would forfeit his rights to the land.

The retention of communal grazing was in keeping with tribal custom and avoided the difficulty of subdividing commonage. Allocating grazing rights for a specified number of animals, rather than for a specified acreage, permitted a great deal of flexibility and made it easier to control the number of livestock in any area by limiting the number of rights sold. Furthermore, it was unnecessary to commit scarce capital to providing fencing and other means of dividing communal land into identifiable holdings.

The act was also revolutionary in that, by attaching a money value to land and by allocating it among individual occupiers, it removed the privilege of free access to land for Africans who wished to settle in a new area. Rights to land were no longer to be among the tribal prerogatives that existed before the act. No longer would any father obtain land for a son who was about to marry by requesting it from the chief. Nor would any tribesman moving to another area be able to acquire a holding merely by submitting to the authority of the new group and paying obeisance to the tribal elders. Furthermore, Africans who lost their positions in urban employment or became infirm or aged would no longer be able to count on the security of an allocation of land in their tribal area, though their families might still take them in and look after them. Money was to be the key to the acquisition of land rights and the price of land rights would be governed by their supply, the quality of the land, its capitalized value, and the demand for land.[13]

It was hoped that the allocation of sufficient land to each cultivator along with consolidation of holdings and the prevention of fragmentation would provide individual families with enough land to sustain themselves without seeking supplementary employment in the wage economy. There would thus be a division of labor between agriculturalists and wage earners. Future generations would either be self-employed farmers or devote full time to wage employment, no longer able to rely on "free" land to sustain themselves when they left or lost their jobs.

The Land Husbandry Act did not establish the size of individual holdings, but section 24 of the act stated that "The Minister . . . may from time to time by notice in the [government] Gazette determine the area of arable land in respect of which a farming right may be granted to a native who is a married man — with one wife. The area so fixed shall in the case of dry farming be not less than 6 acres and in the case of farming irrigable land, may be such smaller area as the Minister may in his discretion fix." [14]

The size of holdings was to depend on climatic conditions. In each area the number of permitted livestock units — a livestock unit consisted of one large animal, or two sheep, or three pigs, or the equivalent in other animals — was to depend on a more complex set of relations. Experiments had shown that one unit could provide enough manure to fertilize an acre of cultivated land. The number of animal units in any area was to be related to the cultivated acreage on the basis of one unit per cultivated acre. But the grazing land required to carry an animal unit also varied according to climatic conditions. The result was that the size "of a full standard holding" depended on the size of the arable holding, the number of cattle required to service the arable holding, and the amount of grazing land needed to maintain the livestock. These relations were to be adjusted according to rainfall conditions. For the standards proposed under the act see Table 6.

Table 6. Standards proposed under Land Husbandry Act, Southern Rhodesia

Average annual rainfall	Full standard holding		Acres of grazing land per animal unit	Approximate total acreage per full holding
	Acres of arable land	Number of animal units[a]		
28 inches or over	8	6	10	68
24–28	8	6	12	80
20–24	13	10	15	160
16–20	12	15	25	390
Below 16 inches	15	20	30	620

[a] One large animal, or two sheep, or three pigs, or the equivalent in other animals.

Source: *What the Native Land Husbandry Act Means to the Rural African and to Southern Rhodesia* (Salisbury: Government Printer, 1955).

Ideally a holding in the 28-inch rainfall area would have 8 acres of cultivable land. The producer's animals would require 10 acres of grazing land per animal unit. His total land requirements would be 68 acres, with the 8 acres of arable land to be farmed under crop rotation, combining a 2-acre fallow with grain and legume crops, which, supplemented by the manure from the cattle, would preserve the nitrogen in the soil. This aspect of the act was aimed at intensifying production by changing the haphazard system of farming, still based on shifting cultivation, to one more suited to a sedentary type of agriculture.

Soil-conserving efforts were also to be included as part of the general task of demarcating arable and nonarable areas and registering landowners. According to the procedure adopted to carry out these tasks, appropriate officials of the Native Affairs Department were to visit each area and draw up a complete inventory of the human and livestock population and the land and water resources of the area. They were to interrogate headmen and villagers and to scrutinize tax registers, in order to obtain as complete a record as possible of the inhabitants and of those absent at the time the count was taken. All data were to be entered on a kraal-appreciation sheet. Thereafter measurements were to be taken of the available acreage and the amount of land cultivated by each family. Livestock were also to be counted. At the end of the count, a register was to be compiled with the appropriate information for each and every village.

Maps were to be prepared for each area with wide use being made of stereoscopic air coverage. Following the initial aerial survey, the land was to be evaluated and classified. Land-use maps were to be provided for each locality. Thereafter plans were to be drawn up for the best physical use of the land depending on its classification. Sites were to be marked for huts and kraals. At the same time grazing areas were to be demarcated, with attention being paid to maintaining a suitable ratio between grazing and arable lands. Roads, bridges, and other communications were to be planned. Mechanical conservation measures were to be undertaken; grass buffer strips were to be planted along the contours; drainage channels, banks, and storm drains were to be constructed.

The massive land-planning operation was to be executed with the aid of tractors and bulldozers. At the same time an assessment committee, which was to include representatives of the African people concerned, was to consider the results of the initial survey. The committee was to make specific recommendations as to the standard amount of arable land for a farming right, the maximum carrying capacity of the reserves for stock, and the standard number of animal units for a grazing right. Once these were agreed upon the appropriate authorities would allocate land to the Africans, and enter the allocations and their location in a registration book. The African producers, where necessary, would then relocate their huts, mark off their holdings in accordance with the surveys and the massive reorganization would be completed. It was hoped that in this rather ingenious manner soil conservation would be achieved, the management of livestock rationalized, and the organization of African agriculture completely changed.

IMPLEMENTATION OF THE ACT

Progress in the implementation of the act has been slow and has lagged behind the projected rate.[15] Originally it was to have been implemented in five years but the period has been extended well into the mid 1960's. Had there been enough land for all families and had the distribution of families been such that the man-land ratios contemplated in the act were in conformity with actual conditions, land might have been distributed according to the formulas of the planners. The assessments undertaken as part of the act indicated, however, that this was not the case. By 1960 it was estimated that there were 359,000 cultivators in the African areas; excluding female cultivators more than 324,000 families were entitled to land rights. If these families were to be given full-sized holdings according to the ideal scale in the act they would occupy 3.1 million acres of arable land. But it is now estimated that only 2.8 million acres of arable land are available in the African areas, so that at best only 212,000 families, or approximately 70 percent of the total number, could receive full-size arable holdings.

Furthermore, it was found that cultivators and families were not evenly distributed throughout the reserves and this has led to considerable variation in the size of holdings in different reserves. In Southern Mashonaland, for instance, there were 79,000 cultivators but only land enough for 32,000 full-sized holdings, while in Mashonaland West there were 45,000 cultivators and land enough for 34,000 full holdings. Disparities also occurred between areas within provincial districts; some reserves in Mashonaland East had land enough to accommodate full-sized holdings for all cultivators with some land to spare, while in other reserves less than 33 percent of the families could have full-sized holdings.

A further difficulty in implementing the program has been the variation in the livestock population, both between and within areas. There are an estimated 1,395,000 animal units in the African areas. The total carrying capacity of all areas — including sections potentially able to support 175,000 animal units once the tsetse fly was eradicated — was estimated to be around 1,677,000 animal units. Animal holdings were unevenly distributed, however: Manicaland was carrying 14 percent more animals than its estimated carrying capacity (121,000 animal units as opposed to a carrying capacity of 106,000 animal units), while Mashonaland West was carrying only 66 percent of its capacity (125,000 animal units as against a carrying capacity of 190,000 units). The situation varied from reserve to reserve within the various provinces. In Manicaland some reserves were 39 percent overstocked but others were 20 percent, 30 percent, and 40 percent understocked. Furthermore, the livestock numbers were not in accord with the ideal ratios of animals to cultivated acreage. In some of the areas there were more acres to be served by animal byproducts than there were animals, while in others the situation was reversed.

In the face of these difficulties the government varied its formulas according to the actual man-land and animal-land ratios in the different reserves. Where sufficient land was not available, tight or intermediate formulas were applied in making allocations, or where there was more land but not enough for all, the acreage held by the larger-scale cultivators was reduced to the standard unit and the "surplus" was redistributed among the remaining producers, even though the resulting holdings were less than the stipulated standard.

In this respect the act had mixed results. In some areas where land was plentiful it was redistributed in accordance with physical criteria so that everyone had the standard acreage. In other areas where land was in short supply the act was applied ruthlessly; the maximum size of any holding was reduced to the permissible limit while any "surplus" land was redistributed to the smaller holdings. Frequently though, especially in the higher rainfall areas where land was scarce, the act merely froze the area of holdings, relocating the sites of holdings to conform with good soil-conservation principles.

The act was not designed to dispossess or to reduce the size of maximum holdings or to be egalitarian. Had there been enough land the authorities would not have cared how large the largest holdings were as long as the smaller holdings were not too small. It was hoped that through enlarging the smallest holdings some stabilization of the population could be achieved; it was hoped, too, that with reasonably sized holdings producers could earn an adequate income off the land and would not seek supplementary employment in the urban areas. The effect of the act, however, was to reduce differences in the size of holdings. Though the total man-land ratios remained the same the distribution of holdings of land and livestock per family was altered.

The application of the act was less egalitarian in its treatment of grazing rights. Where areas were overgrazed the total numbers of livestock were reduced. If the reduction amounted to a fifth of the livestock in an area, it was prorated among cattle owners, a man owning five cattle being forced to sell one, a man with ten selling two, and so on. The reductions were also linked to the condition of the animals. Some owners of older animals, in such poor condition that they would be an obvious drain on the grazing areas, were obliged to sell these animals irrespective of the size of the herd from which they came. Partial implementation has already produced certain economic benefits. There has been a considerable increase in the amount of investment in infrastructure such as roads, water holes, dams, bridges, and culverts. There has also been a large increase in expenditures on soil conservation work: large number of contours, grass strips, ridges, and bunds have been constructed. Some of these improvements could have been made through an ordinary development program, but because they were included within the framework of the act, the location and layout of these improvements has been carried out in a rational manner from a land-use viewpoint.

In addition to increased investment in physical improvements, the act has already created a land market. This has given some producers an opportunity to expand the size of their operations. By the end of 1960, 1,155 farming rights had changed hands at an average price of £5.9s.7d. per acre. Some of these rights were purchased for consolidation of existing holdings. Others were purchased as investments. In addition 13,511 grazing rights had been transferred at an average price of £4.17s.5d. per animal unit. The market is functioning smoothly, and in general the price of land varies according to its productive capacity.[16] These transactions could not have taken place without the partial implementation of the act, and the creation of a land market is one of the most salutary benefits that has come from it. For the first time progressive farmers are able to expand their holdings. The market is replacing allocation according to need with allocation according to use.

SOME REFLECTIONS ON THE NATIVE LAND HUSBANDRY ACT

The Native Land Husbandry Act is a revolutionary act, it represents a change of vast proportions in the lives of those living in the African areas. It strikes at the very root of their system of security. Ideally, change should be introduced after "discovering, assessing and predicting responses of men and women to innovations that go beyond the bound of antecedent convention." [17] Once these responses were known, appropriate policies could be recommended. The administrators of the act, however, felt they could not wait for changes to take place through the slow processes of acculturation nor did they feel that there was time for experimentation. Resources were being destroyed, land was becoming fragmented, and the rate of progress in the African areas was slow. They determined to force the rate and direction of change through massive intervention in the form of a large-scale program of land planning, land allocations, and innovations in tenurial arrangements.

The implementation of the act has had high human costs. Alien concepts have been introduced but not understood; traditional authority over land rights has been usurped by the marketplace.[18] The whole basis of society has been threatened, and security has been undermined rather than enhanced. Because the act has not been understood, and because pressure for its introduction did not come from the Africans themselves, it is viewed as an imposition. This has heightened the sense of insecurity already prevalent because of the land apportionment act.[19] Perhaps more importantly, the implementation of the act is not producing tangible benefits. It has taken away something which, though intangible, is important, and has not replaced it with anything meaningful to most producers. The maldistribution and immobility of the population has resulted in very few producers receiving larger holdings. No land was added to the African areas to permit expanded holdings. There has been no immediate follow-up with programs to raise incomes — no large-scale credit programs, fertilizer or seed distribution programs, or direct subsidies.

In view of the radical nature of the changes to be effected by the act in the lives of an unsophisticated people more attention might well have been given to gaining acceptance of these changes. A more leisurely approach would have permitted experimentation and progress through trial and error. There would have been an opportunity to learn more about the economies of the various reserves and more about the reactions of producers to the proposed programs. Follow-up activities might then have been organized as part of an over-all program to encourage acceptance of the new system. An approach of this kind would have called for the introduction of regional or piecemeal changes rather than a large-scale, once-for-all assault on existing institutions. This piecemeal approach also has merit from an economic point of view.

What benefits will ultimately derive from the implementation of the act remains to be seen. There are, however, questions as to the conceptualization of the Native Land Husbandry Act as an instrument of economic policy. The principal issues are whether the implementation of the act will reduce the outflow of migratory labor, whether it will indeed lead to a substantial increase in agricultural output, and whether the heavy investment required by this program represents the best use of resources.

The heavy emphasis on physical criteria and the use of man-land ratios as a basis for social reorganization may well hinder the attainment of many of the desired ends of the act. As an effort to improve land use, the method of implementation of the act has merit from a soil scientist's point of view. Land classification, with the demarcation of arable and grazing lands, should lead to more rational use of land. The use made of livestock byproducts should build up the nitrogen content of the soil. From an economic point of view, however, the rigid demarcation of land and the association of fixed numbers of livestock with arable acreage is unrealistic. It prevents specialization of production, for it is premised on a pattern of mixed farming throughout the country. This distorts resource use, for the maintenance of livestock on land where crop production is more profitable prevents the most economic use of land. In general, the act has been conceived in a static framework. The "fixing" of ratios of land and livestock is a mechanistic approach which penalizes those who may wish to maximize economic returns from available resources.[20] There is no point in having a rigid ratio of livestock to arable acreage. Small doses of capital, in the form of fertilizer, could free large acreages for arable cultivation. Greater flexibility, permitting the extension of cultivation into communal grazing areas, might lead to increased value of output per acre.

The slowing down of the outflow of migratory labor has been premised on full employment in the African areas. In this regard, there never has been any explanation of the reasons for selecting the particular size of holdings chosen as "economic units" under the act. It appears, however, that the holdings in the various areas were meant to be of a size that would provide full employment for a rural family. This view is given some substance by the 1944 report of the Native Production and Trade Commission, which stated that the director of native agriculture "was of the opinion that if a man and his wife were efficient and hard working they could farm up to 10 acres of arable land in the high rainfall areas and correspondingly more in the medium and low rainfall areas." [21] This view is open to question,[22] but if it is accepted, there is only land enough, under the present system of apportionment, to support 70 percent of the families now in the African areas. Thus, if the present system of apportionment is continued, along with present systems of production, there will still be a "surplus" of labor equivalent to 30 percent of those now in the African areas. Consequently, a large group of producers will still not be fully employed on the land, and so presumably will continue to seek part-time employment in the wage economy.

The framers of the act anticipated an increase in income and projected a rapid increase in output within ten years after the implementation of the act. They projected a rise of 50 percent in crop production within five years and a 50 percent increase in livestock production within eight years. The projected rates of increase in output are more than double the average annual rates of increase for livestock output and almost double those for crop output in the five years preceding the act. These increases would mean a 125 percent increase in average gross output per farmer and a 218 percent increase in net cash income within ten years of the implementation of the act.[23] These very substantial increases are expected to come from a combination of higher productivity per farmer and a higher value of unit output. The expectation is that higher productivity will come in part from changes in the tenurial system and that the "security" of individual ownership of land will encourage a much higher rate of on-farm investment than before.

The assumption that producers will invest at a much higher rate than in the past is open to challenge. While this hypothesis has yet to be studied in detail, there is some experience in Southern Rhodesia to contradict the view that private ownership *per se* encourages greater investment. A small number of privately owned farms have been held by Africans for over 20 years. Private owner-ship has not led to raised levels of output compared with the out-put of communally held farms in the adjacent areas.[24] There are significant differences in the levels of production between farms under differing tenurial systems, but, as will be pointed out in the next chapter, the major determinants lie not in the tenurial ar-rangements but in managerial ability. This merely emphasizes the view that changes in tenurial systems in African agriculture do not in themselves necessarily lead to greater productivity of land nor to higher rates of capital formation.

The implementation of the act will fulfill several important pre-conditions for agricultural development, namely, the freeing of enterprise, the creation of a land market, and the provision of in-frastructure. But the problem of raising productivity is that of converting ordinary native farmers into progressive farmers and an important element in this is an increase in expenditures on de-velopment services. Unfortunately, the resources available for African agricultural development are not adequate to finance the expansion of these services and the simultaneous implementation of the act. The economic problem thus becomes one of establishing a system of priorities between the short-term need to raise output and the longer-term need to change the tenurial system.

The recent pattern of public expenditures has been to place overwhelming priority on expenditures for land reform, land im-provements, and soil conservation. These expenditures in them-selves will not raise the productivity of land or labor. The desired increase in output and incomes will come about only through tech-nological changes at the farm level, and these changes will occur only if there is a development of human skills in agriculture. A better-balanced program would have given more emphasis to in-vestment in human resources to parallel the effort in land reform. As funds are limited, such an approach would stretch out the period of implementing the land-reform program, but it would also have permitted more rational use of resources and eased the im-pact of changes in customary tenure. To carry out a costly land-reform program while neglecting to improve human skills is self-defeating. The two should go side by side. Indeed, as will be de-monstrated in the next chapter, one of the keys to raising over-all productivity in African agriculture is a rise in the productivity of labor.

Chapter 6

Labor: Migrants and Managers

The migratory labor system is one of the salient characteristics of the economies in Southern, Central, and East Africa.[1] Throughout the area African men leave their families in subsistence-producing areas, work in the wage sector, then return to their families for a time before seeking further wage employment. Migrant labor is often seasonal, more frequently though, it is long term. Where there are large well-defined dual economies, as in the Republic of South Africa and Southern Rhodesia, African men continuously circulate between their rural homes and the industrial and agricultural complexes of the country. In the extreme case of the Republic of South Africa, migrants spend close to 60 percent of their working lives (between 16 and 47 years of age) outside the African areas. The annual labor wastage in South Africa due to this system is estimated to be equal to the total annual input of labor.[2]

Men shift back and forth, not only within their own countries, but also across national boundaries. The extent of movement across national boundaries is indicated by the fact, mentioned earlier, that, in 1956, 25 percent of the wage-earning labor force in the Republic of South Africa and 33 percent of that in the Federation of Rhodesia and Nyasaland were migrants who came from outside these countries. Conversely, about half the able-bodied males in the small, relatively undeveloped countries of Basutoland and Nyasaland are migrants working outside of their home countries.[3]

The system has its economic benefits for employers, and also, in the existing circumstances, has attractions for the migrant workers. For the employer — the South African mine operator, for example — it reduces social overhead costs by eliminating the need for family housing and other fringe benefits. The employer can operate on the assumption that the African worker has left his family in a rural area where they can fend for themselves, and wages are often fixed at the level deemed necessary for a single man to maintain himself in an urban area rather than to meet the requirements of a married man and his family. As it is, urban wages for "single" men are low; in Southern Rhodesia only slightly more than a third of the "single" men in Salisbury had gross incomes above the theoretical minimum expenditure on which households can live in health and decency.[4] The system also ensures the ready availability of labor from a stand-by force maintained in the indigenous areas at no expense to potential employers. The presence of such a labor pool, either within the country or in neighboring countries, makes the labor supply very elastic and so exerts a downward pressure on wage levels.[5]

The prevailing circumstances provide an economic inducement for men to work for short periods in the wage economy while leaving their families in the subsistence sector. Cash incomes earned in traditional agriculture are low, but the combination of free land and the security provided through kin groups enable families to maintain themselves at low cost by producing subsistence crops. On the other hand, average returns to African labor in the wage sector are low in relation to the cost of maintaining a family at places of employment.[6] Under these conditions a family's real income is low, if the family as a whole farms, or if they all move into the wage sector. But if the family splits and the male works for wages, while the other members of the family maintain themselves in rent-free housing by producing subsistence crops, total family incomes are higher than if the family remained together.[7]

Migratory labor is an important feature of the economy of Southern Rhodesia. In 1961, 660,000 Africans were in employment there, of whom 300,000 — nearly half — were classified as nonindigenous Africans who had come from neighboring countries to work for relatively short periods.[8] (All but 30,000 of the nonindigenous wage-earners were males.) Very few Southern Rhodesians seek work outside their own country. Within Southern Rhodesia, however, between 45 and 50 percent of the young adult males who reside in the African areas leave home for varying lengths of time to work for wages elsewhere in the country.[9]

This migration has left its mark on the distribution of population in Southern Rhodesia. A demographic sample survey taken at the time showed that in September 1954 almost 75 percent of the African population "resided" in the African areas. However, only 5 percent of the total population of the African areas were adult males between the ages of 16 and 35, though the national average for the indigenous population was 15 percent. Furthermore, the survey indicated that young men made up 18 percent of the indigenous male population in the African areas but 59 percent in the rest of the country.[10]

The population in the African areas is heavily weighted by women, children, and males over 35 years of age. Conversely, the population outside the African areas is predominantly male. Though the number of African families continuously resident in the wage economy is increasing, the European areas still have a very high proportion of men who are separated from their families. An illustration of this is that only 16.5 percent of the men employed in the Salisbury area in 1956 were accompanied by their families.[11]

The average duration of a wage-earner's absence from the African areas is not known. Seasonal outmigration is probably substantial because of the demands for male and female labor in European agriculture, the major employer in the economy. In a study made in 1950 of African farm labor on 80 European tobacco farms, it was found that the average labor force per farm consisted of 73 "long-term" employees and 20 casual or short-term seasonal laborers.[12] All of the laborers were migrants and more than half of the "long-term" employees had worked in their jobs for less than one year, while only one fifth of the labor force had been on the same farm for three years. Thus, unless these laborers were shifting from job to job without returning to their homes, most of them had been away from their homes for less than a year, and few had been away for more than three years.

There have been no studies of the over-all effects of the migratory labor system on African agricultural production. Undoubtedly some of the effects have been deleterious. Men traditionally undertake "heavy work," so their absence would tend to reduce the rate of domestic capital formation and impair some phases of farm operations. Most crops grown in Southern Rhodesia are annuals rather than perennials. The timing of farm operations is therefore important, especially with regard to the onset of the rains. Many migrants attempt to arrange their return to the African areas in time to participate in plowing and land preparation, but the irregularity of the rains frequently confounds these plans. If the advantages of early land preparation are lost, subsequent yields are lower than they might have been. In some areas, too, the absence of males has reduced cultivated acreage simply because families cannot provide the labor required to plant or harvest crops.

Somewhat intangible effects relate to the man's role as decision-maker and innovator. The women who remain in the African areas are conservative. They have not been exposed to the influences of the European economy. They are far less responsive than are males to suggestions for technological changes from the extension services, for they tend to view their task as one of providing subsistence for the family rather than producing a cash surplus. So the absence of the men makes technological change all the more difficult.

Yet the migratory labor system produces some benefits for African agriculture. A spell in the wage economy enables some producers to accumulate capital for on-farm investment. Migrant labor is also exposed to many of the "virtues" of scientific method and timing. Those who retain a residue of the techniques and values of the modern sector of the economy carry this form of "know-how" back to the African areas. As was shown in Chapter 4, the most progressive producers are frequently those who have been in the wage economy for some time. (This form of transfer of knowledge is not confined to Africa; it also appears to be found in countries such as Mexico where the process of learning by osmosis has enabled migrant labor to transfer to Mexico techniques learned in the United States.)

On the whole, however, the periodic and sustained absence of the most productive elements in the labor force must retard agricultural development. Although there is underemployment in African agriculture, it is not necessarily the size of the labor force that is of overriding importance in considering the relation among land, labor, and capital in peasant agriculture. The composition and quality of the labor force is as important as its size. It is true that there can be substitution of labor inputs in many phases of farming operations. Where adult males are the prime movers in expanding acreage, however, their absence restricts the rate of expansion of output, even though women and children may be underemployed. In addition, the absence of males limits current output if they are away at times of peak seasonal labor requirements.

A stabilized labor force with male labor in agriculture fully committed to such work would ease the task of agricultural development. But so long as total family incomes can be increased through migratory labor, males will have reason to migrate. At present the bulk of family income in many African areas comes from supplementary sources rather than from self-employment in agriculture.[13] It follows that one condition necessary for stabilizing the labor force is to raise average incomes in agriculture above the present low levels, so that families can meet their requirements without being forced to separate.

If the number of people engaged in African agriculture were to be stabilized at the current level, increased investment and specific programs for raising productivity might then raise incomes in some areas at a faster rate than population growth. The increase would not be geographically uniform, however. There are regional differences in resource endowment, and it is doubtful whether total output in the drier areas can be raised at a rate in excess of 3 percent per annum.

These drier regions, which are the home of about 30 percent of the African population, are best suited for extensive cattle raising. At present, producers in these areas raise both crops and livestock, despite the fact that crop production is hazardous because of uncertain weather conditions. They cannot rely on crop production to raise their income. Under relatively good conditions a herd of 15 livestock gives a total output of about £25 per year and a return to labor close to 2s. a day.[14] This is well below comparable returns for labor in the wage economy. Furthermore, as is shown in Appendix B, the rate of increase in livestock production has averaged less than 1 percent per annum. Output per animal can be increased through improved breeding, supplementary feeding, better range management, and disease control. Since present methods of production are so haphazard, most of these techniques are more effectively applied if herds are pooled, management centralized, and production rationalized. Yet even a pooling of resources and increased investment will not raise output per animal rapidly. The nature of the livestock industry precludes a sharp increase in output. Even at best average incomes from the production of livestock will rise slowly. At the same time, however, the pooling of resources will "free" underemployed labor. The combination of slowly increasing per capita incomes, a greater "surplus" of labor, and growing needs for cash incomes will increase the pressure on males to migrate.

If the criteria for ideally sized holdings embodied in the Native Land Husbandry Act were to be applied, an additional 10 million acres of land would be needed to provide "full employment" for the present population of the African areas. Though "land pressure" is a potent force in accelerating migration in many areas, it is rather pointless, in the present circumstances, to use such man-land ratios or "employment" requirements in determining conditions that would stabilize the labor force.[15] The important factor is the income that can be derived from the land relative to the income that can be earned through migratory labor. In some areas an expansion of cultivated acreage would raise average incomes, but in many other areas land is not a limiting factor on production.[16] In the drier regions where there is no absolute shortage of land a doubling or tripling of available acreage would yield only fractional increases in income; even if the size of herds were expanded and 20 to 50 acres made available for each additional animal, the marginal rate of return per animal would be extremely low.[17] In some areas more land combined with a concerted agricultural development program would raise average farm income. But as long as 70 percent of the population remains in agriculture, increasing output and incomes at a faster rate than in population growth will become increasingly difficult — as it is, a doubling of the annual rate of output from the African areas would raise output per family by only 3 percent and most of the increased income would be confined to the regions with plentiful rainfall. Even if a large increase in investment in agriculture were made, the maldistribution of the population would lead to disparate rates of growth. A stabilized population in about one third of the African areas would be hard pressed to increase average per capita income from agriculture to the point where it would equal that now earned from agriculture and part-time wage employment.

In the history of most developed economies, the proportion of the population dependent on agriculture for all or part of their livelihood has not been constant. The more usual pattern of development is characterized by a decrease in the proportion of the population in agriculture and an increase in the urbanized population and in the number employed in industry. If this pattern is to be followed in Southern Rhodesia, opportunities to work for wages will have to be expanded and they will have to provide incomes adequate to maintain entire families in the wage economy.

Increased investment, particularly in industry, can expand employment opportunities. The ratio of marginal investment to marginal employment is high, however. One United Nations estimate is that for each person absorbed into nonagricultural employment a capital investment of more than £900 is required.[18] It is estimated that in the Federation of Rhodesia and Nyasaland as a whole, employers directly invested around £300 for each additional employment opportunity created in the manufacturing industry in 1958.[19] Between 1954 and 1960 net output in the Federation's manufacturing sector rose by 12 percent, yet there was an increase of only 2 percent in the number employed in industry.[20] In Southern Rhodesia total investment was at a very high level in the early- and mid-nineteen-fifties, with a peak rate of 62 percent of national income in 1952. During the years from 1951 to 1956 the total number of persons in wage employment rose by an average of 16,000 a year, an increase of 7 percent.[21] Since then, however, the over-all rate of investment has declined, and the rate of expansion of the labor force has remained constant at less than 1.5 percent per annum.[22] Thus, in the early nineteen-sixties opportunities for wage employment are increasing at a slower rate than is the population of the labor pool in the subsistence sector.[23]

Employment opportunities in Southern Rhodesia could be expanded by excluding nonindigenous migratory labor from the country. Nearly half of the employed labor force in Southern Rhodesia is nonindigenous. The exclusion of this labor would shift the incidence of unemployment to neighboring countries, but would create additional employment opportunities for Southern Rhodesian Africans. With the increase in the number of nationals seeking wage employment the government has introduced legislation to give effect to such a policy. Under the Foreign Migratory Act of 1958, the government of Southern Rhodesia is empowered to exclude foreign labor from designated areas. The act, however, would not apply to Africans from other parts of the Federation, who constitute close to 80 percent of the nonindigenous labor force. With the dissolution of the Federation the exclusion of this labor will now be possible if the government wishes to exclude the bulk of the foreign labor. Thus far they have not done so. In addition, the act has not been applied rigorously, because "unemployed Africans in the urban areas are reluctant to take up employment in the rural areas"; foreign migrants are still permitted "to fill the gap that exists." [24] In any event, the exclusion of nonindigenous workers will not necessarily stabilize the labor force. Unless real incomes in wage employment are raised substantially, the positions formerly held by foreign migrants will simply be filled by local migrants.

In view of the slow rate of expansion of employment opportunities in the wage sector, little is to be gained from a policy that increases the number of those dependent on the wage sector without raising average incomes in the country as a whole. Although not intended by the policy-makers, this is what is happening as a result of the rapid implementation of the Native Husbandry Act,[25] which has already turned some migrants into a landless class and will inevitably increase the number wholly dependent on the wage economy.[26] As the act is essentially one for reorganizing land holdings, it will not lead to a total increase in agricultural output. Instead it has shifted underemployed labor in African agriculture into unemployed labor in the wage sector. This process will continue and national resources will have to be diverted to provide the social overhead needed to maintain unemployed labor. This may well result in an increased rate of capital formation in the form of housing and other facilities, but such investments will not represent the most productive use of capital. Consequently, over-all rates of increase in output may well be reduced because of the uneconomical use of resources.

Furthermore, because of the rigidities in the system of land tenure being introduced by the act, Africans in the wage economy, when in need, will no longer be able to fall back on the sustenance previously assured them by tribal traditions. The cost of providing social security will fall on the wage economy or on kin groups in the African areas. Where the incidence is shifted to the wage sector, this will add to the unit costs of labor at a time when employment opportunities are not expanding.

The link between the traditional system of land tenure and widespread migratory labor is an important one. Where an economy is expanding rapidly, the impact of changing customary rights to land can be minimized by the capacity of the economy to absorb displaced labor and any higher costs of social overhead for this labor. But when, as in Southern Rhodesia, the economy is not expanding rapidly, a strong case can be made for adjusting the pace of the change to fit the rate of expansion in the wage economy. In circumstances such as these, a slower piecemeal approach would be more economical than a once-for-all change that has the effect of creating a forced division of labor without increasing total returns to the economy or to labor.

The persistence of the migratory labor system makes the task of agricultural development a difficult one, yet such development is necessary if the rate of migration of male labor from the African areas is to be retarded. When real incomes are raised in agriculture, an increasing number of males will have no economic cause to become migrants. A growing number will then become part of a stabilized labor force committed to agriculture. At the same time, if the wage sector of the economy expands rapidly enough to provide adequate real incomes for an increasing number of families, a growing number of families will also be committed to nonagricultural employment.

There is little reason to believe that, in the short run, a rapid breakdown in the migratory labor system will occur. Lower-cost housing and higher wages in the wage economy will help to stabilize the labor force. There are also possibilities for stabilizing part of the labor force through increasing average family incomes in agriculture in many parts of the African areas. These possibilities will not be realized, however, unless more emphasis is placed on investments that improve the productivity of labor. Some aspects of this problem are discussed in the next part of this chapter.

At present the high rate of labor turnover associated with migratory labor retards specialization of labor within the wage sector. Unskilled laborers who "float" from job to job, from subsistence farming to a range of tasks in the wage sector, have little opportunity to acquire special skills. This applies to the relatively unskilled agricultural labor force as well as to industrial labor. One study of conditions in the labor-extensive tobacco industry cited the lack of special skills among the labor force as a major factor contributing to the decline of output per worker in the decade from 1940 to 1950.[27] The author of this study held that a trained, resident labor force — the antithesis of migratory labor — was necessary to raise productivity. This study, however, did not consider the economics of establishing a trained labor force nor was there any evidence that labor costs per unit of output would decline if such a force were to replace migrant labor.

There is a large amount of underemployment in African agriculture. As was pointed out in the previous chapter, the African areas can provide "full" employment for only 70 percent of those who live in them. Theoretically, almost a third of the population could be moved out of agriculture without depressing output, and the per capita income of those remaining would rise by more than 40 percent. Or the same result could be obtained by adding 10 million acres to the African areas. Regional differences in income levels would continue, however, and there is no good reason to assume that expanding the number of holdings would raise average income levels to a point where the migration into the wage sector would lose its economic attractiveness. Even if all the land in Southern Rhodesia, apart from commercial enclaves, were to be opened for African production, the migratory labor system would continue, as long as producers could raise their family incomes by migrating.

The migratory labor system is one of the factors that make it very difficult to measure changes in labor productivity in the African areas. Given the low income goals of many producers and the excess labor capacity, the services of the migrant can be replaced in some operations by other underemployed workers. The factors of production can be so reorganized that additional labor inputs from those remaining behind may produce the same output as before, though the absence of the men often hinders expansion of production. That is not to say that the marginal productivity of the migratory laborer is zero. Rather, because of work habits and the discontinuous nature of the tasks performed in African agriculture, the number of hours worked by those remaining in the

African areas can be increased when there is a withdrawal of migrant labor. The increase may be enough to produce the same output even though there is a decline in the number of men working. The ratio of marginal product to average product of an hour of work may be much higher than the ratio of marginal to average product per worker.

Changes in the composition of family labor units, shifts in population, and questionable data make it difficult to evaluate changes in the productivity of labor in the African areas. Nevertheless, it appears that productivity has increased slightly between 1948 and 1958. (See Appendix B.) Whatever increases have taken place have come from a minority of producers, however. There has been little over-all change in the output of 70 percent of the families in the African areas; almost all the increases have been produced by 30 percent of the families.

African producers are not homogeneous, nor do they all have uniformly low levels of productivity. There are gradations among them. One significant factor that differentiates producers is the influence of extension education on output. The Native Affairs Department of Southern Rhodesia has classified producers according to the degree to which they have been exposed to advisory services and the use they have made of these services. The classifications are (1) master farmers, (2) plot holders, (3) cooperators, and (4) ordinary native farmers. Master farmers are those who have either trained on existing experimental farms or have followed relatively rigorous methods of farming prescribed by the advisory services, and who have demonstrated their ability to farm well. Plot holders are producers who farm under the guidance of demonstrators or extension officers. They follow prescribed solutions and if they perform satisfactorily, they can qualify as master farmers. Cooperators are those who work in some degree with the extension service, at least to the point where they rotate some crops, use manure or fertilizers, and plant their crops in rows. Ordinary native farmers are those who farm in the traditional way.

Records have been maintained on these classes and the differences in their yields. See Table 7 for the average yields between 1950 and 1956. It indicates that the degree of extension education received by producers and used by them is closely connected with yields. Average yields have fluctuated from year to year, reflecting

Table 7. *Average yields per acre of African producers in Southern Rhodesia having various degrees of extension education, 1950–1956*
(in bags of grain)

Year	Master farmers	Plot holders	Cooperators	Ordinary native farmers
1950	6.6	7.9	4.4	1.5
1951	5.5	4.8	3.0	1.2
1952	7.0	6.6	3.5	2.0
1953	7.5	7.5	4.8	2.5
1954	7.1	6.0	4.5	1.9
1955	6.4	5.5	4.0	2.2
1956	9.0	7.0	4.8	2.5

Source: Prepared from data provided by Native Affairs Department. These figures are not considered to be exact but are useful to indicate relative orders of magnitude.

changes in weather conditions, but in every instance master farmers, plot holders, and cooperators have had significantly higher yields than have ordinary native farmers. In 1956, the last year for which complete data were available, master farmers were producing more than three times more grain per acre than ordinary farmers.

These differences among producers were confirmed by a sample of 485 producers chosen at random in the regions of the country having low rainfall.[28] The average value of their output was £47, of which £25 was from crop production. One third of the farmers in this sample had a total annual output of £20 or less and two thirds had an output of £50 or less. Fifty-five of them were master farmers, plot holders, or cooperators, and the average output of these producers was valued at £108 per holding, of which £59 was from crop production. Thus those who practiced improved methods of farming produced more than double the average value of crop output and a 50 percent greater value of livestock output. They exceeded by far the two thirds of the producers who did not use improved methods of farming, either because they had not been exposed to extension education or because they did not follow the advice of extension officers.

Similar differences are apparent in a smaller sample of fifty-two producers in an area of relatively good rainfall where land is plentiful. The average net value of output of the four or five master farmers in the sample was three and a half times greater than that of ordinary farmers, their average net cash income more than ten times greater.[29]

In 1960 there were less than 9,000 master farmers and around 6,000 plot holders and 90,000 cooperators in Southern Rhodesia.[30] Altogether, about 30 percent of the producers in the African areas followed improved techniques of production. Their yields are impressive and appear to present a *prima facie* case for expanding programs of extension education. An important issue for development policy, however, is whether the influence of extension education is indeed the major variable in explaining differences in yields among the various classes of producers. Higher yields may be the result of greater inputs of labor and capital rather than better farm management; alternatively, higher yields may come at the expense of exploiting natural resources rather than through techniques of production prescribed by the extension service.

Present data are inadequate for isolating the role of extension or advisory services from other factors that influence output. But one rough test of the significance of good farm management is to compare the average yields of farmers who have been exposed to advisory services with those of purchase area farmers. Purchase area farmers have larger holdings than those in the reserves, and these farms have been allocated only to producers who have some capital. Even though the capital requirement is small, the funds available for on-farm investment are undoubtedly larger than those of most producers in the reserves. Purchase area farmers, in short, have more land and more capital than their counterparts in the reserves.

In general the average yield per acre of master farmers and plot holders has been much higher than that of purchase area farmers. A five-year average[31] of grain yield, in bags per acre, demonstrates this:

Master farmers	7.3
Plot holders	6.3
Purchase area farmers	3.8
Ordinary native farmers	2.1

It might be argued that purchase area farmers obtain a larger output (at a lower cost than otherwise) through more extensive use of land than is possible on smaller holdings; that is, marginal returns to land are low while returns to labor are high. The differences in cultivated acreage are so small, however, that this can hardly be a significant factor. Furthermore, there are differences within the purchase areas which point up the importance of management. A survey of 220 purchase area farms indicated that the less successful farmers were not necessarily those who had the lowest levels of investment or the smallest farms. In the words of the author of the survey: "In fact their lack of success rested on poor use of the factors of production at their disposal . . . It is clear, then, that the future success of Purchase Area farms depends very largely on how successful are the measures taken to improve management ability." [32]

Management is important. The level of management depends on individual capacities and knowledge of how to improve techniques of production. Master farmers, some of whom have small plots, some of whom have very little working capital, have higher yields than other producers because they follow proven techniques of production. They rotate their crops as recommended by extension officers and they use available waste materials for organic fertilizers. In addition, they follow advice on the timing of farm operations, an important factor in a country where rainfall is erratic.

It is difficult to improve management and change techniques of production. First, adequate knowledge of the suitable techniques of production must be obtained before the extension service can disseminate useful information. Nothing is more conducive to the failure of an extension program than producers who get poor results after following the advice of extension officers. At present, there is little applied research on the problems of small-scale agriculture in Southern Rhodesia. This lack is particularly significant in connection with the advocacy of new forms of agriculture as prescribed under the Native Land Husbandry Act.[33] The conversion from shifting agriculture to sedentary agriculture requires more continuous cultivation of the soil than in the past. Yet no research has been conducted into the effects of such a change on the soils of the African areas. At least one writer has expressed the view that the result will be an increased rate of soil depletion, the very thing the Native Husbandry Act is intended to end.[34] Without adequate applied research, the consequences of changed agricultural methods will remain an open question until after the new methods have been adopted by producers. By that time the damage to resources may be very great and the confidence of producers in the extension service badly shaken.

Despite the need for research, enough is known so that output could be raised appreciably if producers would adopt changed techniques of production. In the past the process of inducing producers to do this has been slow. In Southern Rhodesia the first major change was the adoption of the plow. (See Appendix B.) This was a self-induced change. In 1927 the government appointed a technical officer to promote the development of African agriculture on an organized basis. Improved techniques were to be extended by African demonstrators. Demonstrators were to be given special training and then sent into the various African areas to establish demonstration plots on cultivators' holdings. Selected cultivators would derive direct benefits from the increased output from the plots, while at the same time the plots would show neighboring farmers the advantages of using improved techniques of production. In addition to supervising demonstration plots, the demonstrators would also help cooperators who wished to adopt new farming methods.

In 1944, the Native Production and Trade Commission examined the results of the demonstration program. They found that after 15 years — from 1928 to 1943 — there were 843 demonstration plot holders and around 3,500 cooperating farmers. Average yields on demonstration plots were five times greater than those produced on ordinary farms. In view of these results the commission was at a loss to understand why more producers had not seized on the new techniques demonstrated:

The results obtained by the demonstrators, when compared with an average return of two bags per acre, were sufficiently startling to justify the hope that practically all the Natives within easy reach of demonstration plots would have clamoured to know the secret. Nothing of the sort occurred . . . In Reserves where demonstrators have been teaching and preaching for ten years or longer, plots cultivated in the old primitive way can still be seen within sight of, or sometimes adjoining, demonstration plots or plots correctly cultivated by a master farmer or co-operator. Several farmers who have cultivated portions of their ground as demonstration plots under the supervision of demonstrators have continued to till the remainder in the primitive manner . . . It is generally admitted that the results have been very disappointing. An admirable scheme of improvement is being wasted, and, if a remedy is to be found, the causes of the failure must be ascertained. Although their methods are primitive, haphazard and often soil-destroying, Native men and women — and particularly the Natives of Mashonaland — are by instinct agriculturists. Natives with no education whatever possess a knowledge of agriculture which, though limited, has served their needs. The failure to follow the new methods cannot be attributed merely to lack of elementary education. Even an uneducated Native can appreciate the advantages of growing without any extra cost five bags of grain where one grew before.[35]

The commission's surprise is understandable, but they made a common mistake in assuming that there are no costs involved in the transfer of techniques of production. The costs that are involved need not necessarily be direct costs. For example, added inputs of unemployed labor may involve high costs to producers in terms of foregone leisure. In addition, changing a system that has provided sustenance, even though its methods are poor, involves an increase in risk and uncertainty. Change tends to disrupt social organization and may require new types of inputs. The farmer's conception of the effects of these inputs on future production and on saving of future inputs may differ considerably from that of an "objective" observer. The observer may assume a very low rate of interest in discounting present inputs, but the farmer may consider the effective interest rate to be very high indeed.

Converting ordinary native farmers into cooperators or master farmers has been a slow process. Up to the present time less than one third of the producers have been persuaded to adopt improved techniques. If there is to be any appreciable increase in African agricultural output, the process has to be accelerated. Accomplishing this will require both an enlargement of the staff engaged in the extension service and a change in methods of extension.

There is no set formula for deriving an optimum ratio of extension workers to farmers, nor is there any magical formula for estimating the finances needed for these services.[36] In Southern Rhodesia the stated ideal was to have — in the higher rainfall areas — ten demonstrators, one African supervisor, and one European land officer per 250,000 acres.[37] Each demonstrator would be responsible for 25,000 acres, 3,000 of which would be arable. He would have to help five to six hundred families. This standard is comparable to the ratios in the United States and the United Kingdom.

Comparisons with advanced countries can be misleading, however. Most producers in the United Kingdom and the United States are literate and receptive to new ideas. (It is worth noting, though, that if the highly literate American producers were to adopt the most modern techniques of production, output could be doubled.) In Southern Rhodesia extension workers are dealing with a conservative and mostly illiterate group. They cannot rely on the media, such as pamphlets and radios, that are usually employed in advanced economies. Information has to be disseminated by word of mouth and this requires personal confrontations. The extension worker in Southern Rhodesia has to provide more information than his counterpart in the advanced economies. He has to advise on prices and price changes and marketing procedures, to instruct producers on the timing of operations, the techniques of production — and other aspects of farming operations — to repeat simple demonstrations many times in order that they may be effective. In addition, if his work is to have any lasting effect he must follow up with repeated visits. This point was forcibly made by the chief native commissioner in 1944:

> If the Demonstrators are withdrawn or moved elsewhere, it will be found that the Plotholders and co-operators, notwithstanding the fact that they have been shown, and have actually carried out the new methods, will slip back into their old ways. It is necessary to put this on record in order that we do not deceive ourselves in dealing with an uncivilised Native population by assuming that because a Native has been taught how to carry out what is "modern," that he will continue to do so as soon as the controlling authority is withdrawn.[38]

Because most producers are unreceptive, extension workers have to devote more time to each farmer than would usually be necessary in more advanced countries. Consequently if any marked and sustained increase in output is to occur, the ratio of workers to farmers must be much higher than is necessary in advanced economies. The personal observations of this author indicate that a reasonable rule of thumb would be to have one such worker for every hundred families.

The method of extension work is important. Undoubtedly output can be increased by compulsion and by applying sanctions against those who do not follow prescribed production patterns, but these methods are not usually part of the accepted philosophy of extension work in most democratic communities. The point is not that there should be free license to destroy natural resources, but rather that excessive regulation and regimentation tend to create hostility toward government officials. For extension workers to assume policing duties would reduce their opportunities for gaining acceptance among producers, and without acceptance, they would find it difficult to overcome the suspicion that is part of reluctance of producers to institute suggested changes.

The tendency in Southern Rhodesia is to restrict rather than to expand enterprise. Compelling farmers to adopt set practices would further this trend. There is no way of ascertaining the extent to which output would rise if compulsion were used, but the cost of introducing such a system would inevitably be high, for a great deal of manpower would have to be diverted to police and regulate farm operations. In addition, the use of compulsion would inevitably alienate producers and so create a difficult atmosphere for promoting development. In the author's opinion these costs are too high to warrant the introduction of compulsion. Producers must retain the freedom to accept or reject the advice given to them, but the government must endeavor to see that the extension service provides them with the opportunity to improve their methods of production.

There is no way to estimate the rates of return from an expanded extension service using the most appropriate methods of imparting information. Nevertheless, there is a strong economic case for expanding the service. The cost of training an extension worker is low and thereafter his salary and maintenance costs about £300 per year. If one extension worker can convert five ordinary native farmers growing maize on forty arable acres of land into master farmers, then, based on average yields, the value added to total output would exceed by several times the annual cost for the worker. Producers would receive increased incomes and the net gain to the economy would far outweigh the marginal cost of expanding the service.

The cumulative effect of expanding extension education and ancillary services would be profound and the larger the program the better. There are, of course, limitations on the extent to which such a service can be expanded. It is conceivable that the service could be enlarged to a point where marginal costs of providing additional workers exceed marginal returns. This is unlikely to happen in Southern Rhodesia in the foreseeable future, however, since financial limitations and shortage of trained manpower are likely to restrict the size of the extension service well below the point of diminishing returns. In the early 1960's, despite strenuous efforts to expand the service to meet the ideal of one worker for 300 to 500 families, there is a shortfall of 30 percent in the number of workers and 60 percent in the number of supervisors. Consequently, the small extension service will have to be used as effectively as possible to yield maximum results while programs are instituted to train additional workers. Demonstrators will have to ration their services if they are to obtain maximum returns from their efforts. If they were to spread their services over all the producers, there would be a high degree of wastage; when many of the producers are nonreceptive marginal returns from extension inputs are low. Returns would be much higher if extension workers were to concentrate on the more receptive producers, to try to convert selected producers into master farmers, and to assist master farmers to improve output. This does not necessarily mean that the less receptive producers should be ignored, but rather that cognizance should be taken of the differences among producers and the dualistic attitudes within the African economy. A strategy should be evolved to cater to both receptive and nonreceptive producers. Such a strategy would make a variety of services available to the farming community as a whole. These services — the introduction of improved seed, for example — would raise output without requiring any fundamental changes in the techniques of production. At the same time special services would be made available to more progressive producers. Such a program would ensure the best use of the limited manpower until such time as the extension service is expanded to a point where it can be used more intensively throughout the area as a whole.

The task of raising labor productivity through improving management is not easy. Many producers are illiterate, conservative, technologically backward, and suspicious. They cannot be converted into enlightened, advanced, efficient producers overnight.

Much depends on the producers themselves, but the able producers must be given the opportunity to change and an essential element in providing that opportunity is the spread of knowledge. Without this there will be little increase in output, despite the large investments being made under the Land Husbandry Act. It is important to recognize that increases in agricultural output depend as much on human factors as on any other factors. Unfortunately, as will be shown in the next chapter, popular preoccupation with expanding physical capacity through the creation of infrastructure has led to a neglect of this vital fact.

Chapter 7

Capital

In the postwar years capital has come to be considered the dominant variable in economic growth. Most theoretical, economic growth models incorporate a concept of a given relation between capital and output. Capital is usually considered to include the value of capital goods at purchase cost or cost of manufacture or building. Output is the "value added" or the value of sales minus expenditures on goods and outside services. Value added may or may not include an allowance for depreciation; that is, it may be gross or net. Once the ratio of capital to output has been established, the ratio can be used to indicate how many pounds or dollars must be spent on capital formation to obtain an increase in national income of one pound or one dollar per year.

There are many ramifications in the measurement, use, and interpretation of capital-output ratios. This is not the place for a discussion of theories of economic growth nor the applicability of capital-output ratios to developed economies. Suffice it to say that many problems attend the valuation of capital and output. The more complex the economy, the more difficult it is to establish the validity of a given relation between the two, but even in simple economies, such as the African farming communities of Southern, Central, and East Africa, it is difficult to establish the relation between capital formation and rates of output.

The difficulty stems in part from the fact that increases in output have occurred in these areas even though the levels of money investment have been very low. This phenomenon raises questions regarding the measurement and meaning of capital and capital-output ratios in relatively backward agricultural societies. In addition, in Southern Rhodesia, when money investments in African agriculture were rapidly increased, almost no increase in per capita output followed. Thus, there is also a question as to what kinds of money investments and capital formation are most appropriate for raising agricultural output. These questions are germane to the problems of agricultural development throughout sub-Saharan Africa.

CAPITAL IN AFRICAN AGRICULTURE

Manifold problems are encountered in assessing the present value of capital based on the discounted value of future output, in estimating the cost of capital, and even in determining what constitutes capital. Frequently the lack of statistics makes it impossible to include some relevant items in national accounts. These problems cannot be treated exhaustively here, but several issues relating to the measurement and conceptualization of capital in African agriculture must be examined.

One issue centers around the definition of "capital" in African agriculture. Capital is usually differentiated from natural resources, which are considered to be "gifts of nature." Land, as a natural resource, is not considered to be capital. More precisely, the inherent fertility of land is not defined as capital, though direct or indirect investments may be required to utilize that inherent fertility; that is, tractors, irrigation works, or roads may be necessary to enable fertile land to be productive. In contrast to "gifts of nature," "capital" is considered to include all forms of reproducible wealth whether used directly or indirectly for the production of an increased volume of output. In this context capital consists of equipment utilized for future production. A closely related concept of capital embraces the notion of the diversion of labor from production for consumption to production for future output. The manufacture of equipment that reproduces wealth requires the efforts of workers who might otherwise be producing for direct consumption. Both concepts of capital imply the need for savings to sustain workers while they create productive capacity and engage in "roundabout" methods of production.

In the African areas of Southern Rhodesia, much of the capital formation that has taken place has involved the direct application of labor to land, to prepare the land for productive use. This is capital formation of the type usually found in simple "Robinson Crusoe" economies. Labor is diverted and productive capacity created for future use even though almost no equipment or reproducible goods are manufactured. If land preparation of this kind is viewed as capital formation, it gives rise to some paradoxes of conceptualization and measurement. These can be illustrated by a hypothetical, microeconomic example that is relevant to much of African agriculture. Two unemployed family groups of the same size might move onto different tracts of land with identical fertility. In the one instance, however, the land is covered with brush; and in the other it is clear and open. The family with the brush-covered field has to clear the land before it can be cultivated. They thus must divert their labor from alternative forms of production for consumption to create productive capacity for future output. During the period required to clear the land they are engaged in capital formation and they have to rely on their savings or surplus to sustain themselves. Once the land is cleared, they can use their labor to produce for consumption or for sale.

In the case where the land was already open and clear, however, the same-sized labor force could be employed immediately in cultivation, planting, and other productive activities. This family would not need to divert labor to clear the land, nor would they have to rely on accumulated savings. (Both families, though, would require some seasonal surplus for the period between planting and harvesting.) No capital formation would occur. In both instances, if a market for land existed, the capitalized value of the land would be increased; but in neither instance is the end product of the labor input usually included in estimates of capital formation.

Apart from conceptual problems there is a problem of measurement of domestic capital formation. As in the hypothetical examples, labor used in the process of land clearing and land improvement in African agriculture is usually family labor or mutual-help parties. Such services are "free" and usually the operations fall outside the exchange economy. The value of the labor inputs is not recorded, nor is there a land market to indicate the value of the end product of the inputs. The result is that this form of capital formation is seldom included in national or regional estimates of capital formation, an omission that can lead to misconceptions about the relation between capital formation and output.

If the government were to import a fleet of tractors to clear and improve land in the African areas, there would then be a clearly identifiable investment in capital goods (though possibly an inefficient use of capital), for a measurable increment in capital formation would be recorded under imports or government investment. Thus a situation could arise where similar outputs were gained off comparable areas; but in one instance, when family labor is used, there would be no record of capital formation, while in the other, when tractors are used, there would be a record. The recorded relation between capital and output would depend on the means used to clear land, and the records would be misleading.

Still another problem of the relation between capital and output in primitive economies relates to the end product of brush clearance. When brush is cleared to improve land, either by hand or machine, the brush is either used directly for firewood or else sold on the open market. The imputed value of firewood produced in the African areas in Southern Rhodesia in 1958 was close to 5 percent of the value of all output from these areas. Yet, since brush is not planted by man and has no value until it is converted into firewood, it is not normally considered to be capital. The result is that 5 percent of the value of output from the African areas comes from the destruction of a "gift of nature" and owes nothing to the rate of capital formation in these areas (though it might represent a disinvestment). Here, again, the relation between capital and output can be misleading, especially if the brush is destroyed by hand and income is created without any apparent capital formation.

There is also a nice question as to whether the end product of some types of land improvements should be considered to be capital formation. In Southern Rhodesia large amounts have been invested in mechanical equipment to correct soil erosion. These investments do not necessarily add to the total productive capacity of an area, but rather they conserve the existing capacity of the land. Hence there could be a question: Do they represent net additions to capital, or are they merely investments to offset the "depreciation" of the land? Conventional economic measurements include these investments as additions to capital, but it might well be argued that this practice is misleading.

Should African cattle be considered as capital? In most advanced economies cattle are defined as capital goods. A period of time must elapse before they become productive. Livestock consume other forms of output and convert them into milk, meat, and hides; their intake is converted to "value added." Furthermore, many cattle are used to provide draft power and so aid in the production of other commodities. They substitute for the machines used in advanced economies. They are often "hoarded" cattle and in this respect are analogous to other forms of hoarded capital. They yield income when sold, or even when they are consumed. Livestock have all the attributes of capital goods when they are viewed as income-yielding assets, but many Africans do not view them in this way. The introduction of the plow in Southern Rhodesia changed the role of cattle in African society by making them useful as draft animals, but even today cattle are not necessarily valued as sources of future income and their present prices do not necessarily relate to anticipated future yields. Instead, many Africans hold livestock as symbols of prestige or as a means of buying brides and enhancing the procreativity of their kin groups. Thus, in some senses, they are clearly capital goods but in others they are not. Perhaps the example of livestock merely indicates that prevailing value systems must be taken into account when relations between capital and output are assessed. In this instance greater efficiency in the use of capital may depend as much on changes in African values as on better techniques of production. If, for example, a radical change in attitudes toward livestock resulted in a higher rate of turnover, that is, if cattle were sold more frequently and slaughtered more frequently, capital-output ratios would be altered.

Livestock represent the largest tangible asset held by Africans in Southern Rhodesia and the yield from livestock has been low. However, even this low yield can be misleading as an indication of the efficiency of the use of capital. Because of compulsory destocking campaigns, which have forced sales, large numbers of livestock have been slaughtered and so output of hides and meat has increased. This increase is in reality a disinvestment in livestock so that a decrease in numbers and value of capital has been accompanied by an increase in output. Unless the circumstances surrounding increased output are fully appreciated, the relation of capital to output will be viewed in a distorted way.

The national accounts of Southern Rhodesia include an estimate of gross fixed-capital formation by sector and type of asset. This estimate includes annual changes in the value of land purchased, land improvements, building and works, plant machinery and equipment. The estimate is broken down by sector: the private sector (persons and companies) and the public sector (government enterprises, local and central administration). The estimates of fixed capital formation in the African areas are almost entirely equated with public expenditures on improvements in these areas, a great deal of which has related to soil conservation.[1]

Partly because of the difficulty in valuation and measurement, it has generally been assumed that there is little private-capital formation in the African areas. In fact, there has been a considerable amount of private-capital formation, particularly in land improvement and on-farm building. As a result, the national accounts underestimate the rate of capital formation and so give a distorted picture of the relation between "capital" and "output" both in the African areas, and in the economy as a whole.[2]

Data are not available for an accurate computation of the extent of capital formation in the African areas. By making some heroic assumptions and extrapolating from certain limited sample data, however, it is possible to make a first approximation. A rough estimate is that in 1957–1958 the gross value of all capital in African agriculture was close to £90 million.[3] The largest single item in this total was livestock, valued at £32 million at the going market price. Next was an estimated £12.5 million for land clearance and £17 million for homes and other on-farm improvements. Most of this £29.5 million would not normally appear in national accounts, particularly if the private sector is considered to make a negligible contribution. The value of roads, dams, and major works was estimated to be close to £20 million; minor equipment and other elements made up the remainder.[4]

If it is assumed that the African areas represent a closed economy, then in 1958 the gross stock of capital goods in the area, with a value of around £90 million, produced an estimated output of £28.4 million (including firewood).[5] This indicates, grossly, a three to one relation between capital and output. If livestock are excluded from the figures, the relation becomes more favorable, which indicates the poor use made of livestock. If the imputed element for direct labor inputs in land clearance is left out, the relation between capital and output is closer to two to one, for the value of capital is diminished but the output remains the same. If the relation considered is that between the gross stock of capital and marketed output, however, the ratio of capital to output is as high as seventeen to one.

These relations are introduced as a matter of interest. They are approximations but they highlight the differences that arise in ratios of capital to output. The ratio could change dramatically if there was a bad season when output dropped sharply. Generally, though, they indicate that a relatively small stock of capital can give the appearance of having a favorable relation to output in an agricultural economy where land is plentiful (even though output is low). The ratio between capital and marketed output, however, is startlingly different from that of capital and total output, which indicates the importance of increasing the values of the output that enters the market.

The ratio of a stock of capital to output tells very little about the average or marginal increases in capital formation needed to produce a given increase in output. Undoubtedly, however, average and marginal rates of domestic capital formation produced much the same amount of output during the years when there was a plentiful supply of land, since most past increases in output came from extending acreage. In other words these were constant returns on investment. Opportunities for this type of low-cost expansion are diminishing. Land has become more fully occupied and the fringes of production are extending into increasingly inhospitable areas. The past "one-to-one" relation between capital formation and output cannot be used as a basis for projecting future needs to produce a given output. Increasing amounts of money investments of one kind or another will be needed to augment domestic capital formation and the rate of money investment in these areas will therefore assume growing importance. It is not only the size of these investments that will be important in expanding output, however. The manner in which the expenditures are allocated between competing ends will also be significant in determining rates of growth of output. As will be shown, there has recently been a substantial increase in money investments without any corresponding increase in output.

One of the development services that has received little attention in Southern Rhodesia is the provision of agricultural credit
to African producers. There are still opportunities for producers
to raise output through better use of labor and better timing of
farm operations without making cash outlays. These opportunities
are diminishing, however, and if per-capita output is to be raised
there will have to be some intensification of production. The
means for intensification — fertilizers, improved seed, insecticides,
equipment — have to be purchased in the exchange economy.

All the available evidence indicates that net returns after cash
outlays for supplies (especially fertilizer) are higher than when
producers do not use these supplies. The most optimistic forecasts
of the incomes that can be earned off a standard holding as defined
under the Native Land Husbandry Act include a large return
based on the use of fertilizers. A holding of eight cultivated acres
with six head of cattle and sixty acres of grazing land is expected
to yield a profit of £98 if the producer uses £22 worth of fertilizer.[6]
However, in 1960 less than 3 percent of the producers in the
African areas used fertilizers.[7]

At present most producers are operating at such a low level of
efficiency that added inputs of yield-increasing supplies could reduce unit costs of production and increase profits, but most producers do not earn cash incomes that permit them to save and accumulate enough to purchase supplies. Nor do they have much in
the way of collateral to offer as security for a loan from commercial sources. Except for the producers in the purchase areas,
they do not "own" the land they are farming so they cannot pledge
it for collateral, nor are their cattle acceptable for this purpose,
since they might die. Most producers do not produce a large
enough surplus so that lenders will accept the pledge of future
earnings against a loan. The only avenue open for the average
producer to acquire capital is through the sale of his labor or his
cattle or by borrowing from public lending agencies created to
meet his needs.

The first such public lending program for Africans was initiated
in 1945. The statutory Land Bank, which provides low-cost loans

for Europeans (usually against mortgages on land), began to make advances to African farmers in the purchase areas (the only Africans who could pledge land). The size and scope of the program was very small; in its first ten years less than seventy farmers received a total of less than £6,000.

In 1958 a program to meet the needs of all African producers was started with the very modest sum of £10,000 and later expanded under a grant from the United States aid program. Even so, by the early 1960's the total amount available for lending had not exceeded £105,000 amounting to less than a few shillings per family in the African areas.[8] This sum is adequate to meet the cash requirements for fertilizers of less than 5,000 producers if they are to match the income goals prescribed for an eight-acre holding under the Native Land Husbandry Act.

There is a pressing need to infuse more working capital into African agriculture and this can only be done through public programs. Unlike similar programs in many other parts of Africa, Southern Rhodesia's very selective program has had few losses.[9] This is all to the good, but the small size of the program is handicapping its effectiveness as a means of promoting development. Credit programs should be incorporated in the general plan for converting ordinary farmers into master farmers; the ready availability of funds is important in inducing the more able producers to adopt improved techniques of production. With the limited funds presently available, the credit program can, at best, reach no more than four or five thousand producers, or less than half of those who are already classified as master farmers and who also require credit facilities.

The lack of resources for expanding credit indicates the imbalance in the present pattern of government allocations. The shortage of credit may well prevent the desired expansion in agricultural output. Increased allocations for credit programs and other development services will not increase the stock of capital in the African areas. They will, however, improve the quality of resources and are important in raising the productivity of the resources already devoted to agriculture. Increased expenditures in development services are a necessary, though not a sufficient, condition for raising the rate of return on past investments as well as on future investments. The added condition is that the producers must be prepared to use these services.

THE PATTERN OF GOVERNMENT EXPENDITURES

The major money outlays in the African areas are made by the government. Before 1940 public expenditures on agricultural development were negligible; small sums were made available for road building, bridge construction, and other minor works such as cattle-dipping pens and small dams. In the nine years from 1941 to 1949 inclusive, expenditure on agricultural development is estimated to have been close to £2.5 million.[10] In the following nine-year period, 1950–1958 inclusive, the level of expenditures increased very rapidly, totaling £15.8 million, a six-fold increase over the preceding nine years. Despite this great increase in expenditures during a period when population rose by around 50 percent, average per-capita output barely exceeded the level attained in the preceding nine-year period. As a result the average and marginal returns on expenditures declined rather than increased.

One explanation why the increased expenditures did not result in increased rates of per-capita output lies in the pattern of the expenditures. As Table 8 shows almost 50 percent of the funds spent in 1950–1958 went for soil conservation, provision of water supplies, and road maintenance and construction; a lesser proportion was for services in connection with the implementation of the Native Land Husbandry Act, such as land allocation, aerial photography, and salaries of surveyors. One fifth of all expenditures was for wages and salaries of personnel, many of whom were engaged in implementing the Native Land Husbandry Act. In brief, the pattern of spending reflected a heavy emphasis on the role of land as a factor in agricultural development.

This pattern is confirmed by the expenditures made under the Native Land Husbandry Act, which between 1956 and 1959 amounted to nearly £5 million. Since 1959 the act has been the major vehicle of African agricultural development and between 1959 and early 1963 more than £11.6 million will have been spent in its implementation. (Part of the capital expenditures are to be financed by a loan of £2 million from the International Bank

Table 8. Direct government expenditures on rural development (excluding ordinary education and health), Southern Rhodesia, 1950–1958 inclusive

	Nine-year expenditure (in thousands of pounds)	Percent of total
Soil conservation	1,119	7
Water supplies	5,060	32
Roads	1,319	8
Fencing	73	1
Agricultural and stock improvement	217	1
Wages and salaries	3,193	20
Dipping and dip tanks	624	4
Marketing	1,357[a]	9
Buildings	647	4
Demonstrations and training	98	1
Grants to native councils	217	1
Experiments and research	165	1
Plant, marketing, and equipment	1,472	9
Other direct expenditures	190	1
Total direct expenditures	15,751[b]	100

Note: Because of rounding, the percentages do not add exactly to 100.

[a] The total marketing expenditure appears in government accounts as £1,957,000, but this includes a bookkeeping item of £600,000, a subsidy for transport charges that is recouped and therefore not counted here as a direct expenditure.

[b] Government accounts show an additional item of £572,000 in indirect administrative charges, not properly included in "direct expenditures."

Sources: Figures derived by author from the annual financial statements of the Southern Rhodesia government and the annual accounts of the Native Production and Marketing Development Fund.

for Reconstruction and Development.) The bulk of these expenditures continue the earlier pattern, the emphasis being on "primary development" (39 percent of the total) and on other investments that relate to expanding the infrastructure and increasing the "physical capacity" for production.[11]

Both in the 1950–1958 period and from 1959 onward the stress has been on investment in land and the reorganization of land holdings. There is a place for these in any development program, but a rapid increase in the stock of capital in any area cannot be accompanied by any comparable increase in output unless the producers in that area know how to use that capital. Otherwise the increase will merely represent excess capacity and both the average and marginal efficiency of the use of capital will decline. At present 70 percent of the producers in the African areas do not know how to use improved land. In addition, although a great deal of the high-cost investment has been for soil conservation, these producers are continuing to use soil-depleting methods of production. The net result may be no increase in output and continued depletion of the soil.[12]

As was shown in the preceding chapter the *sine qua non* for raising African agricultural productivity is to convert as many ordinary farmers as possible into master farmers. The services required to improve managerial ability include research, extension work, and provision of credit. Yet from 1950 to 1958 only 2.5 percent of the total expenditures on African agriculture were directly related to providing these services and only 5.4 percent of the expenditures for implementing the Native Land Husbandry Act from 1959 onward were for the promotion of better farming. Although personnel costs represent around 20 percent of all expenditures from 1950 to date, most of the personnel have been directly concerned with the land rather than with raising the productivity of Africans on the land.

In general the policy-makers in Southern Rhodesia appear to share the common view that capital is of overriding importance in promoting agricultural development. The provision of development services, which constitute investments in human resources, are not considered to be in the same category of importance. The fact that development services are usually financed out of current budgets rather than capital or development budgets reinforces the view that they do not represent worthwhile investments. The neglect of these services, however, represents a gross malallocation of resources.

It is the intention of the government to shift the emphasis from land improvement and primary development to the provision of services as soon as the major expenditures have been made under the Native Land Husbandry Act. But there is a long gestation period in training technical personnel, and provision for training has to be made well in advance of the proposed date of any campaign to expand technical services. As it is, there is a 30 percent shortfall in the extension service and, if the service is to reach the numbers prescribed in the preceding chapter, training facilities will have to be substantially enlarged. For the realization of programs to expand research and to train more farmers, plans have to be made well in advance. It seems fair to state that the general preoccupation with the importance of "capital" and "capital improvement" and with the land has resulted in such plans being assigned a very low priority. This is all the more regrettable because the expenditures required to provide these essential services are not large in relation to those being made under the Native Land Husbandry Act.

TAXES

Between 1948 and 1958 direct taxes collected in the African areas were equal to 60 percent of the direct government expenditures on agricultural development.[13] The government contributed the other 40 percent from general revenues, some of which were provided through indirect taxes by African producers, but most of which was generated outside the African areas. Had revenues from the African areas been greater, there would undoubtedly have been a higher level of expenditure on African agricultural development. As in all economies, the desire for higher revenue through taxation has to be balanced against the effects of the taxes on production, though, as is shown below, it is possible to have taxes that raise revenue and improve resource use. At present, however, the major sources of revenue from the African areas are the poll tax and the levy on agricultural production. The use of these taxes raises several questions as to their economic advantages and disadvantages.

The poll tax was imposed in 1905 and remained at a level of £1 per adult male and 10s. for each wife in excess of one until 1956, when the tax was raised to £2 per male. Almost all able-bodied African men pay this tax; sick and disabled persons, pupils and students; the aged, the infirm, and hardship cases are exempted. All Africans working in Southern Rhodesia pay the tax, though by arrangement with neighboring governments a certain proportion of the taxes paid by "foreign" migrant labor is remitted to the home government. As the tax is purely a function of the size of the working population the amounts collected rose steadily until 1956 and then increased sharply because of the doubling of the tax. (See Table 9.) The extra revenue from doubling the tax was tied to the financing of African education, and the ready acceptance of the increase is an indication of the high esteem placed on education by the African people. (Despite the

Table 9. Southern Rhodesia's revenues from poll tax,[a] *1949–1959*
(in pounds)

Fiscal year	Collected from indigenous Southern Rhodesians	Collected from natives from other countries	Amount remitted to other governments[b]	Total accruing to Southern Rhodesia government
1949	356,371	148,233	59,159	445,445
1950	396,676	138,345	79,766	455,255
1951	358,557	254,241	73,297	539,501
1952	378,267	250,086	79,863	548,490
1953	403,130	173,290	88,217	488,203
1954	436,359	185,205	80,871	540,693
1955	479,422	298,331	168,393	609,360
1956	454,946	265,628	174,531	546,043
1957	861,863	307,403	184,503	984,763
1958	891,178	374,366	202,472	1,063,072
1959	905,720	398,898	194,547	1,110,071
Total	5,922,489	2,794,026	1,385,619	7,330,896

[a] The poll tax was £1 per year for each adult able-bodied male native up to May 3, 1956. Thereafter, it became £2. The second £1 is set aside specifically for education.

[b] Northern Rhodesia and Nyasaland get 17s. 6d. of every £2 which Southern Rhodesia collects from natives who come from those areas. Portuguese East Africa (P.E.A.) gets all of the tax revenue collected from P.E.A. natives who are in the Salisbury area, and half of the revenue collected from P.E.A. natives elsewhere in Southern Rhodesia.

Source: Derived from the annual reports of the secretary for native affairs and chief native commissioner.

increased revenues from these taxes, total expenditures on African education in 1958–1959 and 1960–1961 are still more than double the total revenues gathered from the poll tax.)[14]

The poll tax has the advantage of being relatively easy to administer (though in 1960 only 66 percent of the taxes due were collected because of the difficulties in collecting from migratory laborers).[15] More important, though, the poll tax has the economic merit of being a tax on leisure. As such it increases the aggregate supply of effort in a situation where many resources are underutilized. The poll tax "raises the marginal utility of income (compared to its previous level) while leaving the reward for marginal effort in both the subsistence and money sectors unaltered."[16] The tax creates a demand for money income; the supply of effort to meet that income can come either from increased inputs in the agricultural sector or by males migrating to seek employment in the wage economy.[17] On the other hand, the poll tax is a regressive tax. It is not based on income or on ability to pay. Africans who earn £5 a year pay the same amount as those who earn £300 a year. The tax is not a substitute for the "color-blind" income tax, but the level at which income taxes are levied is geared to European standards of ability to pay. So much so that in 1960 fewer than 200 Africans in the entire Federation of Rhodesia and Nyasaland reported incomes liable for the income tax.[18]

Revenues from the African areas could be increased by lowering the levels at which income taxes are payable, but this would raise innumerable problems of administration, for very few Africans maintain written accounts or could answer to a tax audit. A more appropriate tax might be a combined wealth and income tax similar to that in effect in parts of Uganda. This tax violates many of the canons of tax theory in advanced societies; it is based on local estimates of wealth and income and is assessed and levied at the local level by councils who rely on their personal knowledge as a basis for assessments. Experience in Uganda has indicated, however, that it is an effective tax in closely knit societies where incomes may be low but where evidences of wealth are apparent (particularly in the form of crops). In these circumstances it is possible to make a reasonable estimate of assets and income.

Within Southern Rhodesia a wealth tax, such as a graduated tax on livestock, could improve resource use and raise revenues. It could be levied so as to rise sharply after livestock reach a specified age. A tax of this kind would discriminate against old animals, raise the cost of keeping them, and so encourage producers to sell. Sale of old animals would reduce pressure on limited grazing resources, and make room for the younger livestock that can utilize grazing land to greater economic advantage. The sale of old livestock would also ease conservation problems in the grazing areas. Such a tax should not be too difficult to administer, since a record of all animals is already kept for dipping purposes. Imposition of a tax of this kind, however, would have to be coordinated with the expansion of market facilities. The tax would also encounter resistance because it would interfere with the tradition that makes cattle symbols of prestige. Nevertheless this kind of tax — which has never been tried in Africa or elsewhere — is one that could produce revenues and improve resource use. As such it has obvious merits.

The major agricultural tax in Southern Rhodesia is a levy on the products marketed by African farmers. This tax, which was introduced in 1948, covers a wide range of commodities and livestock and can be as high as 15 percent of the retail price. It is collected directly from African producers and paid into a Native Production and Marketing Development Fund — an important source of funds used exclusively for African agricultural development.[19] Between 1948 and 1958 the levy contributed slightly more than a quarter of the total revenues collected from the African areas. It has been used to service the £2 million loan from the International Bank for Reconstruction and Development for the implementation of the Native Land Husbandry Act.[20]

The levy is deducted at the source on all output marketed by Africans that is handled by statutory marketing boards and marketing agencies. This includes almost all the products and livestock grown by Africans. The use of levies is a simple and effective means of forcing producers to save and insures a steady flow of revenue for planning purposes. The assumption underlying the use of the levy is that Africans are low-cost producers who consume their profits instead of saving and reinvesting in on-farm improvements.[21] By means of the levy the government provides that part of these profits go into a fund to be used for African agricultural development. In effect, the managers of the fund are deciding how these profits shall be used instead of leaving the decision-making to hundreds of thousands of individual producers.

The assumptions underlying the use of the levy as an instrument for promoting development are open to question on several points. The first is whether producers do indeed "consume" all of their surplus. If they do not, this tax policy may well be slowing down the rate of increase in output and capital formation. In a situation where land is plentiful, marginal returns on added cash expenditures by individual farmers may yield high returns; in addition, small cash investments may well complement labor in land clearance so that, if savings are available, the rate of capital formation in African agriculture could well be increased at a faster rate. On the other hand, the transfer of funds to the government may enable the government to invest in expanding infrastructure and add to "lumpy" off-farm capital formation. Where these investments are indivisible, in the sense that only a large-scale investment can yield economic returns, then the use of combined forced savings for off-farm investment may yield higher returns than comparable on-farm investment. No individual producer, for example, could afford to construct cattle dips; these are only economic when they are used by large numbers of producers. Given the same rates of on-farm and off-farm capital formation, however, the question of which has the higher multiplier effect in increasing output is still unresolved. At present there is not enough data to determine the impact of the levy on the rate of agricultural development, but the results of increased public expenditures, including the loan serviced by the proceeds of the levy, do not, as yet, indicate any multiplier effect whatsoever.

Even if producers do not save, there remains a question as to the income effects of the levy. The marginal propensity to purchase consumer goods may be high. The imposition of a levy may be restricting the size of the internal market, and in Southern Rhodesia the major problem of economic growth is not a shortage of capital but a lack of investment opportunities. Any reduction of the size of the internal market can only aggravate this situation. If the withholding of funds from producers results in a merely temporary restriction in the size of the market, to be followed by increased incomes arising from the multiplier effects of the use of the funds, there would be little cause for debate on the merits of the tax. But as has been pointed out, there has been no increase in the average per capita output from the use of these funds.

The levy is inequitable in the extreme. It is imposed on African products but not on European products; there are differential "pay-outs" for identical products depending on the racial origin of the producers. (See Chapter 8.) The logic behind this appears to be that Africans are low-cost producers, relative to European producers, and consequently can bear the incidence of a tax on a unit of output more readily than can high-cost European producers. This is fallacious. Africans may have low cash outlays but their yields per acre are so low that the real costs of production are high. When imputed costs for land and family labor are included in estimating net return to the average producer these returns are close to zero. Thus, in reality, the levy has been applied to high-cost producers and not to low-cost producers. This is an anomalous policy that increases the hardships of the poorest section of the community; as such, it can only add to the incentive for males to migrate and to seek wage employment outside the African areas.

The levy has been advocated by Europeans on the grounds that the benefits from the use of these compulsory savings are desired by those who bear the burden of the tax. The Europeans who advocate this form of taxation do not have to pay it, nor would they readily accept a comparable levy on their own output, even if the combined proceeds were to be used for agricultural development. The incidence of such a levy, they argue, would be unevenly distributed, with the income effect being greatest on those who could least afford it. The contradiction in attitudes toward the same tax on Europeans and Africans is so self-evident that it calls for no comment.

Although the levy on marketed products is relatively easy to administer, it has drawbacks as an instrument of economic policy. In addition to some of the issues mentioned above the levy is a tax on internally consumed products. As is shown in the next chapter, there is a great deal of tax avoidance, so that the tax falls most heavily on those who market legally while the benefits are "indiscriminate." Furthermore, because the tax is on commodities that can be consumed or sold, it discourages producers from marketing their products. It has lowered prices to producers but not to consumers, so there is little to commend it on that score. Finally, perhaps the major weakness in the levy is that an African receives less for an identical product than does a European; this can hardly be conducive to improving race relations.

In different circumstances an alternative, and more useful, tax might be a tax on land. A graduated tax based on the productive value of land would place a high cost on fertile land left unused or used below its rated productive capacity. It would raise the cost of unused land, thereby encouraging more effective use of land, and would increase the pressure on Africans to raise for the market.

Even under normal conditions such a tax would be difficult to apply, but the prevailing system of land tenure in the African areas presents added difficulties. The tax can only be applied when holdings are clearly identifiable, for it is based on the fertility of a particular piece of land. In the African areas holdings are not clearly recognizable nor is too much known about the fertility or productive capacity of most of the land. The application of this tax would have to await the registration and allocation of holdings under the Native Land Husbandry Act, or failing that, the completion of a detailed study of land-use potential that would permit its imposition on a group basis.

Such a tax would have advantages if it were to be applied throughout the country. It would be "color blind" and would encourage all producers to use their land more effectively. It would increase the revenues collected from Africans and Europeans alike, but the incidence would be heaviest on the areas with the most productive land. These are the European areas. Furthermore, the use of a land tax might well force abandonment of unused land in the European areas and so could be a relatively painless method of augmenting the African areas. (In this regard it is relevant to point out that proposals for a land tax submitted to the legislature have never been implemented.)[22]

The problem of raising tax revenues is a vexing one, but taxes have to be considered as more than revenue-raising devices. At present, not enough is known about the impact of taxes on African producers to assess the effect of many of the present or proposed taxes on productivity. As yet there is no way of knowing whether the marginal propensity to consume is high or whether, given added cash incomes, Africans would invest in their holdings. Nevertheless, one factor is apparent — whatever revenues are collected are being squeezed out of poor producers — and so it behooves the government to use these proceeds as effectively as possible.

SAVINGS AND REMITTANCES

In addition to taxes as a source of revenue for government investment in the African areas, Africans also contribute to public and private investment through voluntary savings. The absolute levels of saving among Africans are not large, though the degree to which Africans save out of their meager incomes is surprising. One analysis of a sample of urban Africans states:

> The general picture obtained from this analysis is one of struggle and poverty in a considerable proportion of the sample. To [a certain extent this] is brought about by the level of wages. In its most serious form it arises from the wish of the individual to save . . . it is probable . . .

that the wish to send money to rural relatives, to pay for gifts to urban girl-friends and especially to obtain major items of capital equipment are the principal motives [for saving].[23]

Saving here is, of course, a combination of deferred expenditures for consumption and other goods. By further analysis the average "savings" of an urban African were estimated to be £2 a month, or 16 percent of average incomes of £12, a very high figure, indeed, and certainly one that contradicts the assumption that African workers do not save.

Deposits in post-office savings departments are the most popular form of monetary saving. An intensive propaganda drive has helped to convince Africans that the post office is an institution that is both safe and profitable. The fact that post offices accept very small deposits has also helped their rapid growth in popularity. The number of African depositors increased from 28,000 in 1949 to 129,000 in 1958, with accumulated African savings rising from £72,000 to £2,207,000.[24] Among those who save, the increase in per-capita savings has been from less than £5 in 1952 to £17 in 1958. There is no breakdown that shows whether these savings accounts are those of indigenous or nonindigenous Africans, but the figures clearly indicate a growing tendency to save among Africans.[25] The increase in savings can be attributed primarily to the very rapid growth of incomes in the wage sector, total African wages having risen almost four-fold between 1948–1960. A further factor has been the spread in the number of post offices throughout the country.[26]

Some Africans also make deposits in commercial banks and building societies. Though the number of Africans using banks for savings is estimated to have almost trebled between 1955 and 1960, their total number is believed to be less than one percent of the wage-earning labor force in the country.[27] Banks and building societies play a very minor role as recipients of savings of Africans in the rural areas.

In general, because of the low gross cash incomes in the African areas and an unfamiliarity with thrift institutions, there still is little voluntary saving in public institutions by African producers. There is evidence of hoarding, however, and despite government campaigns, public savings institutions are distrusted and there is still some confusion about the role of "interest" as a factor in increasing incomes. There are no data on the amount of hoarding that takes place, but officials and others claim that it is considerable.[28] It has been observed that after large cattle sales, where as much as £20,000 or more might change hands between buyers and sellers in a single day, there appears to be no apparent increase in the amount of money circulated in the sale area nor in the amounts deposited in the post offices. The assumption is that the money is hoarded.

Hoarding also takes place in relation to livestock. As has been pointed out elsewhere, many Africans tend to build up the number of their cattle for prestige purposes and as a means of demonstrating their wealth. This tradition, which has persisted despite the introduction of the money economy by the Europeans some sixty years ago, involves a form of nonmonetary saving. Cattle are viewed as a store of value rather than sources of income; indeed they have been referred to as banks on hooves. The overall figures for cattle held by Africans and Europeans show that both races hold approximately the same numbers of livestock, but European sales involve a much higher proportion of total holdings than do African sales. In contrast to the Europeans, Africans tend to hoard their livestock, possibly because they do not trust alternative forms of banking.

Remittances from migratory laborers are another source of capital for inhabitants of the African areas, though there is no breakdown of the amounts sent into the reserves nor of the amounts of capital exported from them. A survey of the African market in 1958–1959 indicated that the urban Africans in Salisbury, Bulawayo, Umtali, and Gwelo — the principal cities of Southern Rhodesia — earned a total cash income of £16.6 million. Out of this, estimated expenditures of £15.5 million were accounted for under a variety of headings; £502,000, or 3.2 percent of the expenditures, went to rural areas and possibly some of the unaccounted-for funds were remitted to relatives.[29] These figures include foreign as well as indigenous labor; however, since half of the labor force is indigenous it can be assumed that half of the remittances — around £250,000 — were sent to families in Southern Rhodesia. In addition to remittances, migratory labor also exports capital from the urban areas to the rural areas in the form of durable consumer goods such as bicycles, furniture, and other items. These purchases represent a considerable part of the transfer of wage incomes from urban to rural areas.

Modifications and changes in tax structure can increase the revenues available from the African areas. But these are poor areas: productivity is low, incomes are low, and so are levels of expenditure on nonfood items. Increased savings or tax revenues can only come from reducing levels of consumption but, in many instances, the levels of consumption are so low that little more can be squeezed out unless African producers increase their productivity.

Chapter 8

Prices and Marketing

Prior to the advent of the Europeans and the introduction of the exchange economy, African production in most of Southern, Central, and East Africa was almost entirely for direct consumption. Today, in the early 1960's, African producers are in varying stages of transition between producing for direct consumption and producing for the market. This process of transition is a continuous one, but it is possible to identify four major stages in the move up the marketing ladder:

(1) All production is for direct consumption.
(2) Most inputs are devoted to production for subsistence though there is marginal production for the market.
(3) The greater proportion of input and output is for the market but there is still production for direct consumption.
(4) All inputs are for specialized production for the market, other than minor items for home consumption.

Few producers in sub-Saharan Africa are either at the first stage or at the top of this ladder. There may still be some isolated pockets of producers who are completely out of the exchange economy but the pressures generated by the trader and the tax collector have induced most Africans to produce a salable surplus. Even the primitive Bushmen in the Kalahari Desert market some of their meager output to purchase beads and other trinkets.[1] Yet very few Africans, if any, produce only for the market or mostly for the market. Some — coffee growers in Buganda in Uganda, for example, and coffee and cotton growers in the Lake District of Tanganyika — produce more for the market than for subsistence, but they are exceptions to the general rule. Most producers in Southern, Central, and East Africa are still at the second stage of the marketing ladder, with production for the market being marginal to production for direct consumption.

Many factors influence the division of inputs between production for consumption and production for sale. A few of the sociological factors have been touched on in Chapter 4 and here some of the economic aspects of incentives and marketing will be considered.

Climate and ecology frequently limit the range of crops suited to prevailing sociological and economic conditions that can be grown in an area. Certain crops have attributes that encourage their production. Robusta coffee is an example. It grows on hardy plants that continue to yield income even when neglected; it can be described as a "lazy-man's" crop, for it is not labor intensive.[2] Other food crops — for example, plantains, which provide shade for the coffee — can be intercropped with it, so it is not land intensive. Once coffee has been introduced into an area it spreads rapidly, enabling many producers to move up the marketing ladder without reducing their output of food. Coffee, however, can only be grown in limited areas in sub-Saharan Africa. In many regions, including Southern Rhodesia, the major products grown by Africans are annual crops, which have to be planted and harvested every year. (See Appendix B for lists of the traditional crops grown.) Planting operations for some cash crops frequently conflict with the harvesting or planting of food crops. Furthermore, both food and cash crops grown in Southern Rhodesia have low unit values and are labor intensive, bringing low returns to labor. To encourage producers to move up the marketing ladder in these areas it is important to widen the range of alternatives in output. Although climatic and other physiographic and entomological conditions may preclude the production of any "lazy-man's" tree crops, opportunities do exist for introducing annual crops with higher unit values, which will increase returns to labor and encourage production for the market.

In Southern Rhodesia the recent introduction of Turkish tobacco has resulted in increased output for the market from land and labor that formerly produced only a small marketable surplus. Between 1957 and 1960 average gross value of output per acre from Turkish tobacco ranged from £38. 12s. an acre to £58. 12s. 11d. per acre. This was between five and six times as much as was yielded by the usual pattern of production of low unit value crops. Some producers netted £100 per acre. In 1960 1,500 acres of Turkish tobacco were harvested by some 4,500 producers. If 10,000 acres were planted in tobacco, under favorable conditions the total output marketed by all African producers would increase by more than 25 percent over present levels.[3]

The development services have a direct role to play in encouraging producers to move up the marketing ladder. Applied research is essential in finding new high-unit-value crops to replace or supplement the crops now grown by most Africans in Central and East Africa.[4] Research is also necessary to develop new varieties of established products that can fit into crop rotation plans without conflicts in labor arrangements. Once these new crops or new varieties are available, the extension service is responsible for the dissemination of information about them and the appropriate credit agency has to ensure that producers have adequate supplies to produce them. Thus, there is a close link between the effectiveness of the development services, especially applied research, and the shift of producers into the market. As will be shown, another development service, that of training managers of cooperatives, also has an important role in improving the efficiency of marketing.

INCENTIVES

Even in those parts of Southern, Central, and East Africa where export crops are grown, many producers prefer to leave resources unemployed rather than to increase their labor inputs. Their marginal costs of producing for the market, in terms of foregone leisure, appear to rise so sharply after their immediate needs are satisfied that they voluntarily restrict their inputs of effort. This self-imposed "cut-off" point in production is most common in areas where traditional values are strongest and is one of the elements that contributes to the kinked supply curve for many commodities grown by Africans. (See Chapter 4.) Although this phenomenon of voluntary underemployment may be transitional, it is widespread. If producers are to increase their output and move up the marketing ladder, they must have the incentive to increase their input of effort. This incentive will have to be of the kind that increases the opportunity cost of "foregone income" in such a way that producers will prefer making a greater effort to having greater leisure, that is, the relative values of effort and leisure will have to be changed.

One way to raise the opportunity cost of leisure might be to demonstrate the rewards for greater efforts in terms of the goods that could be purchased through higher incomes. At present in many parts of Central and East Africa the only sources of supply for "incentive" goods are small trading posts. Most of these carry a narrow and uninspiring range of products. The apparent rewards for effort are restricted to the basic necessities of daily life. A wider range of more attractive goods might well raise the materialistic ambitions of producers by visibly demonstrating the rewards for greater effort. Hopefully this "demonstration effect" would spur producers to increase their labor inputs so as to earn high enough incomes to possess these goods. If this view of the importance of incentive goods is valid, then the narrow range of wares now displayed by many undercapitalized traders offers little inducement to increase output. This situation could be remedied by a special credit program to enable selected traders to expand their stocks of exotic consumer goods. Possibly such a program would yield higher returns in the short run than many comparable direct investments in agriculture.

Another approach to encouraging production for the market is to provide an incentive which is more meaningful to producers than higher cash incomes *per se*.[5] The overriding ambition and desire of most Africans throughout Central and East Africa is to see their children educated, though many of them, particularly in the less commercialized areas, do not appreciate the relations among increased output, higher tax revenues, and the provision of educational facilities. In these areas education could be used as an incentive to increase output and sales. This system of incentives could operate at a local level. Production quotas could be assigned to villages or local groups and the local or central government could guarantee that if the quota was exceeded by a given percentage, specified educational facilities would be made available for the families of local producers. These facilities might be in the form of buildings or in the provision of teaching services. (The results of a field experiment convinced the writer of the potential of such an approach. A group of twenty-five producers in the Selukwe area were asked whether they would follow certain specified production patterns in return for a modest bonus payment. The response tended to be negative. When it was suggested, however, that a school teacher would be provided if the producers followed the prescribed practices, the response was over-whelmingly enthusiastic. The salary of the school teacher would have been less than the sum of the bonuses.)

The approaches outlined above are unorthodox and are based on untested hypotheses. Nevertheless, they may be applicable. Generally, though, price and marketing policies are the major instruments for increasing output and sales. In advanced econo-mies most of the theoretical discussion about price policy is con-cerned with resource allocation and maximizing producer incomes. This is just as important in underdeveloped economies, but where the primary need is to pull producers into the exchange economy, to encourage greater inputs and more intensive use of underuti-lized resources, the role of prices may be seen in a slightly different light.

According to one view, an appropriate price policy for encour-aging producers to move up the marketing ladder should take into account the interaction of rising incomes, changing tastes, under-utilized resources, and the irreversible nature of a move out of subsistence production. Such a policy would allow prices to fluc-tuate over a wide range for a lengthy period. It would be more applicable to export crops than to others, especially where oppor-tunities for substitution in output are limited. When sharp changes occur in the terms of trade and prices move upward, producers would receive windfall profits. These profits would raise dispos-able incomes. Producers would spend more on consumer goods. They would acquire new tastes and move up to a higher plateau of living. Once on this plateau, producers would endeavor to remain there. If prices fell, they would increase inputs of underemployed labor and underutilized land in order to increase marketed output and so maintain their level of disposable income. Should prices rise again they would move on to a higher plateau, and so the discontinuous process of upward jerks would continue. Over the long run — provided the trend in prices is upward, alternatives are limited, and the shift out of subsistence is irreversible — there would be a steady increase in production for the market.

An alternative policy, one that is now followed in many parts of Southern, Central, and East Africa, is to stabilize prices. Its origins vary from country to country. In some, prices were sta-bilized to eliminate the alleged high profits made by speculators;

in others — Uganda, for instance — they were stabilized at a low level to hold down producers' incomes and thereby prevent inflation. Almost always marketing boards or statutory marketing agencies have been established to implement these policies. Frequently these agencies have also been used for collecting taxes and levies on peasant products. In some countries, including Rhodesia, the revenue-collecting aspects of the marketing agencies' operations have tended to override their price-stabilizing functions.

The proponents of these policies maintain that stabilized prices induce Africans to send more produce to market. In their view the important factor in encouraging producers to expand output is to reduce uncertainty.[6] As it is, producers have to face many uncertainties and risks in expanding production for the market. Some of these are the "natural" risks inherent in agricultural production, weather, pests, disease, and the like. Others are economic. These include changes in the terms of trade and subsequent fluctuations in prices received by growers. Unlike natural risks, however, some of these economic factors can be controlled. By reducing price fluctuations, it is possible to mitigate one element of uncertainty about returns from expanded production. This, in turn, reduces the effective interest rate when the producer who contemplates making a change discounts the present value of future output. Growers would know that they would receive an assured return for their added inputs of land and labor. As their confidence in the price system increases, they will be encouraged to move into the exchange economy. In short, stable prices are important, for they induce producers to forego leisure by eliminating some of the risk in expanding production beyond domestic food requirements. The level at which prices are stabilized — so important in advanced economies — is not considered to be as important as the need to iron out price fluctuations.

Prices may be important in different periods in the production process. As was suggested in the chapter on the dual economy the supply curve for some products may be kinked or discontinuous. Producers allocate resources to producing foodstuffs regardless of price variations, but, after harvesting, the role of price may be important, as an upward shift in prices increases sales. That is, price does not influence production but does influence sales. This hypothesis was tested for maize and groundnuts for 1948–1958.

(See Appendix C.) The amounts of maize and groundnuts marketed in those years were closely correlated with production, but production does not appear to have been heavily influenced by price. There is some slight evidence that marketings of maize were related to price changes, even though production was not, but there was an inverse correlation between sales of groundnuts and price changes. Thus, based on this analysis, there was a kinked supply curve for maize but a backward-bending sales curve for groundnuts. In general, though, the data are suspect and not too much can be read into these statistical analyses.

As yet there has been little or no empirical study of what constitutes the most appropriate price policy for encouraging African producers to climb the first rungs of the marketing ladder. Most of what has been written in this book and in others is based on untested hypotheses. Gauging the elasticity of supply with respect to price involves complex problems, because conditions vary considerably both within and between regions.[7] Where aggregated data are used they often mask a wide range of responses to price changes and so can be misleading. Furthermore, most of the available data are fragmentary, and the results of analysis tend to be inconclusive. Without good empirical information, policy-makers frequently find themselves in a dilemma as to what constitutes the most appropriate policy for encouraging producers to increase their sales. Nevertheless, as is shown below, even a partial analysis of price and marketing policies indicates some changes that can improve resource use, promote the efficiency of the marketing mechanism, and encourage producers to move up the marketing ladder.

PRICE AND MARKETING POLICY FOR CROPS IN SOUTHERN RHODESIA

Most African producers are at the second stage of the marketing ladder. A few, notably in the purchase areas, are producing more for the market than for direct consumption, roughly in the ratio of 40 percent for consumption and 60 percent for the market.[8] But African producers as a group market only about 20 percent of their total output, including firewood and livestock.[9] These low levels are confirmed by sample surveys. One sample of close to 450 producers in the lower rainfall areas showed that marketed output ranged from 4 percent of the total output in one region to

18 percent in another.[10] A second sample of 50 producers in varying rainfall conditions indicated that the percentage of farm output that was marketed ranged from 10 to 22 percent.[11] At the time both samples were taken many producers had relatively large stocks of grain on hand, earmarked as reserves to meet future requirements for consumption and for seed. The withholding of products from the market can be ascribed in part to traditional fear of famine, but under the prevailing market system the producer may be acting in his best economic interests by not selling all his output.

Price and marketing policies in Southern Rhodesia have not always been arranged with a view to encouraging increased marketing by Africans. Indeed, during the depression and postdepression years Africans who wished to enter the market were discouraged from doing so by a policy designed to curb any African competition that might threaten European interests. After the collapse of world markets during the depression, the government monopolized the major export industry, the corn industry, and instituted a two-price system for locally produced corn. All corn was to be delivered to the Maize Marketing Board and then assigned either to a local pool or to an export pool. The amount allocated to the local pool was the amount deemed adequate to meet local demand. Prices paid for this corn were 30 to 50 percent above world prices, with the incidence of high prices falling on the consumer. The surplus was allocated to the export pool and was sold at whatever price could be realized on the world market.[12]

The method of allocation protected the smaller European producers and discriminated against the Africans. All European producers were given individual quotas for each pool, and the smaller European producers received large quotas — up to 80 percent of all their deliveries — in the high-priced internal market. The internal quotas of large-scale European producers ran around 20 percent of their deliveries. All deliveries by African producers were treated collectively and 20 percent of the total went into the privileged internal market.[13] Superficially this may have appeared to be equitable, as African producers were providing close to 25 percent of all deliveries of corn to the marketing agency.[14] The Africans, however, were small-scale producers. Had they been accorded the same privileges as small-scale European producers they would have received larger shares in the protected internal market. Africans would have received higher prices for eight out of every ten bags of corn instead of for only two. There can be little doubt that the quota system protected small-scale European producers from African competition by restricting African participation in the small but higher priced internal market. By the same token it is unlikely that this system encouraged African participation in the market.

This quota policy has now fallen away completely, and the government's marketing and price policy no longer discriminates against Africans. The major problems in marketing African products stem from the centrally controlled marketing system, which functions relatively efficiently for large-scale producers but not for the much larger number of small-scale producers. In addition, the use of the marketing organization to enforce the levy on African products is leading to a poor allocation of resources and may well be tending to slow down the marketing of African output.

Almost all products grown by producers in Southern Rhodesia have to be marketed through marketing boards or statutory buying agencies which pay guaranteed prices, provide internal market facilities, and undertake the export of surpluses.[15] European producers bulk, bag, and grade their own grain and deliver it to depots established along the main railway line. They are then paid the posted price for their grain or are given a partial payment with the balance to be sent to them after the export surplus has been disposed of and the final "pay-out" has been established. African marketing is done on an entirely different basis. All Africans, except for farmers in the purchase area, deliver their grain in small ungraded lots to the marketing board's agents (usually traders) dotted throughout the reserves.[16] The agents grade and bag the grain and then transport it to the nearest depot. If there is any ancillary pay-out it does not go to individual producers but is put into a development fund.

Payment for the marketing service at the primary buyers' level has been arranged so as to ease administrative problems. The same flat service charges are deducted from the price of each bag of grain purchased by the board's agents. These charges constitute a handling fee and a transport allowance. The trader retains the handling fee but the transport allowance is paid into a Transport

Equalization Fund which subsequently reimburses the trader for his estimated transportation costs. Thus the trader is reimbursed, but the producer has to pay a uniform price for transportation regardless of whether he is one mile or one hundred miles from a grain depot. The price received by Africans for each bag is reduced further by the deduction of a development levy. The proceeds of this levy go into the Native Production and Marketing Development Fund.

One result of this system of deductions is that there is a multi-price pay-out for identical products. In 1960, for example, the posted price for grade A corn was 36s. a bag. This was the price received by European producers who provided their own marketing services. An African producer from a purchase area received 33s. for the same bag of corn if he provided his own services, the 3s. deduction being for the development levy on all African products, marketed through government agencies. Most Africans, however, received 24s. 8d. per bag of corn, after a deduction of 6s. 10d. for transport fees, 3s. for the trader's handling charge, and 1s. 6d. for the development levy.[17] Thus, for the same product, an African in the reserves receives 60 to 70 percent of the price received by a European, provided both are located close to a railhead. The difference is even greater if an extra bonus is paid at the end of the season.

Since 1961 these have seen some modifications in the right of certain Africans to deliver directly to the railhead but the basic marketing system is unchanged and there are still differentials in payout among various types of producers. Such differentials in prices must encourage illegal sales outside the purview of the marketing agencies. It is profitable for many African producers to sell their grain to Europeans at a price above the price they would receive from the marketing board. Europeans, particularly those close to marketing depots, would find it profitable to buy grain from Africans at prices above the prevailing prices guaranteed to Africans, but below the prices Europeans receive when they deliver the grain at the depot. The system of uniformly high transport deductions adds further encouragement for those close to the depots to sell illegally. There is no way of knowing the extent of illegal sales, but the inducement for tax avoidance must be strong. The profits made from illegal sales do not necessarily add to total movements out of subsistence production; they merely provide higher returns for those who market grain illegally. Producers who sell illegally have a double gain; not only do they receive higher prices than those who sell legally, but they also derive benefits from the public expenditures made from tax revenues without having to share the burden of the taxes.

What effect does the system of deductions for services to Africans have on resource use? Do these marketing charges encourage expansion of production for the market?

Between 1950 and 1958, the transport fee rose from 2s. a bag to 6s. 10d. a bag.[18] This increase reflected the rising cost of transport but it was also a result of the increasing radius of transport operations. The equalizing of transport costs has helped producers in the remote areas — those who are more than 160 miles from a depot — to enter the market economy, and production in these areas has increased.[19] If transport equalization was intended to expand marketings, the system has been effective in attaining this goal. The negative effects of the transport levy are difficult to assess. If land was negotiable, and there was a rent on the land, then the impact of uniform prices would be to subsidize land values or to raise rents in the remote areas. There would be no differential in rent due to locational advantages, except to the extent that time in transit is important in marketing perishable products. Other things being equal, remote land would command the same price as land close to the market and all producers could grow the same products having high transport costs and low unit values. This in itself is a distortion of resource use and prevents the specialization of production except in terms of perishability of output. Once land becomes negotiable, uniform transport charges will accelerate the distortion of resource use. Their continuation might well lead to expanded cultivation of bulky low-cost products but would also slow down the rate of specialization of production based on economic criteria.

The present system of marketing charges has the great disadvantage of denying to producers the benefits inherent in a competitive economy without providing compensating advantages other than high-cost subsidization of distant growers. Producers cannot bargain for low-cost transport. The experience of the co-operatives, to be discussed shortly, shows quite clearly that transport costs can be reduced when producers are given the opportunity to bargain for their own transport. The fact that growers are not allowed to deliver their own products and those of their neighbors to the marketing board's depots has a peculiar side effect on resource use. Carts, bicycles, and other means of transport, which are among the major capital investments in African agriculture, are often underutilized. Paradoxically there is "excess capacity" of transportation equipment in areas of general capital shortage. This situation could be changed if producers were to use their own transport to greatest advantage. Such a change would intensify the use of capital and also give some owners of transport an opportunity to accumulate capital that they might then use for investment in their own holdings.

Perhaps the greatest weakness in the present system of a low pay-out to Africans is that it reinforces the traditional disposition of many producers not to market all their output beyond their immediate needs. Almost all the major commodities grown by Africans in Southern Rhodesia are foodstuffs. This is a significant factor that the policy-makers appear to have overlooked in their desire to collect revenue. Unlike producers in Uganda or Ghana whose cash crops are nonedible export crops, African producers in Southern Rhodesia have the option of consuming their products directly, storing them for later consumption, or marketing them, legally or illegally. This range of options is not open to producers of cocoa, coffee, or cotton, the value of which is either the present or future sale value of the crop. With directly consumable foodstuffs, however, the value of a crop can also be measured in terms of its replacement value, that is, the price that would have to be paid if the crop were to be sold and later replaced by foodstuffs purchased in the market place.

The gap between the producers' selling price and the producer-consumers' purchase price is wide, for national policy has been to maintain high internal prices for the principal foodstuffs. There is a substantial difference between the "posted" price for a bag of corn received by producers and the price paid by consumers. When the marketing charges and the development levy are also deducted from the receipts of African growers, the gap widens still further. In 1958–1959 an African producer received 23s. 8d. for grade A corn in a second-hand bag, but he would have had to pay 38s. to buy back the identical bag, and 52s. 6d. for a bag of processed corn meal.[20] As a result, a bag of corn on the farm or in storage had a replacement cost 40 percent in excess of its going sale value. This in itself provides an inducement for producers to retain ample food supplies rather than market them.

The difference between prices received and prices paid is so wide that a series of secondary markets have developed in the African areas. These are governed by local demand and supply and operate within the framework of the existing price structure. It is noticeable that there are seasonal price fluctuations for crops such as corn in these markets — the actual prices paid by African buyers are higher at the end of the season than at the beginning of a season. In both instances, though, the prices are below those that would have to be paid if the corn were to be bought from the official selling agents of the marketing board. Yet, the seller receives more than he would from the board's agents. In such circumstances there is little incentive to market through the board. This encourages tax avoidance, which in turn raises the average fixed overhead costs of the official marketing agency. The burden of these costs falls on those who market legally.

The service deductions have also been used to stabilize the prices of some products. In doing this, however, the government has tended to emphasize stability without adequate consideration of relative prices and their importance in influencing resource allocation and production for the market. This can be illustrated by the price policy for groundnuts. Groundnut production, which is almost exclusively in the hands of Africans, has seldom exceeded 80 percent of national requirements. To encourage production the internal guaranteed price was raised sharply from 1950 levels and was held high throughout the 1950's. As is shown in Table 10, however, the size of the levy was varied so that actual prices received by growers fluctuated within a narrow range well below the level of guaranteed prices.

In the extreme instance, between the years 1951 and 1957, posted prices increased by only 2 percent but the levy was increased by 160 percent. If total deductions, including marketing charges, are taken into account, prices received by producers actually fell by 20 percent between these years.

The manipulations in the levy resulted in a fairly stable price

Table 10. *Guaranteed prices, deductions, and prices received by African producers for unshelled groundnuts, 1950–1959*
(*in shillings and pence per bag*)

	Guaranteed prices	Levy	Total deductions	Prices received
1950	55/6	5/–	n.a.	n.a.
1951	81/6	6/–	17/–	64/6
1952	85/–	8/–	19/–	66/–
1953	85/–	10/6	21/9	63/3
1954	70/–	6/2	17/3	52/9
1955	70/–	6/7	17/7	52/5
1956	75/–	8/4	20/–	55/–
1957	83/–	16/4	28/–	55/–
1958	79/–	12/4	23/7	55/5
1959	79/–	7/9	19/7	59/3

n.a. = not available
Source: Derived from annual reports of the secretary for native affairs and chief native commissioner.

for groundnuts between 1951 and 1959, but the difference between the guaranteed prices and actual prices received was such that it was more profitable to grow crops other than groundnuts — or to sell groundnuts illegally (see Appendix B). Based on actual yields and prevailing prices, the returns per acre of groundnuts have been well below those of the major competing crops.[21] Emphasis on stable prices may well reduce uncertainty and encourage production for the market, but where there are also stable prices for competing commodities, it is not surprising that producers prefer to market those that bring the highest returns.

THE EFFICIENCY OF THE MARKETING ORGANIZATION

An efficient marketing organization is one that maximizes returns to growers by reducing marketing margins without distorting resource use. The present system is not efficient. The prices received by growers are low because of the high marketing charges, quite aside from the effects of the levy. Furthermore, the system has led to distortion in resource use. Nevertheless, it is unlikely that there will be a move away from centrally controlled marketing at the national level. Memories of the collapse of world prices are still prevalent and there is a widespread belief that national control over prices and markets has eliminated the speculator to the benefit of both producer and consumer. Regardless of the economics of this view, the emotional aspects are so strong that whatever improvements are to be made will have to be made within the framework of a centrally controlled marketing system.

The high marketing charges on output could be reduced by a change in national storage policy that would reduce the over-all cost of operating the centrally controlled marketing system. Up until the present the costs of operating this system have been high. The marketing board has estimated that in 1954–1955 the final cost of a bag of corn to the board was 50s. 1d., compared with the guaranteed price of 40s. 6d. paid to producers (excluding deductions on African output).[22] Furthermore, between 1954 and 1958 the average cost of handling corn was close to 10s. a bag, or more than 25 percent of the average guaranteed price to growers in those years. This figure was almost equal to the average government subsidy paid on each bag of corn.

These costs could be reduced if the government changed its policy of holding large stocks of corn as a hedge against disaster or drought. The policy is very costly from an actuarial standpoint, particularly when these stocks are purchased on the national market at prices well above world prices. The board has recognized this and has estimated that the program has added around 10 percent to the cost of every bag of corn sold by the board.[23] If the storage capacity were used to facilitate rapid transit of supplies, especially low-cost imports as they are needed, there could be a considerable saving in overhead costs and a reduction in marketing charges.

At the "local level" the use of the development levy on foodstuffs must encourage illegal sales and lead to an uneven sharing of burdens and benefits within the African areas. While the levy is an effective means of raising revenue from African producers, it is also one factor in raising the replacement cost of foodstuffs. If a goal of policy is to increase the rate of marketing and at the same time to raise revenue, then such a tax should be confined to export crops or to livestock. The replacement value for these commodities is not so important an influence on sales. Even here, however, the amount of revenue raised must be weighed against the influence the levy exerts on resource use.

The most promising institutional approach to reducing marketing costs and raising prices received by African growers is offered by the cooperative movement. Cooperatives, by combining many small-scale producers into one organization, can purchase services that would otherwise be too costly for individual producers. They enjoy a superior bargaining position that enables them to obtain services at a lower cost than the prices charged by the marketing board.

Well-established and expanding cooperatives exist in Tanganyika and Uganda, but in Southern Rhodesia the movement is still limited in size. In 1960 there were only 22 societies with a membership of less than 2,000. The movement is confined to the purchase areas, where producers can make their own arrangements for delivering to the board's depots. The cooperatives already in existence have shown the potential of the movement as a means of reducing marketing costs. Costs of bulking and bagging grain in the best of the cooperatives are less than 20 percent of the fees paid by the board to compensate traders for providing similar services to individual growers.[24] (The cooperatives, of course, absorb the profits that would otherwise go to the traders.) The cooperatives have also bargained for transport on their own account and their bag-per-mile costs have been substantially lower than the allowances provided by the board. In addition to reducing marketing charges well below prescribed levels, cooperatives have also secured higher prices for their grain through improved grading of output. In 1958, for example, four cooperative societies marketed close to 15,000 sacks of grain of which only two were classified as other than top grade.[25] This is all the more notable when it is realized that less than half of the African grain reaching the market is classified as top grade.

Plans are underway to extend the cooperative movement to the reserves and by 1963 close to half the 53 cooperative societies were in the reserves. This should raise producer incomes, for cooperatives provide what appears to be a most effective means of reducing handling charges from producer to the board. The use of cooperatives to bypass traders raises real incomes for some producers in another way; it frees them from those traders who use their present monopoly rights to insist that producers purchase goods at high prices in return for the traders handling their grain.[26]

In the future, when the cooperative movement has become firmly established, it could also be a means of removing some of the costly administrative difficulties of the board. The board will no longer need to deal with large numbers of small-scale traders with all the attendant problems and costs that arise from supervising and handling thousands of returns. By dealing with well-established cooperatives the board's handling charges will be reduced, and when ancillary payments have to be made to African producers, they can be made to the cooperatives. The members of the cooperatives can then determine whether the funds so received are to be distributed among producers or used for the benefit of the group as a whole.

Another important, though intangible, advantage of the cooperative approach is that the members participate in decision-making and in the marketing process. As a result, they have become aware of the problems involved and of the differing costs of various methods used in marketing. This knowledge has led producers to tighten up their own grading systems and work to reduce marketing charges.

Cooperatives should not be viewed as a panacea, but they do provide the institutional framework whereby small-scale producers can be integrated into a commercially oriented market economy. In addition, they may well provide the basis for a new type of socioeconomic organization that can substitute in part for some of the tribal institutions that are being undermined by the Native Land Husbandry Act. However, while recognizing the importance and potential of the cooperative movement it would be folly to consider cooperatives in an amorphous emotional manner. Cooperatives are essentially business organizations, and their principal appeal lies in increasing returns to growers through efficient management.

At present the shortage of trained managers is a limiting factor in expanding the cooperative movement. The training of managers (and of auditors) does not require large capital outlays but is mostly a matter of increasing current expenditures. The increase should be viewed as a development cost rather than as an ordinary cost of administration. Hitherto, as in many other parts of Southern, Central, and East Africa, these expenditures have not been viewed as contributions to development, and the priority given to capital expenditures, which has militated against the expansion of other development services, has also been a factor in slowing down the improvement of marketing through expansion of the cooperative movement.

MARKETING OF AFRICAN LIVESTOCK

The major livestock industry in Southern Rhodesia is cattle raising, primarily for slaughter. Southern Rhodesia has been a small-scale importer of livestock on the hoof from the Republic of South Africa and Bechuanaland and a small-scale exporter of fresh, frozen, and chilled meats. Most of the beef trade is domestic. Internal demand for meat is strong and will increase as per-capita income rises; the income elasticity of meat is high, being around 0.6 for urban African workers, that is, for every 1 percent increase in per-capita income there is an increase of 0.6 percent in meat consumption.[27] The prospects for an expanding internal and export market are promising, provided there is an improvement in the quantity and quality of the livestock marketed by Africans.

Livestock are held by both Europeans and Africans, but African production lags far behind that of Europeans. Africans hold between a third and a quarter more cattle than do Europeans but their sales represent only about a third of the total sales of livestock. Furthermore, as African cattle are usually inferior in quality to those held by Europeans, the proportion of African sales by weight is even lower. In 1955, for example, African sales represented 33 percent of the total number sold but only 25 percent of the total weight.[28]

The difference in the numbers of livestock sold by Europeans and Africans can be attributed to diverse factors. One important factor is that European levels of animal husbandry and range management are much superior. European-held livestock are brought to marketable condition much more rapidly than African livestock so that Europeans produce a larger marketable surplus with a smaller number of animals. Sociological and cultural factors previously discussed also contribute to the low rate of turnover in African-held stock. Many Africans, though not all, still view live-stock as symbols of prestige and regard the numbers held, irrespective of age and condition, to be more important than maximizing the income derived from a herd. Up until 1956, methods of market-ing also contributed to the lag in sales.

In the early 1940's the government established a policy for the "orderly marketing" of African livestock. Its aim was to encourage destocking of overgrazed range land and to eliminate speculation in livestock marketing. The main instrument for executing the policy was the Cold Storage Commission, a statutory marketing organization entrusted with the task of regulating the flow of beef to the market. The procedure adopted was to fix the price of Afri-can livestock on a weight and grade basis and to make it manda-tory for Africans to sell to the commission at these prices. There were to be no sales by private treaty or at European auction sales except by special permits, and these were granted sparingly.

The prices received by Africans for their livestock were estab-lished by the government. There was to be no bargaining as at European auction sales and the Africans had little legal option but to sell to the Cold Storage Commission at fixed prices, with-hold their cattle from market, or sell to African butchers in the African areas. In these circumstances the level of prices fixed by the government was all important in inducing price-conscious Afri-cans to sell their stock. The prices offered for the three most im-portant African grades were respectively 19 percent, 16 percent, and 10 percent below comparable prices in the open European market.[29] The artificial depression of prices did not encourage in-creased livestock sales but it did lead to a considerable amount of illegal traffic with Europeans and others who resold on the open market.

The marketing system for livestock benefited European cattle owners and grazers. In controlling the flow of livestock the com-mission operated a "grazer scheme" whereby surplus stock were leased to European farmers until they were required at a later date. Ownership of these cattle remained in the hands of the Cold Storage Commission. The European "grazers" did not have to make capital outlays to purchase the livestock nor bear any risk of losses due to mortality. They were, however, compensated for the "value added," when they returned the leased livestock to the commission. The value added was considerable. The grading and price system was such that there was a wide spread between prices paid for lower and higher grades. Europeans purchased low-grade, cheap livestock, then returned the fattened animals to the commission. The animals were reclassified into high-priced grades and the European grazers received a handsome profit. Little wonder that a 1956 Commission of Enquiry into the livestock industry stated that the grazer scheme had been useful "in assisting a number of undercapitalized farmers to get on their feet." [30]

In 1956 the marketing system was changed. The market was integrated. Grades were reclassified and prices were raised for the lower grades. African cattle could be sold at auctions in the African areas which were to be open to all buyers on a competitive basis. At the same time the Cold Storage Commission stood ready as a residual buyer, thus providing a floor price for cattle. Grazers who wished to acquire livestock had to buy them in open competition with other bidders at auction sales.

The effect of these changes in policy was to sharply increase the prices paid for African cattle. Average prices rose by 25 percent between 1955 and 1956 and there was a 10 percent increase in the numbers offered for sale.[31] Since then prices have continued to rise steadily, but sales have not. A possible explanation for the decreasing rate of increase in sales was suggested in Chapter 4: commercially oriented producers may have released their livestock in 1956 when prices rose sharply, but the continued rise in prices may have had less influence on the remaining stock owners who were governed primarily by traditional influences.

There are still serious and urgent problems of livestock marketing in Southern Rhodesia and in many other cattle-producing areas in Southern, Central, and East Africa. The persistence of traditional attitudes toward livestock is leading to serious overgrazing and depletion of resources. Expanded market facilities, reasonable price policies, and increased availability of incentive goods will all help to encourage sales. In addition, as was suggested in an earlier chapter, a progressive age tax on livestock might aid in promoting marketing of livestock. Attitudes are changing, but tradition dies hard, and it is unlikely that there will be a rapid, short-run increase in livestock marketings.

There can be no gainsaying the importance of increasing production for the market in African agriculture. With increased marketings the rate of monetization of the economy will be accelerated and the internal market for nonagricultural products, now extremely limited, will grow in size. The efforts of the great bulk of the population will no longer have to be confined to feeding themselves and so there will be more specialization of production and division of labor, further expansion of commerce and trade, and greater opportunity for increased savings and capital formation in the agricultural sector.

Part IV: Conclusion

Chapter 9

Future Prospects
for African Agriculture
in Southern, Central, and East Africa

THE SIZE OF THE MARKET

In the countries of Southern, Central and East Africa that have a heritage of British rule the overwhelming majority of Africans depend on agriculture for their livelihood. Levels of productivity are low and a large share of national resources is used to merely sustain the rural population and provides only a small marketable surplus. Because of this, little "national income," in a monetary sense, is being derived from these resources. The slow rate of increase in marketed output — exemplified in Southern Rhodesia — indicated that African agriculture makes little contribution to raising average per-capita incomes.

In many areas, including Southern Rhodesia, Africans have contributed to economic growth by providing labor to the wage economy through the migratory labor system. In effect, African agriculture has subsidized employers in the wage sector by providing an elastic supply of low-cost labor.[1] This has undoubtedly aided the expansion of the wage sector — especially where there are labor-intensive industries such as the gold mines in the Republic of South Africa — but it has not contributed to the agricultural development. If anything, the migratory labor system has widened the gap between the rates of growth in the wage sector and in agriculture.

In developing economies the relative contribution of agriculture to national output generally decreases as economies grow.[2] Once industrial development begins, the impetus for growth comes from industry. With the exception of the Republic of South Africa, the countries in this region, however, are still heavily dependent on agriculture. Although their future rates of economic growth will inevitably be linked to industrial development and increasing exploitation of mineral resources, at the present time they have still to rely on agriculture to provide the savings to finance growth. In addition, the incomes of those in the agricultural sector determine the size of the internal market for consumer goods and thereby influence the rate of investment in industry. Lack of investment opportunities are greater deterrents to industrial growth than lack of capital. In Uganda, for example, the well-managed and aggressive Uganda Development Corporation has been forced to invest in agricultural development, for the opportunities for industrial development were rapidly exhausted because of the small size of the internal market.[3]

This does not mean that agricultural development should necessarily be given priority in order to develop an internal market for industry. The priorities accorded to different projects in different sectors of the various economies in the region will depend on the goals of national policies and the particular needs of each economy.[4] It is inevitable, however, that high priority be given to projects for raising agricultural productivity, since so high a proportion of national resources are now underutilized and are yielding so small a marketable surplus. Unless African producers increase output for the market more rapidly than the rural population increases, the surplus produced will remain at a low level.

An expansion in marketed output will bring about a greater physical volume of trade in agricultural products. The extent to which that trade increases, however, will depend not only on an expanding supply but also on the growth of demand for agricultural products, either for internal consumption or for export. Rising internal demand will depend on population, growth, increases in the rate and value of per-capita consumption, development of the food-producing sector, the growth of the industrial sector utilizing agricultural products, and the possibilities of substituting domestic products for imports. Increased demand for exports will depend on all the factors that govern the expansion of world trade.

The prospects for the rapid expansion of internal trade in agricultural products are not promising, particularly for foodstuffs. Increases in total population will raise the demand for food, but, as long as most of the population is rural, land is plentiful, and full-time wage employment is scarce, most producers will continue to grow their own food. In Uganda, for example, the relatively prosperous cotton and coffee growers produce their own food rather than specialize in cash crops, and throughout the country as a whole there is a high degree of regional self-sufficiency, with basic diets being satisfied by the localized production of different staple crops. As a result, there is little prospect for any expansion of internal trade in the major foodstuffs. It is unlikely in the extreme that plantains produced in the south could find a market outlet in the north in competition with the staple grains produced there. Local comparative advantages are accentuated by high transport costs for bulky low-unit value commodities such as these staples.

A further limitation on the size of the internal market for foodstuffs in Uganda is the small number of wage earners, less than 5 percent of the total population. These wage earners probably consumed a high proportion of the estimated £8 or £10 million of marketed agricultural output consumed within the country in 1959. The average incomes of wage earners are low, however, and unskilled workers in Kampala — who represent the bulk of the stabilized wage-earning labor force — already spend 58 percent of their incomes on food.[5] In the present circumstances the absolute size of the internal market for staples is severely restricted, and would continue to be so even if prices were to fall. As a result, many producers who do attempt to produce staples for the internal market find that because of the limited market this output remains unsold or, that when it is sold, the total costs of production and distribution are such that returns for effort are zero.[6] In these circumstances the increase in supply does not in itself create demand.

If the example of developed economies is any guide, the most significant increases in demand for domestically produced foods can be expected to come from a relative and absolute increase in the number of families that do not produce food. At present, though, there are more than two food-producing families for each nonproducing family in most of Southern, Central, and East Africa. If the number of wage-supported families were to increase rapidly, trade would increase and the demand for marketed output would increase, but the prospects for this do not appear to be favorable. As has been pointed out, the very high rate of investment in Southern Rhodesia and, more recently, the Federation of Rhodesia and Nyasaland has resulted in only limited increases in the numbers of those who work for wages. Unless there is forced draft investment of the kind found in the Soviet Union it is unlikely that the industrial labor force will expand rapidly.[7] Furthermore, even if the wage-earning labor force were to increase, the number of non-food-producing families would not necessarily expand. If the migratory labor system continued to operate, most African families would not be fully committed to the wage economy and would continue to satisfy their own needs for foodstuffs.

The demand for foodstuffs will not increase as rapidly as the nonfarm population, because the income elasticity of foods is less than unity. Budget studies in Southern Rhodesia and elsewhere indicate that the income elasticity of food is high. These studies also indicate that as incomes rise the pattern of food-consumption changes and bulkier low-cost products, such as those typically produced by Africans, tend to be replaced or supplemented by higher-cost foods.[8] Thus an increase in the average incomes of those in the wage sector will increase total demand for foods but part of that demand will be for "high quality" products. Some of these, such as wheat products, may not be produced locally. This may lead to an increasing propensity to import and reduce the demand for domestic products. It is unlikely, though, that this will be a major factor in determining over-all demand for locally produced foodstuffs.

It might be possible to expand the size of the market for local products by substituting domestic output for imports. There are opportunities for this; for example, sugar might be produced in Southern Rhodesia, wheat in Northern Rhodesia, milk in Uganda. Processed imports might be replaced by establishing local processing industries. The effects of such import substitutions are likely to be limited, however, for agricultural imports represent less than two or three percent of annual food requirements in most of the region.[9] Furthermore, local processing would lead to increased demand for domestic products only if the prices of the processed goods were sufficiently low (or if there was a high level of protection against imports).

In general, the prospects for a rapid increase in internal demand for foodstuffs are not favorable. The large number of subsistence producers, the small size of the wage-earning labor force, and low level of average incomes all point to a small internal market. There is little reason to expect a rapid change in this situation. Nor is there any reason to expect a major increase in the internal demand for locally produced fibers or other products used by industry. The manufacture of fibers, beverages, and some other products might possibly be expanded, but opportunities to establish textile industries or cigarette factories are limited by the small size of the internal market.

The growth of the market for foods and fibers will depend on the rate of nonagricultural development, which is itself limited by the small size of the internal market and the low productivity of African agriculture. Within the existing circumstances in Central and East Africa, there do not appear to be any short-run prospects for rapid industrialization and a sharp increase in the nonagricultural labor force. At the same time, though, there are prospects for raising productivity in African agriculture. If productivity were raised, certain commodities such as corn could find internal outlets as animal fodder and internal demand might be increased to some extent through lowered prices. But, in the main, the increased output would have to be sold in export markets.

World trade in agricultural products has been expanding slowly since the early 1950's.[10] Policies of national self-sufficiency, the rapid increase in agricultural production in the industrialized countries, the expansion of synthetics, and the low-income elasticity and demand elasticity for most agricultural products all militate against any swift growth of world trade in agricultural products, and it appears unlikely that the aggregate demand for African export crops will rise any more rapidly. There are exceptions and the situation varies for individual crops but, in general, the export market is a slowly growing market.

If marketed output from African agriculture is to increase more rapidly than the slow rate of expansion of world trade, African producers will have to increase their share of this market. To do so, they will have to compete with producers in other parts of the world — producers of corn in the United States, of beef in the Argentine, of coffee in Brazil. Where new crops are introduced, such as Turkish tobacco in Southern Rhodesia or groundnuts in Uganda, Africans must compete with established producers on the basis of price and quality. To be successful, they will have to be low-cost, quality-conscious producers.

THE ADVANTAGES OF PEASANT AGRICULTURE

The need to compete in world markets raises the issue of the efficiency of African agriculture and whether peasant production has any advantages in comparison with other forms of production. It is difficult to make quantitative comparisons between different systems because of the lack of data on costs, but the juxtaposition of peasant production and large-scale farming in parts of sub-Saharan Africa provides some insights into their relative advantages and efficiency. Relative efficiency, as the term is used here, is a measure of ability to compete in world markets as well as of capacity to produce a return to factors of production. The linking of these two concepts is important, for they help to distinguish between the viability and the efficiency of peasant production, which have often been confused.

In some instances, peasant agriculture is more viable than large-scale or estate agriculture. This is usually the case when prices of commodities fall sharply and remain depressed. Generally, large-scale production units have relatively high fixed costs in equipment, buildings, and other facilities, as well as large variable costs, mostly for labor. In addition, of course, they are operated for profit. When prices fall sharply, returns may not cover variable costs, and so these costs have to be reduced or the unit will operate at a loss. Variable costs can be reduced by cutting back the size of the labor force and producing less, but this raises fixed costs per unit of production so that there may still be losses on each unit of output. Alternatively, attempts could be made to lower the average wage rate, but wages are usually "sticky" and difficult to force down, especially in politically volatile areas. As a consequence, when prices break sharply and remain low, profits fall to the point where large-scale producers may be forced to cease operation unless they have large liquid reserves. Operators would probably move to alternative employment. In the long run, given a degree of resource mobility and a rise in prices, these estates may move back into production.

Typically, African peasant producers do not have high fixed costs, nor do they have large variable costs in the form of cash outlays. Labor is usually supplied by family members who are sustained by domestic food production, and cash-crop production is marginal to food production. In addition, in many areas, family obligations are reciprocal and mutual and do not center around a cash nexus, so that labor continues to work on despite falling prices and falling returns to labor. Given the limited number of alternative opportunities for employment in most of these areas along with the relative immobility of resources — other than migratory labor — most peasant producers have little option but to continue production. They accept reduced returns to their own labor and management, cutting factor prices to an average unit cost below average unit prices. They continue to produce some crops at well below the break-even point for large-scale units and even, should prices fall further, to a point where imputed returns to labor may be negative. Thus peasant producers are viable when prices fall sharply and remain low.

Experience in Uganda reinforces this view of the relative via- bility of peasant and estate production.[11] In the early 1920's large estates were established in that country to produce tropical prod- ucts. A sharp and sustained break in commodity prices later forced many estate producers out of business, but did not have the same effect on the peasant production of certain tropical com- modities, notably coffee. Peasant producers expanded coffee pro- duction. More recently, since the persistent decline in coffee prices, estate production — which is still minor, being about six percent of total production — has been falling off steadily. Peasant production, on the other hand, has been expanding very rapidly.[12] Thus, because of the nature of the total production unit and the relation between variable and fixed costs, peasant production of coffee appears to have had greater viability than estate production when prices fall sharply.

The viability of peasant production is such that it is question- able whether countries where it is prevalent should join interna- tional cartels that attempt to maintain international prices of commodities, such as coffee, that are in chronic surplus. These cartels usually restrict supply by assigning quotas based on his- torical national shares in a market. In some instances these shares favor countries where most of the exported produce comes from estates. In the absence of cartel arrangements, if prices were to fall sharply, some estate producers would presumably have to halt operations. Where estate and peasant producers compete — as in coffee — this would enlarge the share of the market for the viable peasant producers. Whether or not this would increase total proceeds from coffee sales would depend on the prices received and quantities marketed under a free market and under cartel arrangements.

It may well be that the social product of the economy is enlarged by peasants remaining in production even if prices drop to a point where imputed returns to labor are negative. Lack of alternative employment opportunities would otherwise reduce their marginal productivity to zero, that is, if they were to move out of agriculture, underemployed labor would become wholly unemployed. Where land is relatively plentiful, however, this does not necessarily mean that resources in agriculture are being used efficiently in terms of increasing returns to factors of production. The success of the master farmers in Southern Rhodesia indicates that peasant producers can raise their total output considerably by improving resource management and by adding small increments of capital inputs. The marginal returns from these increments might well raise returns to the producer even though prices are low, that is, producers would operate at a point on the supply curve closer to where marginal costs equal marginal revenues. Peasant agriculture would then continue to be viable, but at the same time resources would be used much more efficiently than hitherto. Peasant producers would then be in a position to be both viable and competitive.

In a period of rising prices, the viable element in peasant agriculture works to its disadvantage in obtaining a larger share of the market. As prices rise for cash crops, they become more valuable in relation to food crops. Because of the traditional fear of famine and distrust of the marketing system, peasant producers are slow to reallocate resources and they continue to produce food for consumption. This limits the opportunities for expanded marketing of cash crops and increased returns to factors of production. Large-scale producers, on the other hand, are by definition profit-oriented, so they will increase production of those crops that maximize returns. Thus, the relative positions of traditional peasant production and estate production are reversed in a period of rising prices.

The present structure and organization of peasant production puts Africans at a disadvantage in expanding crop yields to take advantage of an expanding market. Where land is plentiful, large-scale farmers can expand production and gain advantages through increasing returns to scale. Tractors and mechanical harvesters can be used more intensively. African producers cannot readily expand through more intensive use of labor-saving capital equipment. Most of their production units are too small to reduce costs through the use of heavy equipment. In Uganda, for example, the average size of a cotton holding is six tenths of an acre; little is to be gained by mechanizing cultivation as long as plots are so small.[13] Furthermore, when peasant producers do pool their holdings to extend cultivated acreage by means of labor-saving equipment, problems of vertically integrating production place them at a disadvantage in competing with large-scale producers. Some phases of production, such as plowing, can be expanded rapidly through the use of tractors; others, such as harvesting, are generally more labor intensive. The benefits of extending acreage may be lost unless harvesting is mechanized or there is a large stand-by labor force to meet seasonal needs. In many areas both requirements are lacking. Even if the equipment was available, the technical demands for successful mechanization of harvesting are exacting — uniform spacing, uniform height of plants, and the like. These standards are too demanding for most peasant producers. As a result, they cannot expand their output rapidly when there are opportunities for gaining a larger share of the market. Modern techniques such as those used by large-scale producers cannot be superimposed on traditional systems of production; the entire production process has to be changed to gain the benefits of returns to scale.[14]

Peasant production does have some structural advantages over estate production, particularly where family labor can be used and there are no increasing returns to scale from "indivisible" inputs. The production and processing of Turkish tobacco falls in this category. The major input is family labor, all members of a family contributing their labor to different aspects of production. Labor requirements are such that a family can usually handle one or two acres; more acreage would require a stand-by force to meet seasonal labor peaks. There is no need for heavy investment in managerial training, as the required skills can be acquired relatively easily. Nor is there any advantage to be gained from mechanization, with increasing returns to scale from large-scale "lumpy" investment in machinery. Processing does not require large-scale investment; storage pits can be dug by hand and the tobacco is sun-dried on simple wooden racks. These facilities are "divisible" and can be expanded as required; there are no diminishing overhead costs from increased output but overhead unit costs are constant as production increases. As the market expands, peasant producers are in a position to grow more tobacco by increasing the number of small production units.

In contrast, Virginia flue-cured tobacco, as grown in Uganda and Southern Rhodesia, is better suited to large-scale production. Management is more complex and the necessary skills cannot be easily acquired. Managerial ability is scarce and expensive, and so has to be economized; it is "indivisible," in a manner of speaking, as production and processing are continuous. Management cannot be "spread" over many small operations; it has to be combined with a large-scale operation to retain increasing returns to scale. In addition, in Southern Rhodesia the production of Virginia tobacco depends on mechanization, which assures lower unit costs of overhead as output increases. The same applies to processing facilities, the fixed costs of barns and flues being high.

Because of the indivisibility of inputs and the need for large-scale integrated output, Virginia flue-cured tobacco is not suited for typical peasant production in many parts of Africa. Attempts to produce tobacco of this kind on small holdings have not resulted in a product that could compete in world markets. Low yields relative to high fixed-unit costs, and the poor quality of the leaf due to improper management have resulted in uneconomic production. Experience in East Africa supports this view.[15] Since 1950, a major tobacco company has encouraged production of Virginia tobacco to cater to the heavily protected internal market. The company has several operations in Uganda where selected producers grow tobacco on holdings that vary in size between one quarter acre and two acres. Barns for flue-curing are provided either individually or on a cooperative basis. The result has been a slow but steady increase in output, though yields per acre are still low. The company has provided many services, subsidized fertilizer and equipment, research, and extension workers in a very high ratio to producers. (There are fourteen extension workers for 4,000 growers in the West Nile Province and eighteen to cover 912 growers on 800 acres in Acholi.) Yet, to cover costs of production and leave a satisfactory profit for producers, prices paid to growers are more than one third above comparative world prices. If the government were to have provided these intensive services for so few growers, the overhead unit costs would have been far out of proportion with the returns to the economy as a whole. Furthermore, because of their high costs of production these producers would not have been able to compete effectively on a price and quality basis with large-scale Rhodesian producers.

In general, the poor quality of many peasant products restricts the size of market for peasant output and reduces returns to factors of production. If there is a large element of nonsubstitutability between different grades of a product — as, for example, with products consumed both by humans and by animals — then increased output of low-grade produce will merely force down the prices of that grade without competing with the higher grade. To expand the size of their market and to gain higher returns, peasant producers must improve the quality of their products. They might then be directly competitive with better quality production from large-scale units.

The point can be illustrated by corn production in Rhodesia. In 1957, 44 percent of the corn delivered by small-scale producers to the grain marketing board was classified as Grade A, while 56 percent was classified Grade B.[16] In the same year, however, 97 percent of the produce from large-scale farms was Grade A and only 3 percent was Grade B. Although the difference in price between the grades was only 1½ percent of the value of Grade A corn, peasant producers as a whole received 12 to 15 percent less than large-scale producers received for each 100 bags of corn that both groups delivered to the marketing board. Quality could be raised by using improved seed, better planting techniques, better timing, and better grading. These techniques, if adopted, would raise the value of peasant output, increase returns to factors of production, and improve the competitive position of peasant agriculture.

It is hard to assay the ability of African peasant producers to compete in local and world markets because of the many difficulties that arise in evaluating real costs, apparent costs, costs to individuals, and costs to the nation. Perhaps the situation best can be highlighted by a brief consideration of livestock production in African agriculture. In many areas African-produced livestock are supported by exploitation of natural range cover. Despite this apparently low cost of production, however, the real cost per unit of output may be extremely high. First, poor management and neglect result in a very high rate of calf mortality among African-raised livestock, as high as 25 percent in Uganda, for example.[17] In terms of potential output lost through neglect, real cost to the producer and the nation are high. Second, African producers retain livestock for long periods before marketing them. When the animals do reach the market, despite the long period on the range, their weight and quality are such that returns to producers per pound of meat are low. The rates of return on capital are low and the real interest rate on the use of that capital is high. To these costs must be added the social cost of resource depletion through overgrazing to the point where the natural range cover is completely destroyed.

The demand for lower-grade products may assure prices which, low though they may be, will cover the producers' cash outlay and leave an apparent profit, but because of the real costs involved, the returns to growers should not be confused with returns to society as a whole. There is a distinction between the individual costs of production and the social costs of poor management. If real costs, including the exploitation and abuse of natural resources, are taken into account, then, despite the apparent competitive position of African-produced meat, the net return to the nation as a whole may be very low.

It is impossible to predict whether peasant producers in Africa will succeed in expanding their share of the world market. The various agricultural commodities produced by Africans may or may not succeed in taking a larger share of world trade. Peasant production is well suited for some commodities but not for others. The extent to which peasant production becomes competitive will depend on many factors, including the elasticity of supply, the improvement of the quality of products, the nature of production functions for various crops, and the structure of demand. Tariffs, stabilization programs, and other aspects of trade policy will also affect the growth of the market. It is clear, however, that if peasant production is to be competitive and provide higher returns to growers, unit costs of production must be lowered and quality of output must be improved. This will require a much higher level of productivity than presently exists in African agriculture.

RAISING THE PRODUCTIVITY OF AFRICAN AGRICULTURE

Theoretically it is not possible simultaneously to maximize output per man and output per acre. In much of African agriculture, land is plentiful relative to labor, and so priority should be given to raising output per man. To do this, emphasis in policy should be placed on introducing labor-saving machinery and other means to expand the number of acres brought under cultivation. (Indeed this is what happened in Southern Rhodesia in the 1930's, when the use of the plow became widespread.) At present, however, total factor productivity in African agriculture is so low that there is considerable scope for increasing the productivity of both land and labor, and no great need to stress expansion of acreage.

The major prerequisite for raising productivity in African agriculture is to convert ordinary tribal producers into progressive farmers who use improved techniques of production. Producers must acquire the capacity to use all available resources to greater advantage and must be provided with supplies as and when they are needed. Experience in Southern Rhodesia amply demonstrates that there is little point in having high-cost land-improvement programs or heavy investment in infrastructure if producers do not know how to use expanded physical capacity. To continue investing in land improvement, while neglecting investment in improved farming techniques, is not only self-defeating but also represents a poor use of resources.

Several aspects of the problems of converting ordinary farmers into master farmers have already been discussed in the Southern Rhodesian context. It has been repeatedly stressed that on-farm managerial ability is one of the major factors differentiating progressive producers from others. The opportunity to improve managerial ability can be provided through programs of research, extension, and the provision of credit for supplies. Without these development services even the most enterprising of producers would be hard put to improve his managerial techniques.

One of the major needs to be filled by development services is that of providing and spreading knowledge — the scarcest of all factors in African agriculture. Knowledge — and especially the sort that is developed through applied research — is badly needed to provide a basis for improving management. In the past some very competent research work has been undertaken on the major export crops but little is known about a wide range of technical and economic subjects that influence levels of African agricultural productivity. One area in which research is most seriously needed is that of devising appropriate farming systems for stabilizing African agriculture. If shifting cultivation is to give way to stabilization of production, much more needs to be known about the effects of continuous cropping on the soil, the relation between fertilizers and tropical soils, and the most effective crop rotations for maintaining the soils.[18]

Much needs to be learned about many other topics, including the limiting factors in production. The labor supply offers one example. It is generally accepted that labor is underemployed in African agriculture, but without further research and investigation there is no way of knowing just why this is so. Perhaps labor is underemployed because of uneven distribution in the demand for it; seasonal requirements may exceed the total labor supply available at any one time. It is possible that cultivation has not been expanded in many areas because producers know there would be insufficient labor to harvest a larger crop. There has been almost no research on how labor inputs are allocated and what kinds of labor-saving devices are most effective in spreading the work load over the year. It is highly probable that a great deal of multipurpose female labor is tied down by tedious hand processing in postharvesting operations.[19] If this is indeed so, then the development of simple, small-scale equipment may free a great deal of labor for other activities. In the same vein, little is known about what types of farm equipment — mechanized or otherwise — are most economical in African agriculture.

There are many other areas in which fundamental as well as

applied research is needed. At present, however, the cost of fundamental research is expensive because it immobilizes scarce skilled workers; there is usually a long gestation period before the results of fundamental research can benefit the economy. The most economic type of research would be problem-solving or applied research based on fundamental research conducted elsewhere. It is partly for this reason that applied research is considered to be a desirable element in technical-assistance programs. Further economies can be derived from sharing research results among countries with common problems. At present this is done only on a very limited scale.[20]

Despite the pressing need for research, a considerable body of knowledge about African agriculture already exists. The development agency responsible for spreading this knowledge is the extension service. By and large, the principle of extension is a relatively new one in most countries in Southern, Central, and East Africa. In Southern Rhodesia the first agricultural technician who worked in the African areas was employed in 1924; in Uganda and Nyasaland to this day only the bare beginnings of extension services exist; in Tanganyika and most of the other countries of the general area the creation of extension services is a postwar phenomenon.[21]

The importance of extension education as a factor in increasing output has been amply demonstrated in Southern Rhodesia. One illuminating, though selective, example in Bechuanaland is sufficiently startling to be cited in support of the point. There a recent survey team reported that the extension service was making a successful though limited contribution to the increase in agricultural efficiency. The survey team said that the results achieved before and after instruction by several representative pupil farmers were "more revealing than the fact that maize yields obtained are 10–15 times the African average." The team results reported by the mission are shown in Table 11.

There is no formula for determining the optimum number of extension workers required to promote development. Nor is there any precise knowledge of the relation between expanded extension services and increased output. This relation will vary under differing conditions, particularly with regard to receptivity toward new ideas. In African agriculture, where large numbers of illiterate

Table 11. *Results of extension instruction on four farms in Bechuanaland*

| Farm | Acreage | Gross value of output (in pounds) | |
		Before	After
1	60	45	409[a]
2	25	30	167
3	10[b]	22	85
4	140[c]	210	405

[a] Plus £60 from creaming operations.
[b] Later increased to 20 acres.
[c] With some hired labor.
Source: *The Economic Development of Basutoland, Bechuanaland, and Swaziland: Report of an Economic Survey Mission* (London: H.M.S.O., 1960), p. 166.

conservative producers work on small holdings, requirements may well be greater than in societies where producers are literate and operate on a large scale. In this kind of work the diseconomies of low levels of literacy are great. If all producers were receptive, it would be axiomatic that the larger the number of producers who are reached the better, and so the larger the extension service the better. But if all producers are not receptive and if in spreading the extension service the more receptive producers are neglected in favor of the less receptive, the average return per extension worker would be low. This has been taken into account in the proposed strategy for agricultural development outlined below.

The stress thus far in improving management has been on the acquisition and spread of knowledge about improved techniques of production. But once new information is made available to producers, they have to have supplies in order to apply this knowledge and modify their techniques of production. In many areas where the opportunities for expansion through direct labor inputs are diminishing, the need for these supplies is becoming urgent. In Southern Rhodesia, for example, most producers cannot save enough by reducing their minimal consumption expenditures to acquire the supplies that would enable them to raise productivity. The only way they can obtain production goods such as fertilizers, seeds, equipment, and spare parts is through credit or direct subsidies.

At present much of African agriculture is debt-free. In the view of those who have to cope with problems of severe indebtedness, as in India, this may be a blessing. The absence of usury and usurious interest rates is to be applauded. But it is fair to ask whether development can occur without an expansion of credit whereby low-income producers are able to expand their productive capacity by acquiring seed, fertilizer, implements, and other production goods. This may lead to rural indebtedness but need not lead to a perpetually indebted rural class.

The extent to which credit has been made available to most African producers is severely limited by the orthodox methods pursued in granting credit. Private lending agencies are concerned with profit and they consider most African producers, who have little collateral, to be bad risks. Producers cannot pledge their land, the principal source of mortgage credit in most Western countries, for they do not hold title to it, and their incomes are so low that private agencies are loath to take the risk of advancing credit. Any inclination to lend is further reduced by the fact that many Africans make no distinction between the use of credit for productive purposes and using it for consumption. Finally, even when private lenders are satisfied by collateral arrangements or income prospects, they are likely to discount loans very heavily because of the natural hazards of agricultural production.

In the absence of private lending — other than credit advanced against orders for export crops — the main burden of providing credit has fallen on public agencies. Generally, the creation of public lending agencies to provide Africans with credit is an innovation, and the level of loans that have been made is low. The first program of government lending to Africans in Southern Rhodesia was initiated only in 1958. In Uganda, the first public-lending program of any size was begun in 1954; in Tanganyika public lending commenced in 1947.[22] All these programs are limited in scope and are small in size. In 1959, the average amount of credit available to African producers through public lending agencies in Southern, Central, and East Africa was less than 7d. (or 10 cents) per head.[23] In Southern Rhodesia and Tanganyika in 1958, even though limited funds were available for lending purposes, so few producers qualified as good risks that less than half of the available loan funds could be committed.[24]

The difficulties that public lending agencies face are much the same as those of private lending agencies. Though their interest rates are generally lower, they are governed by many of the same regulations regarding security and risk. In view of the low incomes of producers and the need to induce changes in management techniques, a combination of direct subsidies and low-cost credit may be necessary to infuse capital into African agriculture. Subsidies are perhaps most effective in situations such as that pertaining to cotton production in Uganda, where the spraying of the cotton crop with pesticides could reduce losses to the point where output would rise threefold.[25] If subsidies were provided for sprays and pesticides, the expenditures could be recouped through collection of export duties so that there would be no net loss to the government. At the same time producers' incomes would be raised substantially. Subsidies could also be used to introduce new techniques until such time as farmers were familiar with them. Once the profitability of these techniques had been demonstrated, the subsidies could be reduced, or, if necessary, replaced by extensions of credit.

In other situations, depending on prevailing circumstances, credits or subsidies will have to be provided on a much more selective basis to those who can use them effectively, that is, to farmers who have demonstrated their farming ability. In some areas, the credits or subsidies could be made available in the form of supplies to ensure that the advances are not used for consumption. In any case, if productivity is to be increased, there must be more emphasis on development needs rather than on orthodox banking requirements. One sorely needed change is a relaxation of the rigid requirements for collateral so as to expand the number who can qualify for credit. Where land is not individually owned, livestock are frequently the principal assets held by Africans, but lending institutions have not considered livestock to be suitable collateral for loans. There may be good banking reasons for this, but if the lending system is to be expanded and adapted to African conditions, livestock should be accepted as collateral. Inevitably, the proportions of losses will be high, for many African producers are unfamiliar with the concept of credit, but such losses should be viewed as part of the cost of encouraging innovations. As such, they are not entirely without value to the economy.

Ideally, it would be desirable if credit could be made available to be used under close supervision. This would entail every producer having a "farm plan'" and a budget; credit would be provided to implement that plan. The producer would be assisted by extension agents and others, and his use of credit would be supervised to see that the funds were spent in accordance with the approved farm plan. Programs of this nature ensure that funds are used for the purposes for which they were provided and at the same time producers are assisted in solving their production problems. This type of program is extremely costly in use of trained manpower, however. In Brazil, for instance, where a supervised credit program has been introduced, it has been found that one agricultural expert is required for every thirty farmers cultivating an average of around ten acres. Obviously the manpower is not available for this type of skill-intensive operations in African agriculture.[26]

STRATEGY FOR DEVELOPMENT

The major difficulty in the short-run expansion of development services is not necessarily a shortage of funds. Many African governments, even if they did wish to expand these services, would be limited by the scarcity of trained manpower. Because of this, any long-term program for African agricultural development must provide for building up a cadre of trained persons. This may take many years. In the interim, governments will have to devise an appropriate strategy for using to maximum advantage the limited manpower available. This strategy should take into account the nature of peasant agriculture and the difficulties exemplified by the efforts in Southern Rhodesia of promoting across-the-board changes in techniques of production.

One plan that might be suggested involves a two-tier program. The first tier would provide services benefiting all producers. These services would be ones that do not encompass any fundamental changes in techniques of production. Rather, output would be increased — for example, through the use of high-yielding varieties of seeds — even though producers continued to use traditional methods of production. The use of improved seeds as mentioned in an earlier chapter would require very little in the way of education. Producers would simply replace low-yield seeds with new varieties. If the seeds were distributed effectively the result could well be a substantial increase in output, without any changes in the organization of production.

Other possible services of this type are somewhat analogous to the measures that have increased the rate of population growth in underdeveloped countries. In general, mortality rates have been reduced by exogenous, rather then endogenous, factors. Measures to control disease, such as the use of spraying to eradicate malaria, have frequently been applied without raising the levels of education or changing the habits of the people affected. Losses have been reduced by action beyond the immediate control of the population and requiring no more than minimal cooperation on their part. The same principle should be applied to agricultural output. Locust control by aerial spraying would cut losses and so raise productivity, as would other forms of pest control, including measures to combat livestock disease. If spraying is done by hand rather than by government agents, the cooperation of producers would be needed, but as in the case of introducing improved seed, this would involve little in the way of fundamental changes in methods of production. Such services, together with provision of items such as water supplies and storage facilities, would be available to all producers.

On the second tier of the development program, scarce trained manpower and supplies that can be used to improve individual management techniques would be made available to those who could maximize the use of these services. Only those producers who showed initiative and enterprise and were prepared to change their methods of production would be helped. If they demonstrated the potential to become master farmers, they would be provided with every facility for their managerial ability. The extension service would give them special attention and they would be aided through the waiving of orthodox credit requirements. Loans to these producers would be based on character and ability rather than on the availability of collateral. Such a program would involve a measure of discrimination in the allocation of services and resources between progressive farmers and others. This may be regrettable on the grounds of equity, but there is little alternative if scarce resources are to be used to the best advantage in peasant agriculture. In the long run, as trained personnel become available, these services can be extended to all producers.

The expansion of services, that must be part of any long-run development program, will require trained technical personnel at all levels. As an interim step it may be necessary to create new categories of technicians who have less formal training than is desirable but who can be used as extension agents until such time as persons with more training are available. Possibly the most acute shortage at the present time is in the number of agents who have studied at the university level. In 1961, for example, the University College of East Africa, the major agricultural training center for all of East Africa, had a capacity for graduating twenty-four agricultural students a year.[27] These graduates have to serve a population of close to 20 million, at least 90 percent of whom are engaged in agricultural production.

The urgency of the need to provide additional facilities for specific types of training is also illustrated by the scarcity of veterinarians in East Africa. The number of veterinary officers there is woefully short of requirements, averaging one officer for each 100,000 head of cattle. The comparable figures are one per 3,500 in the United Kingdom and one per 6,000 in the United States. The deficiency is all the more acute because losses through disease are high and because livestock indirectly offer great potential for the growth and diversification of agricultural output. As late as 1960 no course leading to a degree in veterinary medicine was available in any country in Southern, Central, or East Africa except in the Republic of South Africa, where the course was confined to Europeans. A veterinary college has now been established in East Africa.

Increased facilities will provide only part of the solution for expanding the number of trained persons engaged in agricultural work. An additional difficulty is that many Africans are reluctant to enter agriculture as a profession. Only 7 percent of those studying for higher degrees in Central and East Africa in 1960 were studying agricultural sciences.[28] The problem of inducing young men to enter agriculture is not confined to any one region. It is a common phenomenon that young men in many parts of the world prefer to follow nonagricultural careers. Disdain for rural life, low salaries, and the low prestige accorded the agricultural professions all contribute to this phenomenon. Yet there are few areas in the world where agriculture is so important — and where there is such a paucity of trained agricultural scientists — as in Africa.

The expansion of development services does not require large-scale capital expenditures. It is, rather, a matter of small-scale capital expenditures — for dipping facilities, training institutions, rural housing for technical personnel, and the like — and large current or recurrent expenditures, primarily for wages, salaries, allowances, and subsidies. These current expenditures are generally considered to be ordinary rather than developmental costs, and are regarded in the same light as expenditures for administrative services such as police protection or revenue collection. Partially because of this attitude, total recurrent agricultural expenditures are usually low in relation to the importance of the services provided and low in relation to the significance of agriculture as a whole. Agriculture provides one fifth of the gross domestic product in the Rhodesias and Nyasaland and is overwhelmingly important in East Africa, yet current expenditures for agriculture are less than 7.5 percent of total current expenditures in these countries. This contrasts unfavorably with the 12 percent of current expenditures devoted to agriculture in Ghana,[29] which has a gross domestic product smaller than that of the Federation of Rhodesia and Nyasaland but considerably larger than that of Kenya, Uganda, and Tanganyika. The level of these recurrent expenditures is also very low relative to the sums spent on general education.

Undoubtedly current expenditures on agriculture could be increased by cutting back other programs. But in developing economies, where there is strong pressure for expanding social services, it is very difficult for popularly elected governments to do this.

Throughout Africa there is great demand for increased educational opportunities. In Tanganyika and Uganda close to 18 percent of all expenditures are devoted to education.[30] A United Nations Conference on Education in sub-Saharan Africa in 1961 recommended a four-billion-dollar, five-year program to raise school enrollments from 40 percent to 50 percent in primary schools, from 3 percent to 9 percent in secondary schools, and to maintain 2 percent enrollment in higher education. It was estimated that foreign aid of 1.3 billion dollars would be needed to finance this program.[31]

If large funds are allocated for education, less will be available for other activities. In many countries the agricultural sector will have to provide the savings to finance educational programs. To accomplish this, agricultural productivity will have to be raised considerably above present levels. Expanding general education and literacy on the other hand will not necessarily raise agricultural productivity, though it is likely that productivity could be raised by heavier investments in educational activities that are directly linked to agriculture. At present, the general education offered in African schools does not pay much heed to agriculture, and expanding facilities without a change in curricula will probably not enlarge the productive capacity of Africans on the land. This view has been strongly expressed by one writer who holds that: "The African future (and western influence in Africa) depends absolutely on a peaceful yet speedy transformation of African agriculture; and a rural renascence is inconceivable without a revolution in rural education." [32]

One important element in such a revolution would be a recognition of the need to train farmers' sons as well as technicians. Many of those who leave school at any early age are the future generation of farmers. At present there is scant opportunity for young Africans to study agriculture before returning to their farms. Few investments could pay higher dividends. In Southern Rhodesia, for example, the one-year special training courses given on experimental farms are estimated to cost the government £15 a year per man.[33] The cost is low in part because the farmers subsidize their operations through the sale of their own products. At the end of the year, most of the trainees are qualified master farmers. As was pointed out in Chapter 6 the value added to annual output by the conversion of an ordinary farmer into a master farmer far exceeds £15.

FOREIGN AID

One possible way to expand development services without diminishing expenditures on other services is to utilize external aid. The role of foreign aid in promoting agricultural development is too vast a topic to be discussed exhaustively here, but certain aspects of foreign aid that are relevant to the problems of expanding development services can be brought out.

Foreign aid may take the form of either financial assistance — grants or loans — or technical assistance, or it may be a combination of both. Such programs can be multilateral or bilateral. Technical assistance usually makes the services of specialized personnel available to recipient countries. The experts may be advisors concerned with the formulation of development programs, or help in organizing research and training programs, or they can be active in field programs. Most technical-assistance personnel who work on agricultural development act in advisory capacities. There are exceptions, notably in certain types of research work, but generally few of them engage in field work.

Most of the technical-assistance programs that have been concerned with the improvement of agriculture have fallen short of expectations.[34] There are many reasons for this. One is that fluctuations in the aid budgets in the donor countries tend to prevent adequate forward planning. Another one is the difficulty in providing expert personnel who have the required experience and high qualifications. Most experts have short tours of duty, too short for them to be fully effective in a strange environment or to train counterparts who can carry on after the experts have left. Frequently they have no logistic support from the local governments and so they cannot use their expertise to best advantage.

There are exceptions to this rather critical commentary. One successful program of technical assistance is that undertaken jointly by the Rockefeller Foundation and the Mexican government. It could well serve as a model for a program to improve African agriculture. This is a low cost, skill-intensive, multipurpose program of applied research and training.[35] If its end results could be duplicated in African conditions, it would fulfill three important requirements for raising levels of agricultural productivity: the training of scientists and technicians, the production of new varieties of seed adapted to local conditions, and the lifting of the status of agricultural science as a profession.

The Mexican program was initiated in 1941. By mid-1961, between 500 and 600 young Mexicans had received an internship in applied research work and in scientific field work.[36] At least

90 of these trainees have received or are about to receive advanced university degrees in various branches of agricultural science, and 30 of these will be doctoral degrees. Mexico now has the largest cadre of qualified agricultural scientists in Latin America. The program has demonstrated the value of applied research in plant breeding and allied techniques of plant improvement. New varieties of wheat and corn have been developed and disseminated. Their use has been an important element in increasing the production of these two crops and in reducing the former reliance on wheat imports to meet internal demand.[37] In addition, the program has had a subtle but noticeable influence on attitudes toward careers in agricultural science. There is no shortage of applicants to join the training program and Mexico, unlike most African countries, therefore seems to be assured of a steady supply of trained agricultural scientists for the future.

The reasons for the success of the program lie in good measure in the manner in which it was conceived and in the methods used to carry it out. At the outset the goal of the research program was specific; it aimed at eliminating one important and strategic obstacle to the increase of the output of food crops in Mexico. In addition, local personnel were to be trained to replace the foreign experts as the Rockefeller Foundation "phased out" its operations.

The program, operated in close cooperation with the Mexican government, was planned as a long-term venture. This obviated many of the problems encountered in short-term technical-assistance programs. The experts employed by the Rockefeller Foundation were carefully selected on the basis of qualifications and language ability. Thereafter, they were given long-term contracts and were assured of receiving all the logistic support they needed. Whenever possible, a team approach was used to minimize delays due to the absence of one type of specialist. Soil scientists and entomologists have cooperated with biologists, nematologists, and agronomists in searching for solutions to various problems.

The scientists have had a double task of research and training. The methods used for training and the incentives for sustaining interest in agricultural science have been important in making the program a success. Young Mexicans started their training by working side by side in the field with the foreign experts. This procedure discouraged the notion that field work is not the province of the scientist. It also enabled the scientists to watch the progress of their trainees. The more promising were given opportunities to study abroad for degrees. This, in itself, has been a strong inducement for young men to participate in the program. On their return, trainees have continued with their research and field work with the prospects of further study abroad for higher degrees if they showed continued promise. The method of training has encouraged young Mexicans to sustain their interest in agricultural science, and the mixing of field work and academic study has helped change attitudes toward working in the field, a major problem in much of Africa.

Technical assistance of this sort is not a panacea. It would not provide an answer to all of the difficult problems involved in raising African agricultural productivity. Such a program has obvious merits, however. As executed in Mexico, its direct benefits appear to have far outweighed its cost.[38] The program is skill-intensive rather than capital-intensive, and leads to the discovery of new varieties of crops, an important requirement in the strategy of development for African agriculture. The importance of the training aspects is self-evident and the methods used to induce persons to remain in agricultural science and to change their attitude toward agriculture as a profession are clearly relevant to the situation in Africa.

As for financial assistance, the flow of foreign grants and loans to East Africa, the Federation of Rhodesia and Nyasaland and the protectorates in South Africa has not been large. The breakdown of foreign aid in recent years is given in Table 12.

The major international lending agencies concerned with promoting economic development have not been able to make many loans for African agricultural improvement. Up to the end of 1960, the International Bank for Reconstruction and Development had made loans of more than 500 million dollars to all countries south of Sahara, but only two small loans, totaling less than 12 million dollars, had been made for African agricultural development.[39] Major bilateral lending agencies, such as the Development Loan Fund and the Export-Import Bank in the United States, have not made any loans for this purpose.

The reason is not that these agencies do not wish to lend money for development. On the contrary, there is every indication that

Table 12. International economic aid to selected African regions in two recent periods[a]
(in millions of U.S. dollars)

	British East Africa[b]		Federation of Rhodesia and Nyasaland		Basutoland, Bechuanaland, and Swaziland	
	Five fiscal years 1954–1958	Two fiscal years 1958–1959	Five fiscal years 1954–1958	Two fiscal years 1958–1959	Five fiscal years 1954–1958	Two fiscal years 1958–1959
Bilateral						
Grants	83.3	32.9	15.8	4.2	9.4	7.5
Loans (net)	53.6	11.1	51.6	−12.1	12.9	1.6
Multilateral						
Grants	2.1	1.7	0.2	0.1	0.4	0.1
Loans (net)	15.6	—	38.9	18.8	—	—
Total	154.6	45.7	106.5	11.0	22.7	9.2
Average per year	31.0	22.9	21.3	5.5	4.5	4.6

[a] Notice that the two periods overlap. The data refer generally to fiscal years but there are some exceptions which are described in the sources as given below.
[b] Here defined as Kenya, Uganda, Tanganyika, Zanzibar, and Pemba.
Sources: For 1954–1958, United Nations *Statistical Yearbook, 1959*, pp. 421–422; for 1958–1959, United Nations *Statistical Yearbook, 1960*, pp. 432–433.

they would like to make loans to promote development but cannot find "bankable" projects, especially ones that require a loan to meet the foreign exchange component in the project. An important characteristic of a bankable project is that it should "pay for itself." At present, there are few opportunities for large-scale self-liquidating investment in capital works in African agriculture. In a situation where land is plentiful, little is to be gained by substituting capital for land. Nor is much to be gained by loans for large-scale mechanization. Some of the costliest failures in agricultural development — many projects in the Soviet Union and the ill-fated groundnut scheme in East Africa are examples — grew out of a blind faith in the efficacy of capital and machines as a means of raising agricultural productivity.[40] Though it may be socially desirable to ease the drudgery of labor, it is poor economic policy to use high-cost machines to clear land that will yield a low return because producers do not know how to use it.[41]

Expanded development service, not large-scale capital investments, are the prime need for raising agricultural productivity.

But requests for loans for these services do not fall in the category of bankable projects: instead, they are considered under the heading of budgetary support. Most lending agencies are reluctant to provide budget support, for this usually connotes underwriting of normal government expenditures. Such support is not considered to be in the same category as loans for multipurpose dams or public utilities. It does not add to the stock of capital in a country. Without expanded development services, however, productivity in African agriculture will never reach a point where the stock of capital in agriculture is used efficiently.

If foreign loans are to be effective in raising African agricultural productivity, a change in lending policies is required. The emphasis should be shifted to investing in development services. Long-term loans should be made at low interest rates. The lending agencies could devise appropriate procedures to ensure that these funds are used to best advantage. One method might be to station qualified advisors in the recipient countries. These advisors could fill a dual role. They could expand the expertise available in the country concerned and they could hold a watching brief on the use of the loan. Where a loan was not producing satisfactory results, it could be terminated at short notice. This would be feasible, for a loan for current expenditures is easier to terminate than a loan for capital works, since there is no problem of "writing off" whatever fixed investment has already been made.

Grants would be preferable to loans, since the returns on investments in development services might be slow in maturing. The major grant-making agency in the colonial territories of Southern, Central, and East Africa has been the Colonial Development and Welfare Fund of the United Kingdom. Close to one quarter of the grants made by this fund in all of Africa have been for agricultural services, particularly for expanding research and for the provision of water supplies. This is to be applauded, but unfortunately the size of the grants has been very modest.[42]

Hopefully, the new grant-making organizations will be in a position to increase the size and number of grants made for African agricultural development. Hopefully too, they will perceive the need for increased budget support as an essential factor in raising agricultural productivity. Grants for training, credit programs, research, extension, expanding cooperatives, and the provision of other services that fit into the strategy of development would yield far higher returns than capital grants. These grants would be most effective if they were combined with long-term programs of technical assistance, such as the one in Mexico. This can be done if the grant-making agencies have the imagination to see the potential of such an approach.

LAND TENURE

One of the important issues in African agriculture is whether institutional changes in the system of land tenure will raise productivity. There is little doubt that productivity can be increased, through investment in development services, within the existing framework of land holdings. Producers can raise their level of output without "owning" the land they use. As has been stressed in Chapter 5, however, the prevailing system of customary tenure presents obstacles to agricultural development. One major drawback is the absence of a land market. This is inhibiting the commercialization of African agriculture and cost-price rationalization in production, both of which are necessary conditions for rational land use. When land has a market value, it will no longer be a free good and there will be increased pressure to move away from production for subsistence to production for the market. In the long run, land will be used more productively. A further obstacle to growth is that, under most systems of customary tenure, interpersonal distribution of land is based on need rather than use. This penalizes enterprising producers. They cannot expand the size of their operations at will no matter how able they may be. In general, it is the enterprising producers who have provided the growth factor in African agriculture. Enterprise and innovation are scarce, and any strategy of development should support rather than hinder progressive producers.

Any attempt to change the present system of rights to land will disrupt traditional society and have effects that extend beyond the subsistence sector, for this sector is linked to the wage economy through the migratory labor system. Changes in customary tenure will destroy much of the elasticity in tribal society. When land becomes identified as the property of individuals, the traditional right of a migratory laborer to share in the land whenever he is in need will fall away. If he does not own a piece of land, the incidence of maintaining him and his family will be shifted from the subsistence sector to the wage sector. This will raise money outlays on social security and other social overhead in the wage sector and could contribute to raising average unit costs of labor.

Where land-reform programs include the consolidation of holdings, establishment of minimum-size holdings, and prohibition of fragmentation, as in Southern Rhodesia, then there will inevitably be an accelerated displacement of rural population, unless land is extremely plentiful. The displacement will be all the more rapid if it is not accompanied by ancillary programs to change land-extensive techniques of production to land-intensive techniques of yielding increased incomes. This displaced labor will swell the ranks of those seeking full-time employment in the wage sector, but the wage sector may not be expanded at a rate that can absorb this influx. Consequently, an abrupt breaking down of customary rights to land and the creation of minimum-sized "economic-holdings" will shift underemployed labor in subsistence agriculture to unemployed labor in the wage economy.

The wage sectors in most economies in Central and East Africa are not growing rapidly enough to provide full employment for all those seeking employment. Because there has been little investment in the subsistence sectors, wage employment in African agriculture has been slow to expand. In these circumstances, a disruptive and abrupt once-for-all reform program will only add to the ranks of the unemployed and will divert capital to their support. Consequently, as has been suggested in Chapter 5, a selective piecemeal approach to land reform may be the most economic means of balancing competing needs. If the land-reform program were to be confined to limited areas that are relatively advanced, progressive producers would be able to expand their holdings through the market mechanism. At the same time, there would be less displacement of rural labor and most producers would continue to have traditional rights to land. This, in turn, would soften the economic consequences of abruptly breaking down the migratory labor system.

The situation regarding the need for land reform varies from country to country, but in the long run the problem of land tenure and rights to land has to be faced by all of them. If enterprise is to be given an opportunity to express itself, there must be a break with traditional institutions that govern land rights. The distribution of land must be based on use rather than need. Market forces must be allowed to regulate returns to factors of production, including land. The creation of a land market to enable this to happen will disturb the arrangements whereby the tribal system provided security to all at a low level of equilibrium. But if producers want the schools and roads that are among the end products of economic development, they cannot continue to enjoy the luxury of this form of security. The choice should be theirs. If they wish to change the system there will be a great deal of stress and strain. It can be minimized by making the changes slowly but it cannot be avoided. The creation of insecurity is part of the price paid for fulfilling the revolution of rising expectations.

In the final analysis, then, the future of African agriculture depends on the peasant producer himself. In peasant agriculture the producer is the major decision-maker. Development services are necessary for raising productivity, but it is the producer who must take advantage of these services. In this respect the future of Africans on the land depends on the Africans themselves.

Appendices

Appendix A

Methods of African Agriculture, Land Use, and Food Crops in Southern Rhodesia

The two extracts quoted below describe African methods of cultivation, patterns of land use, and food crops. The first was published in 1924, the second in 1953. Both of them describe the practices of the more primitive producers in Southern Rhodesia. As is pointed out in Appendix B, the introduction of the plow brought significant changes in methods of production. The range of products consumed by Africans clearly indicates that official statistics of African output underestimate actual output quite considerably and that the diets of Africans may be much more nutritious than the official production figures would indicate.

EXTRACT I

From *Official Year Book of the Colony of Southern Rhodesia: Statistics and General Information,* no. 1, 1924, published by Authority of the Colonial Secretary (Salisbury: Art Printing and Publishing Works), pp. 66–67.

It cannot be said that the native of Mashonaland is a good agriculturist, his methods are wasteful and in a way ruinous to the future interests of the country. As a rule bush country is selected for gardens, generally in the granite formation where the soil is easy to dig and cultivate. The trees and shrubs are cut down, the stumps of the trees are left standing three to four feet high in the ground, and in the case of very large trees only the top branches are lopped off. The trunks and branches of the felled trees and brushwood and weeds are gathered in heaps around the stumps. The ground is ridged up in ridges about eighteen inches broad, the portion of ground underneath the ridge is not touched with the hoe, the soil from the furrows on either side being placed on top of the ridge. The larger trees are not usually lopped until the ground has been dug. Just before the first rains of the season the brushwood around the stumps is burned and dug into the ground. With the first rains a crop of millet and maize is sown, with pumpkins and gourds around the tree stumps. Ground nuts and beans usually have a garden to themselves, with a few mealies [maize] between the rows. On virgin soil a fairly good crop may be expected the first year, but after three years the land is exhausted, and the native cultivator looks for pastures new. No attempt is made to manure the ground, except with the wood ash and weeds which are dug in. It takes about ten to fifteen years for gardens which have been abandoned to recover and be again fit for cultivation. Rice and sweet potatoes are grown in the vleis, the potatoes being grown on raised beds and the rice in round pits specially dug to retain the water. Here again no manure is used and the gardens have a very short life.

The following cereals and plants are grown by the natives of Mashonaland for foods:—

"Rupoko," red millet (Eleusine coracana).—This is the principal food of the natives of the high veld, and is extensively used for beer making.

"Munga," grey millet (Pennisetum typhoideum).—This grain is mostly grown in the low veld and in parts where there is a poor rainfall.

Maize.—Grown everywhere; before European occupation of country was usually eaten green, roasted or boiled, very little being used in shape of meal.

"Maphundi," Kaffir corn (Sorghum vulgare).—Several kinds of this grain are grown, but not in any great quantity by natives of Mashonaland, the largest crops are seen in the low veld.

Rice.—Two kinds are grown, the red and the white; good crops are grown in the wetter parts of the country.

Beans.—Several varieties of beans are grown, the small spotted brown bean being the most common. Velvet beans are grown by the natives in the low country and used for food in years of scarcity of other foods.

Ground Nut.—This is extensively grown, and is used in the preparation of most of the savouries which the natives eat with their rupoko or munga porridge. They also obtain oil from the ground nut, which is used for cooking and to rub their bodies. The Bambara nut, a kind of ground bean, is grown in certain parts of the country.

Sweet potatoes, pumpkins and gourds, tomatoes (a very small variety), chillies, watermelon and several kinds of cucumbers, are cultivated almost everywhere.

Cassava or manioc is grown by the natives in the low veld, but is not often used as food unless there is a failure of the grain crop.

The sugar cane (Chishona, Ipgha or Magundi) is cultivated for its sweet juice, which is extracted by chewing the green stalk.

The above comprise most of the cereals and plants cultivated by the natives for food.

A great variety of wild fruits and plants are used by the natives as food, or to prepare savouries to be eaten with some of the cereals or drinks.

The following are a few of the fruits used:—Majanji or Mahobohobo (Uapaca kirkiana), eaten as a fruit, but sometimes used in the preparation of a sweet beer.

The fruit of the Mahasha tree, used to make beer.

The fruit of the Baobab tree (Mu-uyu). The seed kernels of this hardshelled fruit, which are covered with a flour-like substance, are put in water and made into a thick gruel.

The fruit of the wild fig, Mukuyu, eaten as fruit, or fermented and mixed with beer.

The Kaffir orange, Matamba, of which there are two kinds, eaten as fruit or made into a drink.

Several kinds of wild plums, Somo and Matondo, the kernels of which are broken open and used as food.

Wild spinach, which grows profusely in old kraals and gardens, is extensively used as a savoury.

The natives have great variety in animal foods. In addition to the flesh of the domestic ox, sheep, goat, pig and fowl, they have the different antelopes, hares, rock rabbits, cane rats, monkeys, baboons, birds of all kinds, six or seven different kinds of caterpillars, many different beetles, locusts and fish. There are, in fact, very few animals that walk, creep, crawl, swim or fly, that are not used by some of the tribes as food. The above list of cultivated grains and vegetables, wild fruits, domestic animals, and wild animals, gives a fairly good idea of the native dietary.

The principal food of the native is farinaceous, usually a thick porridge eaten with some savoury or relish, prepared from some vegetable or animal food. The grains ordinarily used are rupoko and munga, the grain is turned into flour by being ground on flat stones, a small smooth round stone being used to grind with. Rupoko requires no other preparation before grinding, except being winnowed and slightly heated over the fire in a broken pot. Munga is first stamped in a wooden mortar to remove the outer husk, it is then winnowed and ground on the stone. Porridge is also made from the flour of rice and Kaffir corn, but is not as plentiful as the two grains mentioned. Several kinds of beer are made. rupoko being the grain usually used, but in years of scarcity mealies, if available, are used, and if nothing else is obtainable a thick beer is made from mill ground mealie meal which is fermented with yeast made from some fruit juice or sugar. A thick unfermented gruel is made from the flour of the different grains mixed with malt of sprouted grain and is used to feed children and sick persons.

EXTRACT II

The opening paragraphs of an address by D. A. Robinson (Assistant Director, Department of Native Agriculture), "Land Use Planning in Native Reserves in Southern Rhodesia," as printed in *Rhodesia Agricultural Journal,* 50:327–333 (1953). The same piece was issued by the Government of Southern Rhodesia, Department of Agriculture, as Bulletin no. 1730 (1953). The material in small capitals was originally boldface type.

The primitive agriculture of the natives of Southern Rhodesia is based on shifting cultivation. There are variations of this practice in different parts of the Colony, but the following account of the procedure in the Chipinga district will illustrate the system.

SHIFTING CULTIVATION.

The father of a son who is about to marry will obtain permission from the Kraal Head for his son to use the land. While the ground is still workable in April or May, the trees on the selected field are lopped and the branches are piled round the bole. Trees bearing edible fruits, such as *Uapaca kirkiana* (*Muhobohobo*) and *Parinari mobola* (*Muchakata*) are left for food, and others, such as *Gardenia thunbergia* (*Mutara*), are left for ritual purposes. Only men may use the axe, but the women help to pile the wood around the trunk. The axe (DEMO) is hand made, short-handled and kept very sharp. Immediately after this operation the land is hoed by the women and the men help as it is hard, new ground. The soil is left rough.

Some months later, when the wood is thoroughly dry, the piles are burnt and again the land is left alone. After rains have fallen, the seed is sown in December or January and covered by a shallow hoeing, which also helps to mix the ashes with the soil, though no attempt is made to spread the ashes over the field.

A small portion of the land is planted to groundnuts (NZUNGU) and another to bambarra groundnuts (NYIMO) grown separately. On sand-veld soils more NYIMO is sown, while on more fertile soils the greater proportion will be groundnuts. On the larger part of the field a mixture of kaffir corn (MAPFUNDE), finger millet (RAPOKO), bulrush millet (MUNGA), cucurbits (MAPUDZI, MANANGA, MAGAKA, MANWIWA) and cowpeas (NYEMBA) is broadcast and hoed into the soil. Maize (CHIBAHWE) is also grown on the same land mixed with the other crops, but small holes are made with the hoe and several maize seeds planted in each hole. The woman then scuffles soil over the seed with her feet.

One weeding is done in the first season after virgin land is broken up. The work of planting, weeding, reaping, threshing and the making of a new land is carried out communally. The owner of the land invites help and has beer brewed for the working party (NIMBE). Men do help with all these agricultural operations, and most of the labour is done by the young men and women. The older men supervise the work and see that the younger men do a good day's work.

A new field might be about two acres in size. Each year a little more virgin land adjacent to this field is prepared and planted until, after four seasons, the whole area is about four acres. Then a portion of the first prepared land (usually some of that planted to mixed crops) is abandoned and a new piece added each year, so that land is cultivated for four years and then allowed to revert to grass and bush. The virgin land that is broken up each year is first planted to groundnuts, bambarra nuts and sweet potatoes, the latter being planted on ridges made with the hoe. In addition, a patch of vlei land (MTORO) is cultivated, if such land is available. On this wet land early maize and rice are planted. Raised beds are made to grow *Plectranthus floribundus* (TSENZA). The same patch is cultivated year after year and shifting tillage is not practised on this wet land.

After the first trouble-free year weeds begin to grow apace on the dry land and two or more weedings are carried out during the season. The first weeding is not done until the weeds appear to be smothering the crop. No manure is ever applied.

The cultivator does not recognise any definite period of time for his grass and bush fallow. He judges that the land may be used again when the grass is tall and the bush is high. The tall thatching grass which appears last in the succession is *Hyparrhenia* spp. He knows that on poor soil this will take longer than on good soil. Alternatively, the whole kraal moves to a new area after four or five years, this being the more usual custom.

Appendix B

Changes in Output and Productivity in African Agriculture in Southern Rhodesia, 1900–1958

In considering changes in over-all output in the African areas of Southern Rhodesia it is convenient to divide the period under review into two parts, slightly overlapping: 1900–1950 and 1948–1958. The 1900–1950 era was primarily one of expansion of acreage; during the 1948–1958 period intensification of production appears to have assumed some importance.

The information available for the later period is, of course, much more detailed than that for the earlier years. All data utilized in this appendix are derived from official government reports, and at the outset it must be made clear that most of the official estimates of output are based on speculative data contained in reports submitted by native commissioners. These reports are in the nature of informed guesses which are usually summations of the opinions of all the individuals in the district concerned who deal with the administration and development of African agriculture. The small size of holdings, the large amount of intercropping, smallness of staffs, shortage of funds, difficulty of access to some areas, and variations in weather conditions within a district all make precision of estimation extremely difficult. Frequently, too, the absence of a clear definition of what constitutes African output results in a great deal of confusion. Some reporters consider all output produced by Africans in their districts to be African output. Others so regard only the output produced in areas legally recognized as African areas. This excludes the produce of Africans squatting on Crown lands, European lands, and forest lands. Further confusion arises from the shifting of populations and boundaries under the various Land Apportionment Acts.

The estimates of the native commissioners are submitted to the Native Affairs Department and if they appear to be too far out of line with anticipated results they are modified. There is no basis for checking estimates, no over-all benchmarks derived from a census or sample survey, though the abortive agricultural sample surveys of 1947 and 1948 did provide some useful information. Additional data are available from the count of producers and acreage made under the resource inventory undertaken in 1953 prior to the execution of the Native Land Husbandry Act. The statutory marketing boards provide some information on the size of marketings of certain African crops, but the unknown amount of produce marketed outside the aegis of the boards makes marketing data useful only as a very general guide to the accuracy of over-all estimates of production.

In contrast to crops, information about numbers of the principal livestock—cattle—is reliable. The law requires that every animal be dipped, and the administrative procedures ensuring that the law is obeyed have resulted in a carefully kept record of cattle numbers.

With the exception of figures on livestock, existing data give only the most general directions of change and possible orders of magnitude of change. Any refined analysis of the official estimates, especially in the early years, would lend the results a spurious air of accuracy. In the following sections, therefore, only the broadest of changes are considered, particularly for the period from 1900 to 1950.

1900–1950

The major crops produced in this period were food grains: corn (maize), "rupoko" (red millet or *Eleusine coracana*), "munga" (grey millet or *Pennisetum typhoideum*), "maphundi" (kaffir corn or *Sorghum vulgare*), some rice, beans, and groundnuts. In addition small quantities of sweet potatoes, chillies, watermelons, and cucumbers were widely grown. By and large these are still the principal crops, though small amounts of cotton were introduced in the late 1940's.

Estimates of output during the early years are in terms of "bags of grain." To have a comparable series the production of all major crops must be converted to grain equivalents. Estimates of production over the period 1900–1950 appear in Table 13. In very general terms these figures

Table 13. *Average annual production in 200-pound bags of grain or the equivalent, African areas of Southern Rhodesia, 1900–1950*

Years	Thousand bags per year (five-year average)	Index (1900 = 100)	Years	Thousand bags per year (five-year average)	Index (1900 = 100)
1900–1905	193	115	1925–1930	286	170
1905–1910	248	147	1930–1935	269	160
1910–1915	207	123	1935–1940	316	188
1915–1920	248	147	1940–1945	353	210
1920–1925	272	162	1945–1950	410	244

indicate that the average output of "grain equivalents" increased by something like 140 to 150 percent in fifty years, or less than 3 percent per annum. From the incomplete data available it appears that the principal constituents in the increase were corn (maize) and small grains. Corn accounted for about half of the total output throughout the period.

The estimated acreage cultivated in order to produce these amounts increased by about 260 to 270 percent, as shown in Table 14. Cultivated acreage rose at a much more rapid rate than output. Consequently the increases in output must have come from expanded acreage, while yields per acre declined.

Table 14. Land cultivated in African areas of Southern Rhodesia, 1900–1950

Years	Thousand acres (five-year average)	Index (1900 = 100)	Years	Thousand acres (five-year average)	Index (1900 = 100)
1900–1905	592	93	1925–1930	1,303	205
1905–1910	754	119	1930–1935	1,529	241
1910–1915	919	144	1935–1940	1,592	251
1915–1920	1,185	186	1940–1945	1,899	299
1920–1925	1,171	184	1945–1950	2,326	366

It is extremely difficult to gauge whether output per family increased or decreased. Some of the problems of defining changes in labor inputs have been considered in the text of this book. Estimating changes in the labor supply is complicated by the methods of registering population and the fact that although entire families contribute toward output, many African males are away from their areas for part or all of a year. Some of them return for short periods to help with plowing; others return to "rest" and may or may not engage in farming activities. There is no measure of the extent to which those who return participate in production. At the turn of the century, it was estimated that 12 percent of the able-bodied males were away from the reserves for an average of three months at a time. By 1954 the estimate of absent males, presumably gone for a greater part of a year, reached 45 percent of the male population of the reserves. Between 1948 and 1954 the proportion of males away had stabilized somewhat, having increased only slightly from 45 percent to 45.7 percent. (In 1960, an estimated 47 percent of all males were absent.)

Utilizing the available data and adjusting the figures on the basis of the demographic sample survey of 1954, one can say that the *de facto* farm population of African areas rose from 514,000 in 1901 to 1,224,000 in 1950—an increase of something like 140 percent at a time when output rose by 140 to 150 percent and cultivated acreage was extended by 260 to 270 percent. The broad picture that emerges from these estimates is as follows:

(a) Population increased more rapidly than did the expansion of the African areas, even though the African areas were expanded considerably in this period. Available acreage per head declined from around 40 acres to 15 acres.

(b) Output per acre declined. A 260–270 percent increase in cultivated acreage was required to produce a 140–150 percent increase in output.

(c) Acreage cultivated per family rose considerably, with a population 140 percent greater cultivating 260–270 percent more acreage.

(d) Output per family did not increase much, for a 140 percent increase in rural population was accompanied by only a 140–150 percent increase in output.

Thus labor productivity did not increase in terms of output per rural family, even though families cultivated larger acreages. That is, productivity increased in terms of acreage cultivated but not in terms of output.

These phenomena can be explained, in good part, by the technological revolution that followed the introduction of the animal-drawn plow. The plow, one of the very few items of capital introduced into the African areas during these years, was a labor-saving device. It removed some of the restrictions on acreage expansion imposed by the sheer limits of physical endurance; in technical terms it changed the entire production function in African agriculture. In 1900 it was estimated that there was one plow per 200 families; by 1920 there was a plow to every 10 families, and the proportion of families with plows has increased since then.

Draft power replaced hand power and in many areas the burden of the drudgery of cultivation was shifted from women to oxen. Commenting on this, the Morris Carter Commission of 1925 reported that although a larger quantity of land was cultivated by the aid of the plow the yield per acre was often less than it was in the old days when women cultivated the land with the hoe, with a determination and energy which they were no longer inclined to display. Yields probably declined further as the fringes of production extended into less fertile areas.

At the beginning of the century several severe rinderpest epidemics heavily reduced the cattle population. Thereafter, as is shown in Table 15, cattle increased relatively rapidly. Starting at about 55,000 head in 1900, their numbers increased to a million by 1925 and have run between 1.75 and 2 million since 1940.

Table 15. Cattle in African areas of Southern Rhodesia, 1900–1950

Years	Thousand head (five-year average)	Index (1900 = 100)	Years	Thousand head (five-year average)	Index (1900 = 100)
1900–1905	74	134	1925–1930	1,408	2560
1905–1910	198	361	1930–1935	1,698	3088
1910–1915	380	691	1935–1940	1,578	2869
1915–1920	609	1108	1940–1945	1,836	3339
1920–1925	949	1725	1945–1950	1,792	3259

In 1900, with cattle in the ratio of about one animal to ten acres of arable land, the contribution to total agricultural output from this source was very small, probably below 3 percent. In recent years, the value of cattle production has represented about one sixth of the estimated total value of African agricultural output, the ratio of cattle to arable land being about three quarters of one animal unit per arable acre.

Programs to combat livestock diseases reduced mortality rates among cattle. Expansion in cattle population also came at the expense of increasing exploitation of the land by communal grazing, sometimes amounting to misuse. Increased numbers have little relation to labor input, for the labor used in African cattle production is inconsequential. In assessing the increase in productivity of African labor, there is little point in relating increases in cattle numbers to increases in the labor force. Changes in crop production provide a more meaningful measure of labor productivity.

During the period 1900 to 1950, there was little change in the techniques of livestock production and little increase in productivity per animal. The main reason for any lack of progress was, and still is, the family herd system and all that this entails. Many owners regard cattle as a store of value and as a prestige factor rather than as a source of income. Numbers are more important than quality. Herd composition is very poor, with a high proportion of nondescript cattle. There is little supplemental feeding, and during the winter months when the capacity of the range is limited, thousands of animals die from starvation or lack of water. The livestock that do survive are severely stunted and slow to mature.

The poor techniques of animal husbandry go hand in hand with poor range management. Communal occupation of grazing areas remains a barrier to progress, for individual users are slow to recognize any responsibility for the conservation and improvement of lands communally occupied. At the same time, there is no sense of community responsibility for the maintenance of grazing lands.

The broad picture of African farming in Southern Rhodesia during the first half of this century is that of an industry at a very low level of efficiency. During these years African agriculture gained a toe-hold in the market economy, largely through increasing exploitation of the available natural resources. Next to the plow, the most important factor contributing to the modest degree of agricultural advancement was undoubtedly the ox. The use of oxen as draft animals enabled more acreage to be cultivated. In addition, as livestock numbers increased, grazing was extended to take in rough veld and scrub. In this way areas that could not be used otherwise made a contribution to the rural economy.

This was the era of land-use extension and of declining yields. Not only did families take on more arable land and push the growing herds into new grazing lands, but the increasing population also spread out to fill unoccupied areas. A good deal of the limited government effort was absorbed in assisting the process of extending usable acreage through provision of water supplies and other basic facilities. Toward the end of the period the growing pressure of population on the apportioned land began to require intensification of land use. African herds reached the maximum that the unimproved veld could carry, and overstocking became a serious problem. The primitive system of shifting cultivation had required a plentiful supply of land to carry a relatively small rural population. Now more and more rural Africans were seeking part-time work in the towns and in industry. The stage was reached at which it was necessary to set up the framework for more intensive land use.

1948–1958

It was during the period from 1948 to 1958 that the first serious effort was made to introduce purely cash crops such as cotton and Turkish tobacco.

Cotton production rose from 5,000 lbs. in 1947 to 4,000,000 lbs. in 1950, then declined to 4,400 lbs. in 1957 and rose again slightly in 1958. The severe drop was due to the afflictions of insect pests, not an unusual occurrence in areas where cotton is newly introduced. There are many examples of countries where production has risen rapidly for several years and then suddenly declined because of destruction by insects. Usually the early increases in output appear to deny the latent presence of pests, and this leads to neglect of investigation and failure to adopt preventive measures. Doubtless in time a solution will be found to local problems; in the interim, however, production has declined and will lag until new techniques of pest control have been introduced.

Turkish tobacco is an ideal peasant crop. Unlike Virginia flue-cured tobacco, it requires little capital outlay, for it can be sun-dried on wooden racks and cured in underground earth pits. It is a labor-intensive crop and requires limited acreage. In many parts of the country physical conditions are suited to its production, and in some areas income from half an acre of tobacco has far exceeded total income from ten acres of all other crops combined. The government started introducing the crop with a cautious subsidized program in 1952. By 1958 the program had reached only 2,000 growers on less than 1,000 acres of land. Output increased steadily from 1953 to 1957, declined sharply in 1958, but rose again in 1959 and 1960, increasing to 108,000 and 274,000 lbs. respectively. As a larger trained staff becomes available, output of this crop will undoubtedly continue to rise. The opportunities for increasing its production provide one avenue of development that can yield considerable benefits to the African economy, for world demand for Turkish tobacco is strong and is likely to remain so.

Table 16 indicates the trends in the major crops between 1948 and 1958. Production of groundnuts appears to have expanded at a more rapid rate than that of most other crops. This is clearly shown in Table 17, which summarizes annual changes in total output of staple crops, changes in groundnut production, and changes in acreage.

Table 16. Estimated crop production in African areas of Southern Rhodesia, 1948–1958 (in thousands of bags, except for cotton and tobacco)

| Harvest year | Corn[a] (maize) | Products controlled by Grain Marketing Board | | | | | | Wheat[a] | Cotton (thousand lbs.) | Turkish tobacco (thousand lbs.) |
		Munga	Kaffir corn	Rupoko	Beans	Groundnuts	Rice			
1948	1,671.1	682.1	889.0	679.8	242.0	420.5	25.6	11.2	212.6	—
1949	1,487.5	514.6	679.2	617.1	136.9	189.7	16.7	6.4	1,410.6	—
1950	1,835.3	579.2	467.9	574.2	122.5	181.2	9.0	5.6	4,182.2	—
1951	1,278.1	340.5	361.3	415.5	77.2	241.2	1.8	5.5	3,105.5	—
1952	1,973.0	603.9	604.0	677.0	172.0	342.0	13.0	10.0	3,614.0	—
1953	2,787.0	772.5	668.2	849.2	201.4	417.5	26.2	12.5	1,156.1	4.5
1954	3,129.2	821.5	540.2	694.4	156.5	568.8	12.3	18.4	982.5	14.1
1955	2,797.3	675.4	515.0	647.6	137.5	690.7	26.2	18.2	97.2	26.4
1956	3,926.2	978.8	611.6	891.8	148.3	1,028.6	20.3	38.2	25.3	50.0
1957	3,363.4	944.8	505.6	897.3	142.7	1,045.6	23.7	19.2	4.4	78.0
1958	2,847.0	887.2	482.3	917.4	120.8	758.0	23.9	15.0	61.0	47.6

[a] The figures for corn (first column) and wheat are aggregated district estimates.

Marketings of groundnuts rose between 1955 and 1957, prices to growers rising slightly, but the proportion of retentions (the difference between output and sales) rose at a much more rapid rate than did sales.
No reason for these large retentions is apparent, even allowing for a
natural disposition to store stocks. Possibly some groundnuts were
smuggled into neighboring countries where prices were much higher than
in Southern Rhodesia, and some might have been sold on the "black
market," for the structure of deductions made the illegal sale of groundnuts an attractive proposition.

Table 17. Output of all staple crops and groundnuts, and cultivated acreage,
African areas of Southern Rhodesia, 1948–1958

Year	All staple crops (thousand bags)	Index (1948 = 100) All staple crops	Groundnuts	Cultivated land (thousand acres)	Index (1948 = 100)
1948	4,576	100	100	2,621	100
1949	3,627	79	45	2,738	104
1950	3,755	82	43	2,715	103
1951	2,695	58	57	2,815	107
1952	4,358	95	81	2,628	100
1953	5,690	124	99	2,859	109
1954	5,879	128	135	3,129	119
1955	5,434	118	164	3,316	126
1956	7,531	164	244	3,568	136
1957	6,832	149	248	3,210	122
1958	5,972	130	180	3,291	125

The wide swings in production of staple crops, and the substantial
difference in levels of production before and after 1953, can be explained
largely by the influence of weather conditions. This can be demonstrated
by constructing an "index of weather influence" based on the yields of
"ordinary native farmers." These are the farmers who produce in the
traditional ways without the benefits of improved techniques, so that, to
all intents and purposes, their yields are influenced by the weather alone.
The average yields of "ordinary native farmers" and the corresponding
index, which we may call an index of weather influence, appear in Table
18.

There is some disparity between this index of weather influence and
the index of output as shown in Table 17, notably in 1954 and 1957, but
in general, the level of the weather index is much higher beginning in
1953 than in the pre-1953 period, and so is the total output. The weather
alone can be held accountable for raising the yield per acre of all native
farmers by around 15 percent in the years following 1953.

Increases in total output are a function of increased acreage and in-

Table 18. Average yields per acre of "ordinary native farmers"
in Southern Rhodesia, 1948–1958

Year	Average yield (bags of grain)	Index (1948 = 100)	Year	Average yield (bags of grain)	Index (1948 = 100)
1948	2.00	100	1954	1.93	97
1949	1.98	100	1955	2.18	109
1950	1.54	77	1956	2.50	125
1951	1.23	61	1957	1.86	93
1952	2.04	101	1958	2.25	112
1953	2.53	126			

creased yields. During the entire period 1948–1958, acreage rose by about 25 percent (see Table 17). The official estimate of cultivated acreage was scaled down in 1957 to match the inventory conducted in compliance with the Native Land Husbandry Act. After due allowance is made for this, it appears that there was a steady increase in cultivated acreage of less than 2.5 percent per annum. There was a 12.5 percent increase in acreage cultivated under improved weather conditions in the post-1953 period.

If yields had been unchanged, 12.5 percent of the increase in total output since 1953 could be explained by expanded acreage. Because of the weather, however, yields rose by something like 15 percent. Yet the combined effects of better weather and larger acreage do not account for the total increases in this period. Even when allowance is made for errors in the data there remains an unexplained residual in the increased yields in these years.

The explanation appears to lie in the greater productivity of some producers during the good-weather years. It is difficult to estimate average changes in labor productivity, not only because of the problems of measurement outlined earlier, but also because of the shifts in population during the 1948–1958 decade that took place in connection with the implementation of the Land Apportionment Act. Nonetheless, after taking these shifts into account, along with outmigration from the African areas, it appears that population expanded at about the same rate as cultivated acreage, but at a lesser rate than output. More producers were using land more intensively to obtain a greater output.

The increases in output of "ordinary native farmers" have already been discounted in explaining the rise in production during the post-1953 period, their increases being attributable to improved weather conditions. Thus, the additional increases in yields and in labor productivity in the good-weather years must have come from those who are not "ordinary native farmers." These other producers are the cooperators, plot holders, and master farmers. They constitute about one third of the producers. Their absolute numbers have been increasing, and so have their relative numbers, though more slowly: that is, the number of farmers who use improved methods of production is not increasing at a rate much in excess of the increase in farm population. In 1958, 65 percent of the African farmers were classified as "ordinary native farmers," who practice primitive methods of cropping, broadcasting all crops, mixing crops on the same land, and using no manure. Their production techniques are much the same as those described in Appendix A.

The numbers of cattle increased from 1.7 million to 2.07 million between 1948 and 1958. The annual increase in cattle population fluctuated from 18.8 percent in 1949, to 13 percent in 1951 (a drought year), rising to 15.8 percent in 1955 and 18.7 percent in 1958. De-stocking campaigns and the new system of marketing raised sales. Between 1948 and 1958, while African livestock increased by 21 percent in number, sales increased by 39 percent. Even so, the rate of "take-off" is very low relative to European agriculture. The rate of return on capital is extremely low, being less than 6 percent when it could well be more than double that if efficient production methods were used. Furthermore, as far as can be estimated, more than 90 percent of the increased agricultural output in the post-1953 period came from increased crop production and only 9 percent from cattle. This certainly points to one of the weakest sectors in African agriculture, one where there is an urgent need to raise productivity.

Almost all the progress in raising productivity has come from one third of the land-users. As was shown earlier in this book, the output of these producers is far ahead of the mass of the producers; so much so, that the inertia of the great majority of the producers tends to mask the progress that has been made. The differentials in productivity lend support to the belief that there can be considerable progress in African agriculture if more "ordinary native farmers" can be converted into "master farmers."

The level of real incomes of the upper 30 percent of African producers appears to be higher than that of the lowest-paid urban workers. In 1958 average gross (imputed) income per family in African agriculture was around £85; the average income of the upper 30 percent must have been considerably higher than this. (Two acres of Turkish tobacco produce £80.) During 1958 the lowest wage paid to unskilled commercial employees was £78 per year, although the minimum wage was raised to £97 per year for certain categories of employees in 1959/60. No direct comparisons of real incomes can be made because of lack of data on "fringe benefits" provided by employers to urban employees, which frequently include free housing and "rations" or an allowance for rations. Nor is data available on changes in the "terms of trade'" between the African areas and the urban areas on which to base estimates of the changes in real incomes of African farmers.

It does appear, though, that the over-all rate of increase in real incomes has been greater for the lower-paid African workers than for African agricultural producers. The minimum wage for African males rose from 60s. a month in 1948 to 130s. a month in January 1958, a 116 percent increase. The cost of living index for Africans in this category rose by 39 percent during the same period, so the over-all gain of real wages was 67 percent, or more than 6 percent a year.

There is no measure of the changes in real incomes earned off the land between 1948 and 1958. From data on changes in corn production and corn prices, however, it is possible to derive a figure for total corn income. Since corn (maize) is the major product consumed and marketed by Africans, corn income provides a partial indication of annual changes in gross income. The index of changes in corn income for 1948–1958 appears in Table 19. Sharp changes occur in the index between 1951 and 1952 and between 1955 and 1956. In general, however, corn income did not rise as rapidly as wage earnings, and wage earnings in 1958 were higher than those of most agricultural producers.

Table 19. *Index of corn incomes based on price and total production, Southern Rhodesia, 1948–1958*

Year	Index (1948 = 100)	Year	Index (1948 = 100)
1948	100	1953	178
1949	82	1954	171
1950	132	1955	156
1951	81	1956	221
1952	152	1957	193
		1958	159

Note: Production data are given in Table 16. For price data, see Table 20 in Appendix C.

No data are available for reducing gross corn income to net income nor for converting the net income into "real income." Many of the items that go into the cost of living index of African wage earners, however, are also purchased by rural producers—clothes, tea, sugar, and so on. There is no basis for assuming that real incomes in the African areas rose at a faster rate than gross income in those areas. Consequently, if the index of corn income is representative of the rate of change of gross income, then rural incomes increased at a slower rate than wages. Furthermore, since there is a large common component in the cost of living of lowest-paid African workers and rural people, real incomes in the rural areas also probably increased at a slower rate than real incomes in the urban areas.

The trend in wages has been consistently upward and is likely to continue in upward jumps based on statutory action. Rural incomes cannot be raised by this type of action. If rural incomes are to rise more rapidly, there will have to be a rise in total factor productivity. Important elements in raising productivity will be the conversion of more and more "ordinary native farmers" into "master farmers" and the introduction of more highly valued crops. If each farm family grew one acre of Turkish tobacco, other things being equal, average family incomes would rise by close to 40 percent in one year. This would certainly raise average farm incomes above urban wage levels.

A Comment on the Unreliability of Measures of Elasticity of Production and Supply with Regard to Price for Corn and Groundnuts in Southern Rhodesia

Table 20 indicates official estimates of native production, sales, and prices for corn (maize) and groundnuts for the years 1948–1958. I had hoped to use these figures to demonstrate (a) that production is relatively insensitive to price, that is, farmers do not grow these crops with an eye to maximizing profits on the basis of either current prices or those in the preceding sales period; and (b) that sales, on the other hand, are sensitive to price movements. These two conclusions, if supported by the evidence, would lend credence to the observation that there appears to be a discontinuous or kinked supply curve for corn and groundnuts, or alternatively, a sales curve that is not necessarily the same as a total supply curve.

The relation between marketings and price of corn in the current years is indicated by an equation: Sales $= -927 \pm 4.6$ (price) with a correlation (or coefficient of determination) between price and sales of 0.23. This shows that there is an association, but not a very strong one, between sales and price. As price rises, sales increase. As price increases by one unit, marketings increase by 4.6 units. Sales will be -927 units if the price is zero.

Similarly, the simple relation between production and price can be expressed in an equation: Production in period $t = 398 + 8.86$ (price in period $t\text{-}1$) with a correlation of 0.12 between production in one period and the price in the preceding period. This equation indicates that the association between production in one period and price in the preceding period is even weaker than that between current sales and current price. It also indicates, however, that price in the preceding period has a stronger influence on production than does current price on sales. For every unit of price increase in the preceding period, production rises by 8.86 units.

Sales are related to current prices and current production in accordance with the following equation: Sales $= -1428 + 2.98$ production $+ 1423$ price. This indicates that the net response of sales to price change is less than the production response to price changes. Thus, it might be inferred:

Table 20. Native production, sales, and price of corn (maize) and groundnuts in Southern Rhodesia, 1948–1958[a]

	Corn			Groundnuts		
Year	Production (thousands of bags)	Sales (thousands of bags)	Price[b] (pence)	Production[c] (thousands of bags)	Sales (thousands of bags)	Price[d] (pence)
1948	1,671	82	252	378	112	n.a.
1949	1,487	121	264	170	47	n.a.
1950	1,835	124	333	163	57	774
1951	1,278	203	357	217	40	792
1952	1,973	688	408	307	79	759
1953	2,787	898	363	375	143	633
1954	3,129	875	339	511	139	629
1955	2,797	706	335	621	178	660
1956	3,926	1,385	342	925	256	660
1957	3,363	933	324	941	194	665
1958	2,847	533	306	682	69	713

n.a. = not available.

[a] There is some overlap in prices based on a fiscal year and output based on a calendar year, but by introducing the price in the preceding season and relating it to current output some of this error s diminished.

[b] Price per bag received by growers—Grade B corn.

[c] These figures differ from those in Table 16 in Appendix B, as they are based on 200-lb.-bag equivalents rather than the 180-lb. bags used in Table 16.

[d] Price per bag unshelled nuts.

(a) that there is a "normal" supply curve for corn; (b) that production is more sensitive to price than are sales.

When the same analysis is applied to groundnuts, however, a totally different picture emerges. The equations for groundnuts indicate that there is a weak association between production and price in the preceding period and between sales and price in both the preceding and current seasons. In all instances, the relation is a negative one since as price increases, production and sales decrease. This can be summarized in the equation describing the relation among sales, current price, and production: Sales = 268 + 0.17 production − 0.33 price. In the case of groundnuts, therefore, the supply curve is more like a demand curve, or a backward-bending supply curve. In this, it differs sharply from the results for corn indicated by the earlier equations.

On the face of it, then, statistical analysis gives a contradictory picture of production responses to price changes for corn and groundnuts. But these results cannot be given too much credence. In the first place, any analysis depends on the reliability of the data. As has been pointed out in the preceding appendix, the data on production are not reliable. In addition, many sales go unrecorded.

The use of simple correlation analysis to determine elasticities of supply is based on a set of assumptions that are remote from reality.

There is no point in discussing these assumptions in detail here, but in general, they postulate an unchanged set of conditions governing the relation between price and other factors during the ten-year period. Furthermore, what is being measured is not necessarily a supply curve. The average prices each year represent the intersection of supply and demand for that year. Supply has shifted markedly from year to year because of the weather, and at the same time demand may have changed because of changes in the prices of competing foodstuffs. Thus, the path traced by the annual intersection of supply and price is not necessarily a supply curve; it may well be a curve that reflects the intersection of annual shifts in supply and demand.

For these reasons the results must be held to be inconclusive. If acreage data and other information were available, a more elaborate set of relations could be introduced so as to take account of the variables that do influence supply. The present data are such that this would be pointless.

**Notes
Index**

NOTES

Chapter 1: Africans, Europeans, and the Land

1. For further information see *Land Reform: Defects in Agrarian Structure as Obstacles to Economic Development* (New York: United Nations Department of Economic Affairs, 1951) and the section on Africa in the 1958 report, *The State of Food and Agriculture* (Rome: Food and Agriculture Organization of the United Nations, 1958).

2. The figures for average per capita incomes are approximate and only indicate rough orders of magnitude. The South African figure is based on an estimate of the net national average income per person in 1959 and is taken from the estimate of geographical income in the South African Reserve Bank *Quarterly Bulletin of Statistics* (Pretoria), March 1960. The Central African figure is based on an estimate of the net national income per head as presented in the *Statistical Abstracts* compiled and issued by the Central Statistical Office in Salisbury. The figures for East Africa are based on per capita geographic incomes as derived from the *Statistical Abstracts* of the East African Statistical Department of the East African High Commission in Nairobi. These estimates for East and Central Africa include a large and arbitrary component for subsistence production.

3. S. H. Frankel, "Capital and Capital Supply," a paper delivered at a meeting of the International Economic Association in Addis Ababa in July 1961. This paper and others on the economic development of Africa are to be published in 1964 by the Oxford University Press.

4. Information derived from the *Statistical Abstracts* of the Central Statistical Office (Salisbury) and the East African Statistical Department (Nairobi).

5. Author's estimate based on correspondence with various persons in these countries.

6. These figures are derived from estimates prepared by Dr. E. J. Berg to be used in a forthcoming book on labor problems in Africa. For a concise explanation of the many factors that have led to the growth of the migratory labor system in sub-Saharan Africa, see the article by Berg "Backward-Sloping Labor Supply Functions in Dual Economies: The Africa Case," in *Quarterly Journal of Economics* 85:461–492 (August 1961). This article includes a review of much of the literature on this subject.

7. These are estimates indicating orders of magnitude. Population data are not very reliable and there are special problems in defining "rural dwellers." The principal sources used for deriving these estimates are the *Report of the Commission for the Socio-Economic Development of the Bantu Areas* (Pretoria: South African Government Printer, 1956), popularly known as *The Tomlinson Report* and hereafter cited as such; the

Nyasaland *Report on the Census of 1945* (Zomba: Government Printer, 1946); the *Monthly Digest of Statistics*, compiled and issued by the Central Statistical Office, Salisbury; the *East African Population Census, 1948* (Nairobi); and the *Quarterly Economic and Statistical Bulletin* (Nairobi). The latter two are both issued by the East African Statistical Department of the East African High Commission.

8. Data derived from various sources. See Montague Yudelman, "Problems of Raising Agricultural Productivity in South, Central, and East Africa," in *The Transfer of Technology*, to be published by the Duke University Press in 1964.

9. R. W. Stephens, "Population Pressures in Africa South of the Sahara," *Population Research Project Bulletin* (Washington, D.C.: George Washington University Press, 1959).

10. John Phillips, *The Development of Agriculture and Forestry in the Tropics: Patterns, Problems and Promise* (New York: Frederick A. Praeger, 1962), p. 178. Referring to the tropics in general, Phillips stresses that they are "not rich storehouses capable of high yields even from fairly well-informed practices in agriculture and forestry."

11. *The Tomlinson Report*, p. 58.

12. *Basutoland, Bechuanaland Protectorate & Swaziland: Report of an Economic Survey Mission* (London: H.M.S.O., 1960).

13. Author's estimate based on estimates of value of subsistence production relative to value of marketed output: *Statistical Abstracts*, Central Statistical Office (Salisbury), and *Statistical Abstracts*, East African Statistical Department (Nairobi). See also K. C. Abercrombie, "The Transition from Subsistence to Market Agriculture in Africa South of the Sahara," *Monthly Bulletin of Agricultural Production and Statistics*, Food and Agriculture Organization of the United Nations, vol. X, no. 2 (February 1961).

14. Tanganyika: based on figures in the IBRD (International Bank for Reconstruction and Development) report, *The Economic Development of Tanganyika* (Baltimore: Johns Hopkins Press, 1961). South Africa: based on figures from *The Tomlinson Report*. Northern Rhodesia: based on an estimate provided by Economic Adviser. Southern Rhodesia: see Chapter 4. Uganda: based on figures in the IBRD report, *The Economic Development of Uganda* (Baltimore: Johns Hopkins Press, 1962).

15. See "Work and Wealth," in *The Bantu Speaking Tribes of South Africa*, Isaac Schapera, ed. (London: G. Routledge & Sons, Ltd., 1937), I, 166. See also Elizabeth Colson, "Native Cultural and Social Patterns in Contemporary Africa," in *Africa Today*, C. G. Haines, ed. (Baltimore: Johns Hopkins Press, 1955).

16. As quoted from *East Africa Royal Commission, 1953–1955 Report* (London: H.M.S.O., 1955), p. 23.

17. G. B. Masefield, *A Short History of Agriculture in the British Colonies* (London: Oxford University Press, 1950), gives a description of the early methods of cultivation in Rhodesia.

18. Information provided by the Department of Agriculture, Entebbe, Uganda.

19. See Appendix A for the food-consumption habits in Southern Rhodesia.

20. See *Communal Land Tenure*, an FAO land-tenure study, prepared by Sir Gerald Clawson (Rome: Food and Agriculture Organization of the United Nations, 1950).

21. Ministry of Economic Affairs, *Report on an Economic Survey of Nyasaland, 1958–1959* (Salisbury: Government Printer, 1959), p. 41.

22. *East Africa Royal Commission, Report*, p. 323. For a strong dissent from this particular viewpoint, see the article by M. J. Herskovits, "Economic Change and Cultural Dynamics," in *Tradition, Values, and Socio-Economic Development*, Ralph Braibanti and J. Spengler, eds. (Durham, N.C.: Duke University Press, 1961).

23. For a fuller discussion of these topics, see the second part of W. K. Hancock, *Survey of British Commonwealth Affairs*, vol. II: *Problems of Economic Policy, 1918–1939* (London: Oxford University Press, 1942), and Lord Hailey, *An African Survey*, revised 1956 (London: Oxford University Press, 1957), chap. xi.

24. See E. A. Walker, *The Great Trek*, 3 ed. (London: Adam & Charles Black, Ltd., 1948) and S. D. Neumark, *Economic Influences on the South African Frontier* (Stanford, Calif.: Stanford University Press, 1957).

25. Kenneth Ingham, *A History of East Africa* (London: Longmans, Green & Co., 1962).

26. For a fuller discussion of some of these factors, see Margery Perham, "White Minorities in Africa," *Foreign Affairs* 37:637–648 (July 1959).

27. For an incisive examination of this problem of the evolution of the philosophy of economic development in the Republic of South Africa, see S. H. Frankel, *The Tyranny of Economic Paternalism in Africa: A Study of Frontier Mentality, 1860–1960*, supplement to *Optima* (Johannesburg, December 1960).

28. For a fuller discussion, see E. M. Brookes, *The History of Native Policy in South Africa from 1830 to the Present Day*, 2 ed. rev. (Pretoria: J. L. van Schaik, 1927).

29. Selby Ngcobo, "The Urban African Worker" (unpublished ms., Salisbury: University College of Rhodesia and Nyasaland, 1961).

30. See *The Tomlinson Report*.

31. *East Africa Royal Commission, Report*, p. 19.

32. *Report on the Agricultural and Pastoral Production of Southern Rhodesia, Northern Rhodesia and Nyasaland 1957–1958* (Salisbury: Government Printer, 1959), p. 6.

33. This data comes from the author's private correspondence.

34. IBRD, *Economic Development of Tanganyika*.

35. Estimate made by author.

36. See Hailey, chap. xi, for a fuller exposition of this.

Chapter 2: The Economic and Social Background

1. Most of this description is derived from a mimeographed paper by V. Vincent and R. G. Thomas (in consultation with R. R. Staples), "The Agroecological Survey; Part I of An Agricultural Survey of Southern Rhodesia," available at the Federal Ministry of Agriculture, Salisbury.

2. *Ibid.*

3. For a more detailed description of the bioclimatic regions of Southern Rhodesia, see John Phillips, *Agriculture and Ecology in Africa* (New York: Frederick A. Praeger, 1959).

4. Sir Edgar Whitehead, "Southern Rhodesia," *International Affairs* 36:188 (April 1960).

5. Mimeographed release from Central Statistical Office, Salisbury, Oct. 17, 1962. A preliminary figure of 3,610,000 was announced in a release June 21, 1962.

6. Estimate in *Monthly Digest of Statistics* (Salisbury: Central Statistical Office), December 1962, p. 1.

7. *Demographic Sample Survey of the Indigenous African Population of Southern Rhodesia, 1953/55* (Salisbury: Central Statistical Office, 1956), pp. 1–8.

8. *Monthly Digest of Statistics,* December 1962, pp. 1, 2. The figures on natural increase (table 3 in the source) are for calendar years; the population (table 1) is estimated to have risen by 26,000 between June 30, 1955, and June 30, 1957.

9. *Ibid.,* p. 3.

10. Gertrude Caton-Thompson, *The Zimbabwe Culture* (Oxford: At the Clarendon Press, 1931).

11. For a fuller description of this early period, see Philip Mason, *The Birth of a Dilemma: The Conquest and Settlement of Rhodesia* (London: Oxford University Press, 1958).

12. The Matabele gave the name Amahole or "slaves" to the tribes they displaced, which are now called the "Mashona" by European ethnographists. The bulk of the Africans in Southern Rhodesia are Bantu but they can be grouped into two main divisions — those who speak Chishona (the Mashona) and those who speak Sindbele (the Matabele). The Chishona speakers account for about three fourths of the population. Tribal differences are of very little account today, for legally and administratively all language groups are treated the same. The greatest divergence among the Africans of today is that between the educated urban dweller and the unsophisticated tribal African.

13. Charter of the British South Africa Company, October 29, 1889. Copies of the charter are available in the library of the legislative assembly, Salisbury.

14. These figures are those given in a memorandum by H. Wilson Fox, an adviser to the company, in "Problems of Development and Policy" (1910). The memorandum is available in the Central African Archives in Salisbury.

15. H. Wilson Fox, "Land Settlement in Rhodesia by Europeans," memorandum also in Central African Archives.

16. C. H. Thompson and H. W. Woodruff, *Economic Development in Rhodesia and Nyasaland* (London: Dennis Dobson, Ltd., 1954).

17. An interesting view on this point is that expressed by the chairman of the company on the occasion of the company's fiftieth anniversary: "Those connected with the British South Africa Company may derive a not unworthy satisfaction from the reflection that they have disproved the text-book maxim that a trading corporation cannot govern; and they have shown that, if it be true that the functions of government and commerce are incompatible, in their case at least, it is the commercial interest and not the work of administration and development that has suffered. Whatever may be the theoretical objections to its dual nature, the last of the great Chartered Companies may await with confidence the judgment of history on its public achievements." From the *Times* (London), May 18, 1960.

For a critical view of possible conflict of interest between directors and senior officials of the company as administrators and shareholders, see L. H. Gann, *The Birth of a Plural Society: The Development of Northern Rhodesia under the British South Africa Company 1894–1914* (Manchester University Press for the Rhodes Livingstone Institute, 1958), pp. 48–49.

18. Colin Leys, *European Politics in Southern Rhodesia* (Oxford: At the Clarendon Press, 1959), p. 13.

19. Henry Clay, *Report on Industrial Relations in Southern Rhodesia* (Salisbury: Government Printer, 1930).

20. See the *Report of the Urban African Affairs Commission, 1958* (Salisbury: Government Printer, 1959) for a succinct description of economic development in this period.

21. See Thompson and Woodruff, *Economic Development in Rhodesia and Nyasaland*.

22. Figures provided by the Central Statistical Office, Salisbury.

23. The 1958 national accounts for the Federation of Rhodesia and Nyasaland showed that gross domestic capital formation in the Federation declined; however, in 1958 capital expenditure was still relatively high, being 33 percent of the GNP compared with corresponding ratios of 43 percent and 39 percent for 1956 and 1957. A great deal of this investment was in forms of production that either have small spread effects on the country (copper mining in Northern Rhodesia) or in large public works. The share of domestic capital formation attributable to the public sector was 34 percent in 1956, 38 percent in 1957, and 48 percent in 1958.

24. For an analysis of some of the effects of the Common Market, see Arthur Hazlewood and P. D. Henderson, *Nyasaland: The Economics of Federation* (Oxford: Basil Blackwell, 1960).

25. Department of the Treasury, *Review of the Economy of Southern Rhodesia for the Year 1960* (Salisbury: Government Printer, 1961).

26. *Ibid.*

27. *Ibid.*

28. The United Nations with its large Afro-Asian bloc must be included as one of the important external forces that is creating pressure for change. For an illustration of the role of the United Nations as an agent exerting pressure, see R. R. Ballinger, "South Africa and the Wider World," in *Looking Outwards: Three South African Viewpoints* (Johannesburg, South Africa: South African Institute of Race Relations, 1961). See, too, United Nations, General Assembly, 17th Session, *Agenda Report of the Special Committee on the Situation with Regard to the Implementation of the Declaration on the Granting of Independence to Colonial Countries and Peoples,* U.N. doc no. A/5238 (October 8, 1962), chap. ii: "Southern Rhodesia," pp. 56–147.

29. The franchise in Southern Rhodesia has always been "color blind," but in compliance with Cecil Rhodes' dictum, that government should be in the hands of civilized persons, the qualifications for the franchise have been set at a level which enables almost all Europeans to qualify and very few Africans to do so. Less than 1000 Africans were registered to vote in the late 1950's. The constitution of 1963 enfranchised many more African voters so that 15 out of 65 seats in the enlarged legislature could be won by Africans provided the enfranchised Africans exercised their right to vote.

30. The words "master" and "servant" are used in the Masters and Servants Act of 1891, which was derived from a similar act of 1856 in the Cape of Good Hope. This act, still on the statute books, paternalistically protects an African servant if, among other things, the master fails "to supply his servant with good, bedding or other articles stipulated in his contract of service." Under the act, however, a servant could be charged "for insulting his master, neglecting his master's property and deserting from his master's service."

31. As cited in W. K. Hancock, *Survey of British Commonwealth Affairs,* vol. II: *Problems of Economic Policy, 1918–1939* (London: Oxford University Press, 1942), pt. 2, p. 101. Italics mine.

32. *Ibid.*

33. For a fuller exposition of this and many other features of the relations between Europeans and Africans, see Leys, *European Politics in Southern Rhodesia.*

34. *Ibid.,* p. 272.

35. Sir Edgar Whitehead, "Southern Rhodesia," *Journal of International Affairs* 36:194 (April 1960). Italics mine.

36. *Report of the Secretary for Native Affairs and Chief Native Commissioner for the Year 1954* (Salisbury: Government Printer, 1955).

37. *Review of the Economy of Southern Rhodesia* (1960).

Chapter 3: Land Apportionment

1. Quoted by permission of the author, P. Laundy, from an unpublished manuscript (Salisbury, 1959).

2. Charter of the British South Africa Company, October 29, 1889.

Copies of the charter are available in the library of the legislative assembly, Salisbury.

3. *Report of the Southern Rhodesian Native Reserve Commission of 1915* (Salisbury: Government Printer, 1916).

4. This order-in-council of 1898 also specified that mineral rights on native lands were to be retained by the company but the company was to compensate any Africans moved off the land as a result of mineral exploitation. Section 83 of this order introduced the Cape Clause, the wording of which is essentially the same as in the text on pages 63-64.

5. N. Sithole, *African Nationalism* (London: Oxford University Press, 1959).

6. *Report of the Secretary for Native Affairs and Chief Native Commissioner for the Year 1920* (Salisbury: Government Printer, 1921), p. 1.

7. *Report of the Land Commission of 1925* (Salisbury: Government Printer, 1926), p. 4.

8. Commenting on this a subsequent government commission pointed out that "towns are not born by a simple administrative decision to send numbers of people to a particular locality," *Report of the Urban African Affairs Commission, 1958* (Salisbury: Government Printer, 1959), p. 28.

9. The Land Apportionment Act of 1941. A copy of this act is available in the library of the legislative assembly, Salisbury.

10. *Second Report of the Select Committee on Resettlement of Natives* (Salisbury: Government Printer, 1960).

11. The requirements for acquisitions in the purchase areas were to be the same as for Europeans wishing to acquire Crown land. These conditions were: (a) an agreement of lease for a period of five years; (b) after the period the lessee may apply to have the agreement of lease changed to an agreement of purchase; (c) after an agreement of purchase has been entered into, all rent paid in terms of the agreement of lease is regarded as part of the purchase price; (d) freehold title is granted when the final payment of the purchase price has been made.

12. An undated interdepartmental memorandum on this subject stated: "It is a reasonable assumption that recent unrest and strikes amongst the Natives can in part be attributed to the increased settlement of Europeans and the constant issue of notices of ejection on Natives from land which quite wrongly but by mere effluxion of time they have come to believe belongs to them. The rural Native must be assured now that he will be given land — the Native Department is at its wits end to provide land and in the meantime the European having acquired land is becoming more and more irate at not being able to utilize such land owing to the presence of Native tenants and even squatters and their livestock."

13. *Report of the Urban African Affairs Commission* (1958), p. 122.

14. The Land Apportionment Act of 1941 in section 41 stated that "no Native may lease, use or occupy land outside such area which falls within the jurisdiction of local authority." This denies Africans the right to occupy premises outside their segregated areas. In recent years, however, provision has been made for certain exempted classes. These are: (a)

persons engaged as professors, lecturers, teachers or students at the multi-racial University of Salisbury, (b) a person practising as an advocate, (c) a visitor, ordinarily resident outside the Federation, who is on a *bona fide* visit to the territory or is in transit through the territory.

15. See *Report of the Urban African Affairs Commission* (1958), p. 37.

16. "African Tragedy" in *Africa South* 1:59–67 (April–June 1957), esp. p. 67.

17. *East Africa Royal Commission, 1953–1955 Report* (London: H.M.S.O., 1955), p. 60.

Chapter 4: The Dual Agricultural Economy

1. *Report on the Agricultural and Pastoral Production of Southern Rhodesia, Northern Rhodesia and Nyasaland 1956–1957* (Salisbury: Government Printer, 1958), p. 4.

2. *Report on the Agricultural and Pastoral Production of Southern Rhodesia, Northern Rhodesia and Nyasaland 1959* (Salisbury: Government Printer, 1960), p. 19.

3. *Report of the Secretary for Native Affairs and Chief Native Commissioner for the Year 1960* (Salisbury: Government Printer, 1961), p. 22.

4. See charts 1–8, "Population and Livestock Concentrations in Native Reserves and Special Native Areas" in *Report of the Secretary for Native Affairs and Chief Native Commissioner for the Year 1962* (Salisbury: Government Printer, 1963), pp. 20–38.

5. Information provided by Native Affairs Department.

6. *Report on the Agricultural and Pastoral Production of Southern Rhodesia, Northern Rhodesia and Nyasaland 1957–1958* (Salisbury: Government Printer, 1959), p. 3. European-owned cattle were 2,074 million, African-owned 1,506,000.

7. The average of 480 per head is for Matabeleland, 280 per head for Mashonaland is based on tables on livestock production in *Report on the Agricultural and Pastoral Production of Southern Rhodesia, Northern Rhodesia and Nyasaland 1960* (Salisbury: Government Printer, 1961).

8. *Report of the Secretary for Native Affairs* (1960), p. 37. Thus, close to 70 percent of the cultivators were not livestock owners.

9. Information provided by Native Affairs Department.

10. *Report on the Agricultural and Pastoral Production of Southern Rhodesia* (1960), p. 6.

11. *Sample Census of African Agriculture of Southern Rhodesia* (Salisbury: Central Statistical Office, July 1961). This survey indicated an average acreage under cultivation of 8.1 acres. The same crops were grown throughout the country, though more corn was grown in the wetter areas.

12. Based on unpublished district returns made available by the Native Affairs Department.

13. *Report on the Agricultural and Pastoral Production of Southern Rhodesia* (1959), pp. 8, 9.

14. Data derived from unpublished manuscript in the Central Statistical

Office (1958). The largest single item of expense was labor which accounted for 30 percent of total expenditures.

15. *Report on the Agricultural and Pastoral Production of Southern Rhodesia* (1959), p. 12.

16. Between 1953 and 1958 the number of tractors in use increased from 7,318 to 10,327. The African labor force in that time ranged between 194,000 and 204,000. There is no data on average wage levels but limited interviews indicate that European producers were substituting tractors for cattle-drawn plows because of a rise in wage levels, unreliability, and shortage of labor, a wish to free grazing lands for other forms of production, and because mechanization permitted better timing of farm operations (e.g., tractors could be used for night plowing).

17. In 1960, 8,704 cultivators used 2,400 tons of fertilizer compared with more than 100,000 tons in the European areas. Only 592 bags of hybrid maize were distributed in the African areas. *Report of the Secretary for Native Affairs* (1960), pp. 48 and 79.

18. Information provided by Native Affairs Department. There was a slightly wider range in a sample of 50 holdings taken by the writer. The range was £4 to £85, with an average of £28 per holding. The upper quartile in the distribution of this sample had investments of £45 on holdings of close to 11 acres each.

19. *Report of the Secretary for Native Affairs* (1960), pp. 50–54.

20. This estimate is based on 1958 average prices and 1958 value of output and does not include any return on animals for providing draft power or manure.

21. *Report on the Agricultural and Pastoral Production of Southern Rhodesia* (1957–1958).

22. *Report of the Secretary for Native Affairs* (1960), pp. 98–99, figures for 1958.

23. Based on relative gross value of crop output of cultivated acreage in 1958.

24. Data derived from unpublished manuscript in the Central Statistical Office (1958). Realized incomes to farm operators totalled close to £9 million, or an average of £1,300 per farm operator.

25. *Report on the Agricultural and Pastoral Production of Southern Rhodesia* (1956–1957), p. 24. Volume of crop production quadrupled and that of livestock production doubled in this period.

26. J. H. Boeke, *Economics and Economic Policy of Dual Societies as Exemplified by Indonesia* (New York: Institute of Pacific Relations, 1953). For a very cogent dissenting opinion on his theory, as it applies in Indonesian circumstances, see Benjamin Higgins, "The 'Dualistic Theory' of Underdeveloped Areas," in *Economic Development and Cultural Change* 4:99–115 (January 1956). See, too, in the same journal a spirited defense by J. M. Van Der Kroef, "Economic Development in Indonesia: Some Social and Cultural Impediments" 4:116–133.

Other writers have applied various aspects of economic theory to dual economies. W. A. Lewis's classical growth model, for example, is based on the existence of subsistence and capitalistic sectors of the economy with a different level of average income in each sector. See W. A. Lewis, "Economic Development with Unlimited Supplies of Labor," in *The Manchester School of Economic and Social Studies* 22:139–191 (May 1954). For a careful study of this aspect of the dual economy and the impact of dualism on wage levels in Central Africa, see W. J. Barber, *The Economy of British Central Africa: A Case Study of Economic Development in a Dualistic Society* (Stanford, Calif.: Stanford University Press, 1961), especially chap. vii.

27. Boeke, pp. 2 and 3.

28. Boeke, p. 293.

29. These extracts are quoted from the *Official Report on Debates of the Legislative Assembly* (unrevised), vol. 48, no. 43 (Salisbury: Government Printer, 1960). The figures in parentheses denote column numbers in official reports.

30. W. A. Lewis, *The Theory of Economic Growth* (London: Allen & Unwin, 1955), p. 22.

31. H. Myint, "An Interpretation of Economic Backwardness," in *Oxford Economic Papers* (Oxford, England), July 1954.

32. For a discussion of the problems of motivation, see W. E. Moore, *Industrialization and Labor: Social Aspects of Economic Development* (Ithaca, N.Y.: Cornell University Press, 1951), p. 153.

33. The persons in the sample could well change their opinions as the influence of the money economy becomes stronger. Their responses were certainly influenced by such noneconomic factors as a strong desire to join their families and to return to a familiar environment where they are masters in their own homes. Finally, it must be stressed that these were migratory laborers, the same test applied to fifty permanently urbanized workers who had their families with them might have produced a different result. The permanently urbanized worker might think of returning to the indigenous area to retire but might well have no target income in mind.

34. The data on expenditures on European agriculture were compiled from various sources: annual financial reports, loan accounts, and records of legislative voting.

African agriculture is one of the major residual responsibilities of the constituent governments of the Federation of Rhodesia and Nyasaland. In 1957–1958 total expenditures on all aspects of African agriculture represented about 15 percent of the total expenditures to be defrayed from loan and revenue funds in Southern Rhodesia. This was less than the amount allocated for education and less than the amount allocated for police services. It is difficult to compare amounts allocated for African agriculture with proportionate amounts allocated for various items in Southern Rhodesia by the federal government. However, it appears from the 1957–1961 Federal Development Plan that the proportionate expenditures on railroads and power are much greater than those for African agriculture. See *Estimates of Expenditure to be defrayed from Revenue*

Funds and from Loan Funds During Year Ending 30 June 1958 (Salisbury: Government Printer, 1957) and Federal Government of Rhodesia and Nyasaland, *Development Plan 1957–1961* (Salisbury: Government Printer, 1957).

Chapter 5: Land Tenure

1. Philip Mason, *The Birth of a Dilemma: The Conquest and Settlement of Rhodesia* (London: Oxford University Press, 1958), pp. 100–101.

2. J. F. Holleman, *Shona Customary Law with Reference to Kinship, Marriage, the Family, and the Estate* (Cape Town: Oxford University Press, 1952).

3. See Appendix A for a description of "Agricultural Methods and Food of the Natives of Mashonaland," circa 1924.

4. *Report of the Mangwende Reserve Commission of Inquiry, 1961* (Salisbury: Government Printer, 1961), p. 37. This is an excellent report and bears the imprint of Dr. Holleman, the leading authority on Mashona Law.

5. *Ibid.*, p. 18.

6. This approach was recommended in Colombia by an economic survey mission but it was considered to be too difficult to implement in a country at Colombia's level of development. See the report by the IBRD (International Bank for Reconstruction and Development), *The Economic Development of Colombia* (Baltimore: Johns Hopkins Press, 1952).

7. These are systems of tenancy where tenants are compensated for land improvements such as those in the United Kingdom.

8. The first approach to providing greater security of tenure by introducing cadastral surveys, written contracts, and title deeds was made in 1930, following the recommendation of the Carter Commission Report of 1925 that land be provided for nontribal occupation in the native purchase areas.

9. See the Natural Resources Act.

10. Extract from the *Report of the Natural Resources Board for 1954*, quoted in *What the Native Land Husbandry Act Means to the Rural African in Southern Rhodesia: A Five Year Plan that will Revolutionise African Agriculture* (Salisbury: Government Printer, 1955), p. vi.

11. *Report of the Secretary for Native Affairs and Chief Native Commissioner for the Year 1947* (Salisbury: Government Printer, 1948).

12. Rights could not be pledged or attached for debt. (This is viewed as an important safeguard for a "backward people.") A holder may nominate his successor upon death.

13. Some social anthropologists have felt that this act has ignored and threatened the life of tribal communities in its desire to save the soil. Thus Holleman, in his *African Interlude*, has pointed out that the act has interfered with existing social organizations and the divisions of land have destroyed existing authority. In his view the new economic structure is being based on an unstable social basis. This, of course, is one of the intractable problems of "modernizing" tribal society where such

modernization requires rapid change. His plea that such change is undertaken with the advice and guidance from social anthropologists appears to make eminent sense. See J. F. Holleman, *African Interlude* (Cape Town: Nasionale Boekhandel, 1958), esp. pp. 205–209.

14. There were to be special allowances of land for additional wives, for widows, and headmen.

15. Information on the implementation of the act is derived from the *Report of the Secretary for Native Affairs and Chief Native Commissioner for the Year 1960* (Salisbury: Government Printer, 1961).

16. *Ibid.*, see p. 29, table 11. Average prices of land varied from £3.12s. an acre to £11.11s. 11d. per acre while grazing rights varied in price from £2.7s. 4d. per animal unit to £15.0s. 0d.

17. M. J. Herskovits, "Economic Change and Cultural Dynamics," in *Tradition, Values, and Socio-Economic Development,* Ralph Braibanti and J. Spengler, eds. (Durham, N.C.: Duke University Press, 1961), pp. 114–138. The author is particularly critical of "culture-bound" economists who transfer their notions of what is required for economic development — as learned in advanced economies — while ignoring the economic patterns of the indigenous peoples who are to change their ways. He recommends that the approach to these problems be through cultural dynamics and a cross-cultural approach, since economic development is an acculturative phenomenon. Change should come through acculturation whereby the indigenous society molds its institutions to meet changing needs. No one can deny the validity of this view. All that can be said is that if there is to be change then due weight must be given to the "social costs" of the change. All development involves costs — including "social costs." The difficulty here is twofold: Can a government stand by and see resources being destroyed while waiting for the acculturation process to work? And how does one measure the social costs of destroying tribal agriculture?

18. It was assumed that an understanding of the nature of the changes would come about as a result of consultations, but in at least one area a commission of inquiry found that while the act had been explained it was not understood and this had heightened the community's sense of insecurity. See *Report of the Mangwende Reserve Commission of Inquiry* (1961), pp. 170–173.

19. In this regard it is worthwhile noting a 1944 report which stated: "Some of the Natives, particularly those with a smattering of education, are very suspicious of the motives behind the present drive by the Native Agriculture Department to improve the productive capacity of Native lands. They *fear that any success will be a reason for depriving them of portion of the Reserves* set aside for them or a ground for refusing their demands, which are insistent, for an extension of the Reserves." *Report of the Native Production and Trade Commission, 1944* (Salisbury: Government Printer, 1945), p. 25. Italics mine.

20. This fixing of ratios of livestock to arable land was premised on the assumption that all cultivators owned livestock. Only after a count of livestock owners, as part of the implementation of the act, was it dis-

covered that, in fact, some 60 percent of the cultivators did not own livestock.

21. *Report of the Native Production and Trade Commission* (1944), p. 27.

22. My own estimate, based on a sample of 50 holdings, is that under present circumstances, 16–20 acres of land is the cultivated area that provides "full employment" for an African family with present techniques of production.

23. There is a wide discrepancy between my estimates and the official estimates of gross value of production, though there is only a slight difference in cash sales. The anticipated increase in value of subsistence production is a puzzle. According to figures provided by the Native Affairs Department, the average annual income of an African farmer was expected to change as follows:

	Old conditions	New conditions	Increase
Gross value of production	£40	£90	£50
Value of production for consumption	£23	£40	£17
Cash sales	£17	£50	£33
Cash costs	£ 6	£15	£ 9
Net cash incomes	£11	£35	£24

Commodities are valued at farm prices which are projected to increase slightly over the period under review. These estimates include an increase in the output of Turkish tobacco but generally they are based on higher output of existing crops and livestock.

24. In interviews with those who had farms in purchase areas the reasons given for purchasing farms were varied. They included such statements as "less crowded," "more room," "less interference from authorities," and similar answers. They were seldom couched in terms of opportunities to increase incomes, though this may have been implied in the other answers. In general it may be pertinent to point out that a major source of "insecurity" is the fear of being displaced through government action. Despite these observations it does appear that economic considerations do play an important role. For example, in 1960 there were 3070 applicants for purchase area farms; however, 40 percent of the farms made available in 1960 were not taken up by Africans even though the purchase prices and terms of purchase were extremely reasonable. The conclusion to this paradox is: "It would appear that, despite the land hunger among the African people they are still highly selective in respect of the land they are prepared to occupy and pay for," *Report of the Secretary for Native Affairs* (1960), p. 125.

Chapter 6: Labor: Migrants and Managers

1. Writing in *Migrants and Proletarians: Urban Labour in the Economic Development of Uganda* (London: Oxford University Press, 1960),

p. 129, Walter Elkan points out that: "In Europe the growth of towns was associated with the growth of a new category of people, the urban industrial working class. In Africa too, towns are growing rapidly, but although some of their houses may be built to last a lifetime, those who stay in them seldom stay so long; sooner or later they return to their original homes."

2. *Report of the Commission for the Socio-Economic Development of the Bantu Areas* (Pretoria: South African Government Printer, 1956), popularly known as *The Tomlinson Report* and hereafter cited as such.

3. *Basutoland, Bechuanaland Protectorate & Swaziland: Report of an Economic Survey Mission* (London: H.M.S.O., 1960) and Arthur Hazlewood and P. D. Henderson, *Nyasaland: The Economics of Federation* (Oxford: Basil Blackwell, 1960). Migratory labor provides an important source of "capital inflow" in some countries. In 1957, 12 percent of all African personal incomes in Nyasaland were in the form of emigrants' remittances. In Bechuanaland, in 1958, the inflow of funds from migrants was equal to one fifth of the value of that country's total exports.

4. *Report of the Urban African Affairs Commission, 1958* (Salisbury: Government Printer, 1959), appendix II.

5. W. J. Barber, *The Economy of British Central Africa: A Case Study of Economic Development* (Stanford, Calif.: Stanford University Press, 1961).

6. An important factor in reducing real incomes in the wage economy is the high cost of family housing (where such housing is readily available). See Ellen Hellman, "Urban Areas" in *Handbook on Race Relations in South Africa* (Cape Town: Oxford University Press, 1949). See also *East Africa Royal Commission, 1953–1955 Report* (London: H.M.S.O., 1955), chap. xix; and the *Report of the Urban African Affairs Commission* (1958).

7. The stress here and throughout this chapter is on economic rather than social factors. There are noneconomic factors that might encourage migration such as an excursion into the wage economy taking the place of valor in battle. (Cf. Isaac Schapera, *Migrant Labour and Tribal Life: A Study of Conditions in Bechuanaland Protectorate* [London: Oxford University Press, 1947].) Then, too, males might *not* migrate for "patriotic reasons," even though they might stand to gain from such a migration. (See P. H. Gulliver, *Land Tenure and Social Change among the Nyakyusa*, East African Studies no. 11, East African Institute of Social Research, Kampala, Uganda, 1958.) In my view, however, the major force that encourages migration is an economic one: the push of low agricultural incomes and the pull of the need to earn a higher level of income to meet expanding needs.

8. Department of the Treasury, *Review of the Economy of Southern Rhodesia for the Year 1960* (Salisbury: Government Printer, 1961), p. 7.

9. The exact numbers of migrants at any one time are unknown but this is the best estimate available. It is based on demographic sample surveys; see the *Demographic Sample Survey of the Indigenous African*

Population of Southern Rhodesia 1953/55 (Salisbury: Central Statistical Office, 1959). In some areas, particularly during drought periods, as many as 93 percent of the men have been reported as being absent; see the *Report of the Secretary for Native Affairs and Chief Native Commissioner for the Year 1947* (Salisbury: Government Printer, 1948).

10. *Demographic Sample Survey* (1953/55).

11. *Report of the Urban African Affairs Commission* (1958), p. 18.

12. "Native Labour in Agriculture," Government of Southern Rhodesia, Department of Agriculture, Bulletin no. 1523 (May–June 1950), reprinted from the *Rhodesia Agricultural Journal* 67:234–252 (1950).

13. The *Report of the Mangwende Reserve Commission of Inquiry, 1961* (Salisbury: Government Printer, 1961), p. 30, states: "Although their exact proportions are unknown, there can be little doubt that wage earnings now form a major part, if not the bulk, of the income of rural-based families." See Appendix B for a comparison of rates of growth of agricultural incomes and urban wages.

14. "Cattle in the Lower Rainfall Regions of Southern Rhodesia: Economic Aspects," mimeographed paper for internal distribution, Native Affairs Department, Salisbury.

15. See Gulliver, *Land Tenure and Social Change among the Nyakyusa,* and *Outline of Agrarian Problems in Nyasaland* (Nyasaland: Government Printer, 1955).

16. In many of the medium rainfall areas output per family tends to rise as acreage increases, up to about 16 acres. With a smaller acreage, output per acre rises; the intensification of production gives higher returns per acre but not high enough returns to labor to compensate for the smaller acreage. Land and labor combine in a classical production function where diminishing returns to labor with "constant capital" set in at about 16 acres. Returns to labor are highest at about 16 acres but tend to fall below 16 to 20 acres after which returns to land do not rise sufficiently to offset lower labor incomes. See "Cattle in the Lower Rainfall Regions of Southern Rhodesia."

17. The rate of increase in income per animal is not a cash increase but is a prorated value added. It is not realized unless animals are sold. The rate of "value added" varies according to the age of the animal and prevailing market prices. As is pointed out in Appendix B, the growth rate in the livestock industry as a whole is very low.

18. *Economic Development of Under-developed Countries: International Flow of Long-Term Capital and Official Donations, 1959–1961,* U.N. doc. no. A/5195 (New York: Secretary General, United Nations, 1962).

19. The ratio of marginal investment to marginal employment will depend on many factors — such as the extent of infrastructure and the nature of the industry — and the proportions of the factors. This figure of £300 is based on data derived from national accounts and provided by the Central Statistical Office. The evidence indicated that either there is a substantial time lag between investment and employment effects or

despite the low price for labor industrialists are substituting capital for labor. For example, the motor-vehicle industry reported an increase in capital expenditures of £2 million without any increase in employment.

20. "Problems of Economic Development of the Federation of Rhodesia and Nyasaland," by W. L. Taylor of the University College of Rhodesia and Nyasaland. This paper was delivered at a meeting of the International Economic Association in Addis Ababa in July 1961. It and others from this meeting will be published in 1964 by the Oxford University Press. The author concludes that manufacturing industry can be only of limited assistance in absorbing surplus labor with present techniques of production.

21. *Report on the Census of Africans in Employment Taken on 8 May 1956* (Salisbury: Central Statistical Office, November 1957).

22. Between 1958 and 1960 the number of Africans in wage employment rose from 627,000 to 642,000. *Review of the Economy of Southern Rhodesia* (1960), p. 6.

23. *Ibid.*, p. 30. Between 1954 and 1960, 107,000 Africans entered the wage economy but the subsistence population rose by 283,000.

24. *Ibid.*, p. 8.

25. Initially the act was intended to force a division of labor between those in African agriculture and those in the wage economy, but by 1961 the *Report of the Secretary for Native Affairs and Chief Native Commissioner for the Year 1960* (Salisbury: Government Printer, 1961) was specific in stating that "a large number of the families on the land [will] have to supplement their incomes from other sources," p. 22.

26. In the Mangwende Reserve with a population of from 50,000 to 60,000, it was assumed that there was ample land for all producers. After 87 percent of the land had been allocated according to the prescribed formulae, more than two fifths of the adult males who were registered taxpayers in the area had been rendered landless by the act. These taxpayers were ward members who were away or had been away for some time when the allocations were made. Many of them were young unmarried adult males who had not established a family. See the *Report of the Mangwende Reserve Commission of Inquiry* (1961).

27. "Native Labour in Agriculture."

28. See "Cattle in the Lower Rainfall Regions of Southern Rhodesia: Economic Aspects," pp. 3 and 5.

29. *Report of the Mangwende Reserve Commission of Inquiry* (1961), pp. 31 and 32. Comparable figures were:

	Average net values	*Average net cash incomes*
Master farmers	£62	£40
Plot holders and cooperators	£28	£ 6
Ordinary farmers	£17	£ 3½

30. *Report of the Secretary for Native Affairs* (1960), p. 78.

31. This information comes from a mimeographed paper, "African Re-

settlement and the Native Purchase Area Problem" by the economic advisor to the Native Development Fund (Salisbury, 1958). These yields are for all grain and pulse crops.

32. Arthur Hunt, *Native Purchase Area Farms: An Economic Appraisal* (Salisbury: Native Affairs Department, April 1960), p. 20.

33. J. F. V. Phillips, *The Development of Agriculture and Forestry in the Tropics: Patterns, Problems and Promise* (New York: Frederick A. Praeger, 1962), esp. p. 147.

34. Ken Brown, *Land in Southern Rhodesia* (London: Africa Bureau, 1959).

35. *Report of the Native Production and Trade Commission, 1944* (Salisbury: Government Printer, 1945), p. 25.

36. U.N. doc. no. A/5195, *Economic Development of Under-developed Countries: International Flow of Long-Term Capital and Official Donations, 1959–1961,* p. 4. There is a widespread belief that "the under-developed countries should annually spend an amount equal to one per cent of their national income on agricultural extension services and research." This formula is widely used in development planning, but, conditions vary so much from country to country it seems rather ridiculous to apply the same yardstick to — for example — India, Paraguay, and Libya.

37. "The Work of Agricultural Demonstrators in Southern Rhodesia," in *Tropical Agriculture,* Journal of the Imperial College of Tropical Agriculture 31:110–111 (April 1954), Government Printing Office, Trinidad.

38. *Reports of the Secretary for Native Affairs and Chief Native Commissioner for the Years 1941, 1942, 1943, 1944 and 1945* (Salisbury: Government Printer, 1947), p. 165. The tone of the quotation reflects the prevalent attitude but the substance of the comment is the point of interest.

Chapter 7: Capital

1. Information provided by Central Statistical Office. See also their *Monthly Digest of Statistics,* "Supplement on National Income of the Federation, 1954–1958," January 1960 (Salisbury: Central Statistical Office), pp. 15–16.

2. The writer believes that the Central Statistical Office is one of the best statistical offices in Africa. Its difficulties stem from a shortage of staff and some of the peculiar problems of estimating the value of capital formation in the African areas. For example, there is no market for most of the land in the African areas and so little basis for estimating changes in land improvements in these areas.

3. The method used to obtain this estimate was as follows: (a) livestock were valued at current prices; (b) an estimate was derived from the average cost of major and minor roads and these were valued accordingly by multiplying mileage with average cost per unit at 1958 prices; (c) land clearance was estimated to cost £3 an acre, the 1958 price for

such clearance. Improvements through irrigation were valued at £10 per acre (conservation work was not included); (d) the average value of equipment was based on 1958 prices and the amount was based on the extrapolation from a limited number of samples; (e) housing was valued very arbitrarily, as were other improvements, and estimates as to numbers of houses and bins and other improvements were based on regional samples; (f) major equipment for road building and soil conservation was not included (to prevent double counting) nor was any estimate made for housing provided for extension officers. Schools, mission stations, and similar institutions were not included, as they were not considered to be associated with African agricultural output; (g) water holes and bore holes were valued at costs of development.

This method leaves much to be desired; it is a first approximation in the absence of detailed information and is presented as such.

4. The problem of estimating changes in gross fixed-capital formation is compounded by an absence of "land purchases" in the African areas.

5. This estimate is not to be accepted uncritically. It is only an order of magnitude based on the official estimate of value of output as presented in Chapter 4.

6. "Broadsheet No. 3" (November 1958), Information Services Branch of Native Affairs Department, Salisbury. This is an optimistic estimate. It excludes imputed costs of labor and depreciation.

7. *Report of the Secretary for Native Affairs and Chief Native Commissioner for the Year 1960* (Salisbury: Government Printer, 1961), p. 48. A total of 8,704 farmers were reported as using fertilizer, a 100 percent increase over the preceding year.

8. *Ibid.,* p. 92.

9. *Ibid.* The average repayment of all loans is 72 percent of the loans made.

10. Figures derived by the author from government financial statements.

11. The breakdown of expenditures between 1959 and the end of 1962 is as follows:

	£ thousands
Primary development	4,519
Application of the Act	1,366
Auxiliary services	2,713
Staffing — transport and housing	3,074
	11,672

Only £530,000 has been allocated for the "promotion of better farming," which includes items such as fencing, equipment, livestock, seed, fertilizers, and wages; £116,000 has been allocated for the expansion of research and training facilities. In contrast, 11.8 percent is to go for surveying, resettlement, and afforestation, 39 percent for primary development, while transport and staffing are to account for 21 percent of the expenditures. Thus, all in all, only 5.4 percent of total expenditure under the act is to be for the improvement of management.

12. A further reason for the low return associated with the increased expenditures is that some of these expenditures were used for "ideological" purposes rather than for production purposes. Many Africans were "resettled" in accordance with the dictates of the Land Apportionment Act. Many subsistence producers and squatters were transferred from the European areas to relatively distant areas. This transfer required large direct and indirect public expenditures. Most of these expenditures — other than limited sums earmarked for resettlement — are included in the over-all estimates of expenditures in the African areas. Although there is no breakdown of the amounts allocated for this purpose, the total cost of resettlement is generally estimated to be close to £250 per family, much of this outlay going for the preparation of settlement areas. About £3 million, or close to 20 percent of the total expenditure was used to relocate subsistence producers. But moving subsistence producers from one area to another, where they continue to subsist, adds nothing to total output. Thus, while these investments led to a redistribution of the population, they yielded very little return on the outlay of public funds.

13. Estimate made by writer by comparing tax revenues as reported in financial statements and reports of the Secretary for Native Affairs. This excludes local council taxes, dog taxes and vehicle taxes, all of which are small. It also excludes matching grants made by the government to district and other councils.

14. In 1958–1959, £2.5 million was spent on African education and total tax collection from poll taxes was only £1.1 million. See also the *Report of the Secretary for Native Affairs* (1960), p. 13.

15. *Ibid.* Males are registered for tax purposes in the area where they attain manhood so that it is difficult to keep track of migratory labor for tax collections.

16. P. T. Bauer and B. S. Yamey, *The Economics of Under-Developed Countries* (Cambridge, Eng.: University Press, 1957), p. 195.

17. In a survey made in Bechuanaland in 1947, 40 percent of the 297 males interviewed reported that they left home to seek work in the Union of South Africa because of the need for money to pay taxes. This is discussed in a chapter on the economic causes of labour migration from Bechuanaland in Isaac Schapera's, *Migrant Labour and Tribal Life: A Study of Conditions in Bechuanaland Protectorate* (London: Oxford University Press, 1947).

18. Information provided by Revenue Department in Salisbury.

19. The levy is varied by commodities and by year and is used for purposes other than raising revenue, for instance, to "stabilize" prices (see Chapter 8). In general the levy has been at around 10 percent of the retail price of taxable commodities.

20. Revenues from levies have risen from £136,000 in 1949–1950 to a peak of £743,000 in 1957, falling off to £476,000 in 1959. Fluctuations in weather conditions have influenced tax receipts on crops but revenues from livestock have risen consistently from £76,000 in 1949–1950 to £347,000 in 1959.

21. See the *Report of the Secretary for Native Affairs and Chief Native Commissioner for the Year 1948* (Salisbury: Government Printer, 1949), p. 26. "It is the policy of the government to relate prices of agricultural produce to the costs of production of European produce, but there is no discrimination between prices paid to European and Native producers. Generally speaking Native producers do not plough back as development capital anything like the same proportion of their returns as European producers do. The Act thereby provides for a contribution from Native producers towards the capital development of their areas by means of a levy on certain products marketed by them.

The whole of the levy or pooled funds are to be returned indirectly and collectively to all Native producers by applying the whole of the new fund to the improvement of production and the provision of better marketing facilities."

22. A Land Tax Act was introduced in 1928 and amended in 1929–1931. It provided for an annual tax of one percent of the unimproved value of all taxable land. This act, No. 3 of 1931, was suspended by the governor's proclamation, No. 16 of 1931. Its operation can be restored in the same manner.

23. *Report of the Urban African Affairs Commission, 1958* (Salisbury: Government Printer, 1959), p. 184.

24. Information provided by the Federal Ministry of Posts, Salisbury.

25. The propensity to save is a puzzle. Individual deposits have increased, but there is currently no source of data for establishing the relation between increased savings and increased incomes. Urban samples indicate that the proportion of money saved by the poorest groups is much higher than that saved by more affluent groups. Could it be that the poorer groups still retain unsophisticated tastes or do they feel the need to save as a means of providing against future unemployment? It may be that their wants are still on a low level and that their next level of wants includes relatively "lumpy" expenditures for which they are saving. There is no credit available for most low-paid urban workers who wish to purchase items such as furniture, bicycles, and the like.

26. The term "post offices" as used here includes the makeshift offices usually found in trading stores where Africans can deposit savings, buy stamps, and the like.

27. Estimate provided from local sources.

28. *Report of the Secretary for Native Affairs* (1960), p. 11.

29. "The African Market in Salisbury, Bulawayo, Umtali and Gwelo," in *Monthly Digest of Statistics,* January 1960.

Chapter 8: Prices and Marketing

1. E. M. Thomas, *The Harmless People* (New York: Alfred Knopf, 1959).

2. Production of coffee in Uganda is estimated to require only 80 man-days per year compared with cotton which requires 140 man-days per year. See the IBRD (International Bank for Reconstruction and

Development) report, *The Economic Development of Uganda* (Baltimore: Johns Hopkins Press, 1962), p. 122 in the Uganda version.

3. Figures from *Report of the Secretary for Native Affairs and Chief Native Commissioner for the Year 1960* (Salisbury: Government Printer, 1961), p. 47.

4. Attempts are being made to introduce coffee, sugar cane, and tea into the African areas but thus far these crops have not been produced by Africans. *Ibid.*, p. 45.

5. The principle of "meaningful'" incentives has been used to encourage producers to shift into sparsely settled areas in Tanganyika. It was found that making relatively high-grade cattle available for purchase by those who moved provided the strongest incentive. See G. A. Bridges, *Planning Land Settlement Schemes with Special Reference to East Africa* (Addis Ababa: Economic Commission for Africa, Food and Agriculture Organization of the United Nations, 1961), p. 11.

6. J. R. Raeburn, "Some Economic Aspects of African Agriculture," *The East African Economics Review* (Nairobi) 5:45 (December 1958).

7. In Uganda, for example, the differences in attitudes toward the market between nearby regions such as Buganda and Karamoja is pronounced. The Ganda are market-oriented, the Karamajong are not. Indeed, as the Karamajong raise only livestock and as their present money needs are still limited, the problem of overgrazing in these areas may be more easily solved by lowering prices of livestock than raising them. There is reason to believe that there is a backward-bending supply curve for livestock at this time and that lower prices would induce increased sales.

8. Arthur Hunt, *Native Purchase Area Farms: An Economic Appraisal* (Salisbury: Native Affairs Department, April 1960).

9. See Chapter 4 on the dual economy and the *Report of the Secretary for Native Affairs* (1960), table 6.

10. See "Cattle in the Lower Rainfall Regions of Southern Rhodesia: Economic Aspects," mimeographed paper for internal distribution, Native Affairs Department, Salisbury.

11. Sample taken by author.

12. Relative prices for a bag of corn were as follows between 1931–1932 and 1936–1937:

Year	Local selling price	Export price
1931–1932	9/2	5/2
1932–1933	8/7	5/1
1933–1934	9/6	6/10
1934–1935	10/5	6/4
1935–1936	10/–	5/11
1936–1937	10/6	7/8

Source: *Report of the Grain Marketing Board for the Period 1 April 1952 to 31 March 1953* (Salisbury: The Rhodesian Printing and Publishing Co., 1954), p. 3.

13. In accordance with the Maize Control Act of 1931. In 1934 the act was amended: Europeans who delivered less than 100 bags of maize had a quota of 75 percent of their deliveries in the high-priced internal market; those with 200–300 bags had a quota of 70 percent, and so on up to 6,000 bags where the quota was 25 percent. The African quota was not to rise above 25 percent.

14. Figures derived from the *Report of the Grain Marketing Board for the Period 1 April 1951 to 31 March 1952* (Salisbury: The Rhodesian Printing and Publishing Co., 1953). This report gives an excellent summary of marketing problems between 1933 and 1953 and much of the material used here is from that report.

15. In most cases the guaranteed prices for domestically produced commodities are tied to the landed costs of imported supplies. The major exceptions are corn which, up until recently has been heavily subsidized with internal prices based on "average costs of production," and Virginia flue-cured tobacco, the price of which is freely determined by the export market.

16. Corn can be bought directly from Africans by miners and prospectors and by rural Africans who need it for their own consumption. In 1957 these sales were required to be registered with the Grain Marketing Board to stop avoidance of payment of the development levy.

17. See Table 1: "Maize Producer Price Structure, 1960 Harvest" in *Report of the Secretary for Native Affairs* (1960). Africans in the purchase areas and members of cooperatives pay a higher levy than do other Africans.

18. Annual reports of the Secretary for Native Affairs and Chief Native Commissioner.

19. This is difficult to establish with precision. District data provided by the Native Affairs Department indicate, however, that there have been increasing deliveries of grain to the board from the outlying areas.

20. See *Report of the Grain Marketing Board for Period Ending 30 June 1958* (Salisbury: The Rhodesian Printing and Publishing Co., 1959), p. 18.

21. In 1958–1959 it was estimated in an unpublished paper that returns per acre for groundnuts were 60 to 70 percent below those for competing crops, corn and millet. These results are confirmed by samples taken by the author.

22. *Report of the Grain Marketing Board for Period Ending 30 June 1958*, p. 30.

23. *Ibid.*

24. Handling charges per bag of grain in the best of the cooperatives were 5*d.* a bag compared with the 3*s.* paid to traders by the board.

25. *Report of the Secretary for Native Affairs and Chief Native Commissioner for the Year 1958* (Salisbury: Government Printer, 1959), p. 96.

26. *Report of the Native Production and Trade Commission, 1944* (Salisbury: Government Printer, 1945).

27. See *Monthly Digest of Statistics* (Salisbury: Central Statistical Office), January 1960, p. v.

28. *Commission of Enquiry into the Livestock Industry* (Salisbury: Government Printer, 1956), p. 4. Average cold-dressed weight of European-owned livestock was 582 pounds compared with 391 pounds for African stock. In 1960 less than 8 percent of the 213,000 head of cattle sold were in the "good" grades. The vast majority were low-grade animals.

29. Data derived from information provided by the chief economic advisor to the Ministry of Native Affairs. The economic evidence as presented by the chief economic advisor was an important factor in securing a change in the marketing system.

30. *Commission of Enquiry into the Livestock Industry*, p. 11. The system had a double edge: the Land Apportionment Act made land relatively plentiful for Europeans and so gave them ample opportunity to operate as grazers. Conversely Africans were forced to sell their livestock partly because of a relative shortage of land allocated to them under the Land Apportionment Act.

31. See the Annual Reports of the Secretary for Native Affairs and Chief Native Commissioner for the years 1956–1960.

Chapter 9: Future Prospects for African Agriculture in Southern, Central, and East Africa

1. See W. J. Barber, *The Economy of British Central Africa: A Case Study of Economic Development* (Stanford, Calif.: Stanford University Press, 1961). The migratory labor system also affects the productivity of labor in the wage economy but this aspect of the economy is not considered here. See also Sheila Van der Horst in *South African Journal of Economics* 25 (December 1957) and E. W. Stanton, "Native Labour on Repetitive Work," *Race Relations Journal* 16 (Johannesburg: Institute of Race Relations, 1949), and Selby Ncgobo, "The Urban African Worker" (unpublished ms., Salisbury: University College of Rhodesia and Nyasaland, 1961), chap. i.

2. T. W. Schultz, "Connections Between Natural Resources and Economic Growth," in *Natural Resources and Economic Growth*, J. J. Spengler, ed. (Washington, D.C.: Resources for the Future, Inc., 1961).

3. IBRD (International Bank for Reconstruction and Development), *The Economic Development of Uganda* (Baltimore: Johns Hopkins Press, 1962), part II.

4. See G. F. Papanek, "Framing a Development Program," in *International Conciliation*, no. 527 (New York: Carnegie Endowment for International Peace, March 1960). The usual criterion for establishing investment priorities is to determine which investments will add most to the national income. By this criterion it might be appropriate, in those countries that have dual economies, to concentrate investment in the European areas, where additional investment will give the greatest returns. But the spread effects of investments also have to be considered,

and as has been shown, investments in the European areas have done little to promote development in the African areas except by the drawing-off of migratory labor. It is this writer's view that, given proper direction, the marginal increments of input in the African areas in Southern Rhodesia can yield high returns.

5. Estimate derived from data provided to the author while in Uganda by the Government Statistical Office.

6. This is literally correct for producers of perishable crops such as vegetables in the Kigezi areas of Uganda. These vegetables are of good quality but there is no market for them in Uganda and transport costs are too high for their export.

7. This is not to say that there should be no "unprofitable" investment in industrial development, but this is not the place to take up various theories of industrialization, balanced growth vs. the "big push," and the like. For a discussion of this see the citations in G. F. Papanek, "Framing a Development Program."

8. See the *Urban African Market in Salisbury*, Central Statistical Office.

9. United Nations *Economic Bulletin for Africa*, "African Statistics Annéxe" (Addis Ababa: Economic Commission for Africa, Food and Agriculture Organization of the United Nations, 1961), vol. I.

10. To analyze projected trade conditions for each and every commodity would be a major exercise in itself. The *general* conclusions presented in this paragraph are a synthesis of many studies which are unanimous in finding that there will be a slow expansion of international trade in most temperate and tropical products of the kinds grown in Southern, Central, and East Africa. For a general summary of short-term prospects see *F.A.O. Commodity Review 1962*, special supplement: "Agricultural Commodities Projections for 1970" (Rome: Food and Agriculture Organization of the United Nations, 1962).

11. See Walter Elkan on "Uganda" in *Economic Development: Analysis and Case Studies*, Adamantios Pepelasis, et al., eds. (New York: Harper and Brothers, 1961), and C. C. Langley, *Crops and Wealth in Uganda*, East Africa Studies, no. 12 (Kampala: East African Institute of Social Research, 1959).

12. *The Economic Development of Uganda.*

13. *Symposium on Mechanical Cultivation in Uganda*, J. L. Joy, ed. (Kampala, 1960).

14. There are also sociological problems of partial mechanization where the value system is not changed completely. If the man's role in the production process is mechanized but the woman's is not it adds to the burdens of the women and creates friction in the family group. Then, too, the role of mechanization cannot be appreciated as a factor in raising productivity without changes in attitude toward the market. According to one report on Uganda, for example: "It seemed that the Bunyoro were not using mechanization to increase their agricultural potential but rather in all probability to increase their leisure. In itself this is not a bad

objective but it is perhaps not a high priority for a developing country."
Symposium on Mechanical Cultivation in Uganda, p. 7. See also K. D. S.
Baldwin, *The Niger Agricultural Project* (Cambridge, Mass.: Harvard
University Press, 1957).

15. Information provided to the writer by the East Africa Tobacco
Company of Uganda and the government of Uganda. See also *The Economic Development of Uganda.*

16. *Report of the Secretary for Native Affairs, Chief Native Commissioner and Director of Native Development For the Year 1957* (Salisbury: Government Printer, 1958).

17. See *The Economic Development of Uganda,* also *Basutoland, Bechuanaland Protectorate & Swaziland: Report of an Economic Survey Mission* (London: H.M.S.O., 1960).

18. John Phillips, *The Development of Agriculture and Forestry in the Tropics: Patterns, Problems and Promise* (New York: Frederick A. Praeger, 1962), p. 147. The relation between development of new techniques of production and apparent land pressure is highlighted in the report of a recent survey mission to Tanganyika. Even though over-all population density in Tanganyika is low and Africans were only cultivating about 10 percent of the total land available to them, the system of shifting cultivation required several acres of bush fallow for every area under cultivation. As a result, 30 to 40 percent of the land that could be used was left idle for at least a year. IBRD, *The Economic Development of Tanganyika* (Baltimore: Johns Hopkins Press, 1961), p. 84.

19. Studies made in the former Belgian Congo indicated that "38 percent of the total labor time in the production of the major food crops was for operations of threshing, grinding and the like that were postharvesting but pre-consumption operations." These labor requirements could be reduced considerably by simple technological changes. See B. F. Johnston, *The Staple Food Economies of Western Tropical Africa* (Stanford, Calif.: Stanford University Press, 1958).

20. For further information on this point see "The Organization of Research," in Lord Hailey, *An African Survey,* revised 1956 (London: Oxford University Press, 1957).

21. See *The Economic Development of Tanganyika; The Economic Development of Uganda; Basutoland, Bechuanaland Protectorate & Swaziland;* various reports of the Director of Agriculture in Nyasaland; and the *Report of the Commission for the Socio-Economic Development of the Bantu Areas,* popularly known as *The Tomlinson Report.* As the spread of the democratic process undermines the authority of chiefs, their power to command producers to increase output diminishes and persuasion has to replace the dictates of chiefs. This is an important facet of the increasing significance of extension work. See "Cotton and the Uganda Economy 1903–09," by Cyril Ehrlich in the *Uganda Journal* (Kampala) 21 (September 1957).

22. This excludes loans made to cooperatives. See *The Economic Development of Tanganyika* and *The Economic Development of Uganda.*

23. Based on estimates of credit available apart from lending through cooperatives.

24. *The Economic Development of Tanganyika.*

25. *The Economic Development of Uganda.*

26. H. Belshaw, *Agricultural Credit in Economically Underdeveloped Countries* (Rome: Food and Agriculture Organization of the United Nations, 1959). This valuable study provides many insights into problems of providing rural credit, but unfortunately the author did not concern himself with African problems.

27. Information provided through correspondence.

28. *Final Report of the Conference of African States on the Development of Education in Africa* (Addis Ababa: United Nations Economic Commission for Africa and UNESCO, May 1961), p. 8. (The Republic of South Africa is excluded.)

29. M. Yudelman, "Some Aspects of Agricultural Development in Sub-Saharan Africa," paper delivered at a meeting of the International Economic Association in Addis Ababa in July 1961. This paper and others on the economic development of Africa are to be published in 1964 by the Oxford University Press.

30. Estimate derived from *The Economic Development of Uganda* and *The Economic Development of Tanganyika.*

31. *Final Report of the Conference of African States.*

32. Thomas Balogh, "What Schools for Africa?" *New Statesman* 63:412 (March 23, 1962).

33. Estimate of cost provided by Native Affairs Department for 1958.

34. These impressions are based on the author's observations in various agencies and in different parts of the world.

35. For further information see: The Rockefeller Foundation, "Program in the Agricultural Sciences," in *Annual Report, 1960–1961* (New York: Office of Publications, 1961). Some of the economic benefits of the program are assessed in "The Impact of Agricultural Research on Mexican Wheat Products" by N. E. Borlaug in *Transactions of the New York Academy of Sciences,* series II, vol. 20, no. 3 (January 1958). See also, A. T. Mosher, *Technical Co-operation in Latin American Agriculture* (Chicago: University of Chicago Press, 1957), p. 106. As a former official of the Rockefeller Foundation, the author has had opportunities to observe this program at first hand.

36. Information provided in private correspondence.

37. The new varieties of wheat were one of a series of factors that led to increased wheat production. Others were the expansion of acreage suitable for wheat, heavy investment in irrigation, and high internal prices for wheat. Nonetheless, without the new varieties of wheat the large increases in production would not have occurred, for the new varieties not only gave larger yields but also were disease resistant. The research program was an important link in a chain of factors that enabled production to be increased.

38. It is difficult to estimate the direct costs of the Mexican program.

Some costs were borne jointly by the government of Mexico and the Rockefeller Foundation and some were spread over various activities. The Foundation's direct contributions to the corn and wheat breeding and to the training program are estimated at less than $7 million up to mid-1961. Although it is also difficult to estimate the value of direct benefits from the program, it certainly has been an important factor in reducing a $60 million wheat import bill to zero, to say nothing of the indirect benefits from the training program and the value of increases in corn production.

39. L. Rist, "Capital Inflow into Africa," paper delivered at a meeting of the International Economic Association in Addis Ababa in July 1961. This paper and others on the economic development of Africa are to be published in 1964 by the Oxford University Press.

40. See N. Jasny, *The Socialized Agriculture of the USSR* (Stanford, Calif.: Stanford University Press, 1949). See also in S. H. Frankel, *The Economic Impact of Underdeveloped Economies*, esp. chap. viii, "The Dongwa Experiment: Lessons of the East African Groundnut Scheme" (London: Oxford University Press, 1955).

41. The following examples illustrate the relatively high cost of mechanized land clearance: (1) In Southern Rhodesia it costs approximately £18 an acre to clear land by machine at Gokwe, compared with £3 an acre by hand (author's estimate). (2) In the ill-fated "groundnut scheme" in Tanganyika it was anticipated that clearance by machine would cost about £3 an acre. From incomplete data the actual cost appears to have been around £25 an acre. (H.M.S.O. Report no. 7030. Final costs are author's estimate.) (3) Tsetse-fly eradication in Uganda is estimated to cost £250 per square mile (see *The Economic Development of Uganda*, p. 215). (4) In Bunyoro in Uganda "a satisfactory system of land clearance" reduced costs from £45 to £15 per acre, but "even at a cost of £15 per acre . . . it is impossible for this cost to be borne by farm revenue accounts over a short period." (*Symposium on Mechanical Cultivation in Uganda*, p. 69.)

The problems of relocating Africans on cleared land are lucidly discussed by G. A. Bridges who concluded that: "It would seem wise to initiate settlement schemes only where there is serious over-population which cannot be reduced by the introduction of improved techniques, better seeds, fertilizers . . ." (in other words by improving management). See *Planning Land Settlement Schemes with Special Reference to East Africa* (Addis Ababa: Economic Commission for Africa, Food and Agriculture Organization of the United Nations, 1962). The dis-economics of large-scale mechanization of clearance in nonindustrialized societies are discussed with special reference to the groundnut scheme by S. H. Frankel, *The Economic Impact of Underdeveloped Economies*.

42. L. Rist, "Capital Inflow into Africa."

Index

BOOKS PREPARED UNDER THE AUSPICES OF THE CENTER FOR INTERNATIONAL AFFAIRS, HARVARD UNIVERSITY

Published by Harvard University Press

The Soviet Bloc, by Zbigniew K. Brzezinski, 1960 (sponsored jointly with Russian Research Center).

Rift and Revolt in Hungary, by Ferenc A. Váli, 1961.

The Economy of Cyprus, by A. J. Meyer, with Simos Vassiliou, 1962 (jointly with Center for Middle Eastern Studies).

Entrepreneurs of Lebanon, by Yusif A. Sayigh, 1962 (jointly with Center for Middle Eastern Studies).

Communist China 1955–1959, with a foreword by Robert R. Bowie and John K. Fairbank, 1962 (jointly with East Asian Research Center).

In Search of France, by Stanley Hoffmann, Charles P. Kindleberger, Laurence Wylie, Jesse R. Pitts, Jean-Baptiste Duroselle, and François Goguel, 1963.

Somali Nationalism, by Saadia Touval, 1963.

The Dilemma of Mexico's Development, by Raymond Vernon, 1963.

The Arms Debate, by Robert A. Levine, 1963.

Africans on the Land, by Montague Yudelman, 1964.

Available from Other Publishers

The Necessity for Choice, by Henry A. Kissinger, 1961. Harper & Brothers.

Strategy and Arms Control, by Thomas C. Schelling and Morton H. Halperin, 1961. Twentieth Century Fund.

United States Manufacturing Investment in Brazil, by Lincoln Gordon and Engelbert L. Grommers, 1962. Harvard Business School.

Limited War in the Nuclear Age, by Morton H. Halperin, 1963. John Wiley & Sons.

Counterinsurgency Warfare, by David Galula, 1964. Frederick A. Praeger.

People and Policy in the Middle East, by Max Weston Thornburg, 1964. W. W. Norton.